Communications in Computer and Information Science   **809**

Commenced Publication in 2007
Founding and Former Series Editors:
Alfredo Cuzzocrea, Xiaoyong Du, Orhun Kara, Ting Liu, Dominik Ślęzak,
and Xiaokang Yang

More information about this series at http://www.springer.com/series/7899

Massila Kamalrudin · Sabrina Ahmad
Naveed Ikram (Eds.)

Requirements Engineering for Internet of Things

4th Asia-Pacific Symposium, APRES 2017
Melaka, Malaysia, November 9–10, 2017
Proceedings

 Springer

Editors
Massila Kamalrudin
Universiti Teknikal Malaysia Melaka
Melaka
Malaysia

Sabrina Ahmad 🆔
Universiti Teknikal Malaysia Melaka
Melaka
Malaysia

Naveed Ikram
Riphah International University
Islamabad
Pakistan

ISSN 1865-0929   ISSN 1865-0937 (electronic)
Communications in Computer and Information Science
ISBN 978-981-10-7795-1   ISBN 978-981-10-7796-8 (eBook)
https://doi.org/10.1007/978-981-10-7796-8

Library of Congress Control Number: 2017963759

Printed on acid-free paper

This Springer imprint is published by Springer Nature
The registered company is Springer Nature Singapore Pte Ltd.
The registered company address is: 152 Beach Road, #21-01/04 Gateway East, Singapore 189721, Singapore

Preface

Requirements Engineering (RE) is now a well-established discipline of research and practice in software and systems development. The importance of developing and following effective RE practices has long been recognized by researchers and practitioners alike. In the Asia–Pacific region, RE is also receiving more and more attention due to the increasing reliance on software-intensive systems.

The Asia-Pacific Requirements Engineering Symposium (APRES) is a focused intellectual forum for in-depth discussion of all issues related to RE. It aims to bring together researchers and practitioners from industry, academia, and government to share the state of the art and practice in RE and explore emerging challenges in RE innovation. It also aims to foster collaboration among the RE community of researchers and practitioners in Asia and Oceania. Following the success of APRES 2014 in New Zealand, APRES 2015 in China, and APRES 2016 in Japan, the fourth edition of APRES (APRES 2017) took place in Malaysia, specifically in Melaka the historical city of Malaysia.

Responding to the growing trend toward interconnectivity, the discussion at APRES 2017 addressed the changing work practices and challenges of RE in response to the Internet of Things (IoT). This year, we accepted 11 full papers and five short papers. All papers were carefully reviewed by at least three Program Committee members and detailed constructive feedback was provided to the authors. We also had participants and presentations from Australia, Malaysia, Pakistan, Japan and Korea.

APRES 2017 was held for two days during November 9–10, 2017. The symposium hosted two keynote speakers who each presented a topic relevant to the current development of RE. The first speaker, Professor Didar Zowghi from Australia, highlighted the sociotechnical perspectives in RE, while the second speaker, Professor Madhusudan Singh from Korea, discussed Blockchain Technology in RE. Both topics are relevant to the changing work practice and research in RE.

The paper presentations at APRES 2017 were organized into five main topics, i.e., big data, cyber security, crowd-sourcing, automation, and requirements challenges. APRES 2017 also attracted a good number of participants and enriched the overall offering of the conference for the discussions of real-world problems and sharing of industry experiences and practices in RE.

Our greatest thanks go to the authors and presenters whose contributions made APRES 2017 a success. We are grateful to the Program Committee members for their thorough and timely reviews of the submissions. We thank the Steering Committee for their valuable guidance.

   Our thanks also go to Springer, publisher of the APRES proceedings, for their continuous support. Finally, thanks to EasyChair for making the conference management such an efficient task.

   We hope you all enjoy the APRES 2017 proceedings.

November 2017   Massila Kamalrudin
                                                              Sabrina Ahmad
                                                              Naveed Ikram

Organization

General Chair

Massila Kamalrudin   Universiti Teknikal Malaysia Melaka, Malaysia

Program Co-chairs

Naveed Ikram   Riphah International University, Pakistan
Sabrina Ahmad   Universiti Teknikal Malaysia Melaka, Malaysia

Program Committee

Jim Buchan	Auckland University of Technology, New Zealand
Tony Clear	Auckland University of Technology, New Zealand
Didar Zowghi	University of Technology, Sydney, Australia
Mikio Aoyama	Nanzan University, Japan
Muhammad Ali Babar	Adelaide University, Australia
Muneera Bano	University of Technology, Sydney, Australia
Aditya Ghose	University of Wollongong, Australia
Seok-Won Lee	Ajou University, South Korea
Lin Liu	Tsinghua University, China
Stuart Marshall	Victoria University of Wellington, New Zealand
Mahmood Niazi	King Fahd University of Petroleum and Minerals, Saudi Arabia
Xin Peng	Fudan University, China
Shahida Sulaiman	University Teknologi Malaysia, Malaysia
Haiyan Zhao	Peking University, China

Organizing Committee

Kamal Zuhairi Zamli	Universiti Malaysia Pahang, Malaysia
Dayang Norhayati Abang Zawawi	Universiti Teknologi Malaysia, Malaysia
Rodziah Atan	Universiti Putra Malaysia, Malaysia
Sharifah Mashita Syed Mohamad	Universiti Sains Malaysia, Malaysia
Badariah Solemon	Universiti Tenaga Nasional, Malaysia
Mazlina ABD. Majid	Universiti Malaysia Pahang, Malaysia
Norazlina Khamis	Universiti Malaysia Sabah, Malaysia
Nurazlina MD Sanusi	Universiti Teknikal Malaysia Melaka, Malaysia
Rosmiza Wahida Abdullah	Universiti Teknikal Malaysia Melaka, Malaysia

Safiah Sidek	Universiti Teknikal Malaysia Melaka, Malaysia
Noorrezam Yusop	Universiti Teknikal Malaysia Melaka, Malaysia
Halimaton Saadiah Hakimi	Universiti Teknikal Malaysia Melaka, Malaysia

Abstracts of Keynote Talks

Old and New Directions in Requirements Elicitation Research and Practice: A Sociotechnical Perspective

Didar Zowghi

University of Technology Sydney, Australia

Requirements elicitation is the most communication rich and iterative activity in requirements engineering that relies heavily on the skills and the cooperation of all stakeholders. It represents an early but continuous and critical stage in the development of software systems. Requirements are elicited rather than just captured or collected and there are elements of discovery, creativity, emergence, and development in the whole elicitation process. All these diverse elements have presented many challenges for requirements elicitation research, training and practice. In this keynote, I will look at the past and present directions of research and practice in requirements elicitation and highlight the thorniest issues revealed and addressed so far. I will argue that we do not have any real theory that can adequately explain the requirements elicitation process. I will then review some of the important lessons that I have learnt from my two decades of requirements engineering research to posit that ultimately this theory would have to be a "reconciliation of social and technical". I will also speculate a sociotechnical approach that could address the fundamental challenges of requirements elicitation.

Role of Blockchain Technology in Requirement Engineering

Madhusudan Singh

Yonsei Institute of Convergence Technology

In the requirements elicitation phase of requirements gathering, a lot of information is collected and documented from the stakeholders and customers. The information is sometimes miscommunicated due to inconsistency, incompleteness, non-verifiability and difference of opinion among different stakeholders. Every new discussion with customers, and stakeholders brings up new ideas, which is very challenging for the requirements engineer to maintain the consistency and verifiability with the previously recorded information. Neither the customers nor stakeholders account for what they said, what they are saying and what they actually want. Using the systematic manual analysis or an executable model to check requirements is not enough. There is an emergent need of an open transparent and verifiable platform network like blockchain for customers, stakeholders, and requirements engineers for communicating, collaborating and collecting their ideas, thoughts and requirements clearly and coming up to a consensus. This will help requirements engineer to clearly analyse and elicit verifiable, traceable, comprehensible requirements for the system, which can maximally comply with the needs of all the customers and stakeholders involved with the software system. Therefore, Blockchain can play a very important role in requirements engineering domain. The blockchain technology has four key points (Consensus, Cryptography, Smart contract and ledger) they can build the secure distributed and decentralised bond during the requirement engineering process. In this keynote, I will discuss followings:

1. Introduce Requirements Engineering with Blockchain technology.
2. Blockchain based Requirements engineering for software engineering.
3. Blockchain based Security requirements challenges and solution for software engineering.
4. Discuss the blockchain based requirement engineering for emerging technologies (Artificial Technology, IoT, Big data etc.).

Contents

Requirements Challenges

Automation

Big Data

Big Data Services Requirements Analysis

Affan Yasin[1], Lin Liu[1(✉)], Zhanqiang Cao[1], Jianmin Wang[1],
Yingbo Liu[1], and Tan Sheau Ling[1,2]

[1] School of Software, Tsinghua University, Beijing 100084, China
linliu@tsinghua.edu.cn
[2] Ecogeneration International PTE Ltd., Singapore, Singapore

Abstract. The development of the Internet and cloud computing has set up a matured environment for developing and deploying big data services. The main objective of requirements engineering for big data is to capture big data service users' needs and provider's capabilities, and to identify value added service use cases for big data technology in a given organizational context. Major objectives may include: collect real-time data about the world, search for useful information in large data sets, gain insights about given problems by data analytics, predict possible trend of interesting subjects, and make decisions for the next immediate actions. In this paper, we propose a big data service requirements analysis framework, which aims to provide useful guidelines for eliciting service requirements, selecting the right services architectures and evaluate the available technological services implementations. For services under operation, we suggest data analysis to service logs to elicit user's changing needs, to evaluate the run-time service performance and to check compliance to general standards and domain-specific regulations. Example cases from eHealth and industry 4.0 are discussed to illustrate the proposed service requirements framework.

Keywords: Big data · Requirements · Services engineering · Process
Case study

1 Introduction

Big data services are artefact centric, process-oriented in nature. A nice analogy is that "data is the running water, and software are the pipes, reservoirs and functional units along the way". The objective of services computing in the big data era, is to develop service pipelines processing large volume data on demand. The major challenges are reflected in two aspects: on the one hand, the big data services should address the actual needs of stakeholders, which requires to develop right services to process the right data, and calls for an integrated engineering lifecycle. On the other hand, there are abundant amount of data generated during the services engineering lifecycle, in other words, "data about the pipes", which may also require insights for better services development and operations.

Big data services often refer to a wide variety of outsourceable functions to the cloud. It can range from supply of data, to the supply of analytical software tools, with which to interrogate data and providing reports. Service providers may provide services as online dashboard or control panels, or offline consulting services. It aims to help

M. Kamalrudin et al. (Eds.): APRES 2017, CCIS 809, pp. 3–14, 2018.
https://doi.org/10.1007/978-981-10-7796-8_1

general users and developers facing difficulties in making selections among the existing big data packages. We argue that requirements have to be analysed properly, including: (1) identify valuable use cases; (2) check the availability of core data sources; (3) support the selection of big data service architecture; (4) define right service process and deployment strategy; (5) build self-adaptive services run-time monitoring mechanism.

Service engineering in big data era has to address two major challenges: data life cycle management with integrated development environment and service life cycle management including run-time behaviour data analysis tool. Extracting common patterns in the big data services development and operation, we built an integrated big data service requirements analysis framework. Domain-oriented big data services requirements can be intuitively expressed as: (1) the definition of data services process models, through the reuse of the existing business process model and services specifications; (2) the specification of available data sets and required data transformations; (3) the specification of algorithms needs for generating required services outcomes; (4) the level of performance, security protection and user experience are identified. Then, appropriate service components and corresponding optimal configurations are selected based on domain knowledge [7].

The remainder of the paper is organized as follows: Sect. 2 reports the background and related work. Section 3 introduces our big data requirements elicitation framework, describes how we scope a given application, analyse the raw data and mapping them into a feasible big data solution. Section 4 presents the requirements representations and aspects unique in big data applications. Section 5 presents a general framework for requirements consolidation at run-time, e.g. requirements discovery by process mining, variability detection by diagnosis and comparison, identification of requirements by change prediction and recommendation of alternatives. Section 6 introduces example cases, and Sect. 7 concludes the paper and discuss future work.

2   Background and Related Work

With the growth in popularity of big data technology, we receive constant requests for building sustainable big data service platforms, encourage the rapid development and delivery of expected infrastructure and results with minimum efforts. However, big data is inherently complex, volatile, lack of correlation, and value scarce, which makes it difficult to form standardized and systematic technological solutions. In order to address the diversified requirements of big data processing in different application domain, services engineering in big data era has to address the major challenges of big data life cycle management with integrated development environment and run-time service optimization tool [23].

The quick adoption of big data technology is explored in many industry sectors. There are a few related accounts on big data services requirements in industrial white papers [3, 18] and in research literature [26]. General requirements analysis activities for business analytics projects are discussed in [3, 5]. Requirements for big data analytics in the healthcare domain are facing the processing of abundant clinical data accumulated in daily practice [4, 11, 12, 16, 19, 21, 24, 27], if big data services are used, practitioners will only need to worry about the business and clinical value of these resources besides renting the cloud-based storage and analytics engines. Even the costs of HIPAA compliance and data protection is at the providers' stake [14], as it is stored in their server, hence their responsibility.

Amazon's Amazon Web Services (AWS) and Google's AdSense and AdWords are well-known and widely used by thousands of small to medium sized businesses across the world. The primary reasons for its adoption is to host data infrastructure, target marketing at relevant niches for potential customers. Key success factors also due to easy integration, maximum availability and efficient data analysis. Take the example of Cenique, a Hong Kong-based company helping clients conduct instore-advertising and analysing audience behaviour, whose adoption of AWS services eventually contribute to assessing the user trend by gathering user data using nine metrics to get the maximum insight of the data and user behaviours[1].

Anyone can analyse data if he invests time learning to use cheap off-the-shelf hardware and open-source software, while companies spend money on software components and infrastructures for commercial big data initiatives. When a big data services is used, the service providers set up the environment and leave the service users free from the technical jargons and only concentrate on the business issues. In the process mining domain, open source process mining platform is widely used across different domain [1, 2, 9, 13, 28], which can be transformed into online services for wider industrial adoptions. In order to address the diversified requirements for life cycle management of big data in different application domain, encourage its rapid development and delivery of expected values with minimum efforts, innovative engineering methodology and integrated inquiry life cycle for potential big data applications are in dire needs.

3 Big Data Services Life Cycle Support Needs

This paper discusses big data requirements in the context of an integrated big data applications design and development lifecycle, supporting data collection and cleaning, integration and storage, analysis and presentation, support high-level, domain-oriented requirements description framework describing the complex business needs. The development environment supports the construction of big data application systems from the service components according to the user's needs. It has the main functions of system design, script generation and automated deployment. The software life cycle support includes: design, development, operation and optimization of big data application systems, operation analysis tool to support the self- adaptive and self-optimization of applications. The use of machine learning, data mining, correlation analysis, information visualization and other technologies, high performance computing, analysis of data generated during software life cycle, such as: log, system configuration, deployment scripts, performance indicators, extract useful information. The formation of big data requirements knowledge base helps practitioners to optimize the design decision-making and the operation of the services and applications.

---

[1] https://aws.amazon.com/solutions/case-studies/big-data/.

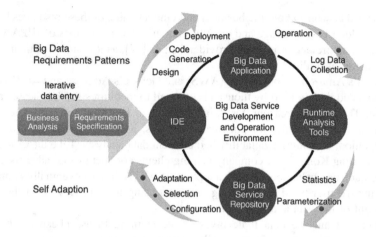

Fig. 1. Big data application systems lifecycle support

The work is carried out stepwise as shown in Fig. 1, including four parts: big data services repository, integrated development environment (IDE), runtime analysis tool and big data applications. The main contents include:

- Automated big data services component selection according to the user needs;
- Capacity planning and recommendations of big data system hardware according to the user;
- Initial configuration and optimization of big data software service parameter according to the user needs;
- Dynamic update of data resources, update big data service repository based on domain, parameter-based configuration knowledge and the users' feedback.

The operation of the big data service repository is divided into three stages, train and preparation phase, usage and operation phase and adaptation and optimization phase, as shown in Fig. 2. Prior to use, we first train the component selection decision tree and the performance model, initialize the software configuration rule base; training results can be used in component selection and parameter configuration; in the subsequent usage stage, the selection decision tree, the performance model and the software parameter configuration rule base can be updated iteratively according to the users' feedback.

In the usage phase, the first step is to obtain the user needs according to the standardized user requirements indicators. Through a friendly web user interface, the user can answer a series of questions raised by the big data component service archive to generate the quantitative service requirements index. In the second step, the user can select the appropriate big data system components according to recommendations. In the next step, the required hardware resource is allocated according to pre-trained performance model and the user's performance indicators, the user can modify or confirm the hardware resource configuration directly. The fourth step is the initial parameter configuration of the big data service application. The optimal initial parameter configuration is calculated through rules in knowledge base, which is then confirmed or modified by the user. The fifth step is to generate a deployment plan, including system selection, hardware resource configuration checklist, the initial software parameter configuration for each big data system component; then submit it to the automatic deployment tool to generate big data system. The self-adaptive, self-optimization support are reflected in the derivation of the index and parameter from business requirements, the automated selection of components, the automated code generation of big data application systems, the automated system deployment, and the runtime log analysis to adaptive adjustment and cross-layer optimization.

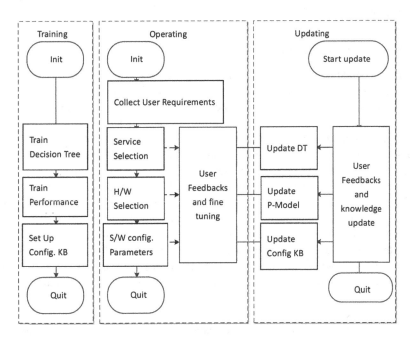

Fig. 2. Big data service repository management support

4 Requirements for Big Data Services

Questions to be asked in the current landscape of big data services requirements analysis include: (1) What is the business objective and use case to serve? It has to be born in mind that there are many "pseudo-requirements" in big data projects. There are many projects start with the "how" without first considering the "why". Big data service has to solve real-world problems, so one has to establish why there is a particular need for business to allocate time and resources to it. (2) What data is available? Does it serve its purpose? What data has to be to collected? How is the data quality? It is utmost important to identify the right data sources in the target organization. As the current status is that business processes are inherently dispersed, heterogeneous, and autonomous, so the data collection, interpretation requires considerable effort without support from automated tools. Due to the heterogeneity and uncertainty in data collection, analysis, mining stage, data quality is a general challenge that everyone has to face. (3) What data mining algorithms and machine learning model to use? Only if the business objective and data resources are identified, it is possible to build or select the right analytical services. This paper proposes a requirement driven approach for big data application services development and run-time services support platform, covering the entire big data life-cycle: collection, storage, computation, analysis, visualization, as well as the service engineering life cycle, including: design, implementation, operation and optimization, forming a self-adaptive, self-optimizing solution. We have applied the proposed techniques in specific application domains such as industry 4.0, and healthcare as illustration and validation.

4.1 Requirements Elicitation

Requirements elicitation is the entry point of big data application system development for a user, which covers the four aspects of big data requirements: identification of business use cases, sequence of actions performed by an actor, based on which architecture capabilities are planned; identification of data objects, based on which the end-to-end procedures and capabilities are planned, architectural design based on requirements both functional and non-functional. User requirements are collected through a simple, intuitive, easy to use interface, and provide input to the follow-up step of services selection and parameter configuration. The purpose of requirements analysis is to identify big data components in the inventory, and to determine appropriate hardware configuration and software system components. In due process, experienced users can further improve the recommended systems components and parameters, making the system capacity in line with requirements. For advanced users who are familiar with the various big data system components, he can also choose to skip requirements acquisition and analysis, directly make paradigm selection and parameter configuration.

Big data system development platform is user-oriented, so user requirements need to be expressed precisely. First, it has to capture the various kinds of resources and services in the big data application system, such as hardware resources, software resources, domain knowledge, configuration parameters, performance indicators, etc. The scope will cover the typical big data application system functional requirements, such as business content and data objects, operational procedures and non-functional requirements, such as user population, data volume and performance requirements.

From the operating environment point of view, it is necessary to support the requirements definition of a single type of resource, as well as multiple types of resources. It is necessary to support definition of the input/output data clearly, and also the temporary intermediate data. From an operational point of view, it is necessary to support the accurate expression of the various types of hardware resources, software resources, domain knowledge, configuration parameters and performance indicators, as well as the above resource-based abstract/fuzzy expressions. It is necessary to support the expressions of common basic temporal operational order relationships, such as: sequence, synchronization, and also other high-level control flow structures, such as, parallel and recursive structure.

4.2   Big Data Services Requirements Catalogue

By summarizing the practical experience of major big data service providers' capability descriptions and their various service usage scenarios, we identified 26 big data application requirements indicators covering following aspects: requirements type, data type, business process, and performance index, as shown in Fig. 3. There are 14 indicators related to components selection: type of storage, data consistency management strategy, data types, scale of single file or data record, data arrival mode, data schema characteristics, query types, computation types, analytics types, query response time, calculation response time, analysis response time, system availability, and whether data is imported. Based on the above requirements indicators, a big data services component selection decision tree is constructed for data storage, data processing and analytics. In our current system, the C5.0 algorithm is adopted to construct the decision tree. When building a decision tree, use a known set of data, including selection results under different conditions. The system has built-in the initial knowhow to build the decision tree. The system also supports the user to insert new knowledge. When the user changes the result of a certain selection, the resource library will receive the corresponding feedback, a new knowledge entry (as training data) will be added to the knowledge base and the decision tree model will be updated according to learning result.

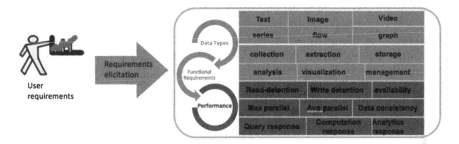

Fig. 3. Big data services requirements catalogue

5   Service Requirements at Run-Time

When the big data application is running, the runtime data management system collects the data generated by the major services in real time and simultaneously performs data storage and indexing to meet the management requirements of massive operational data. In addition, the data stored in the framework will be entered into the parameter recommendation system, to feed historical data for learning purpose.

5.1   Runtime Service Monitoring

This section proposes a big data services optimization method based on monitoring and log analysis. By collecting the operation log of big data application services, analysing the services resource usage and computing ability bottleneck, the service resource deployment is iteratively improved. Introduce the systematic data mining method to analyse the data of the big data application execution process, update the corresponding model knowledge in the big data component library, and provide guidance for the system configuration of similar load, and static resource allocation is avoided while optimizing the application efficiency. For example, during 2012 to 2014, China Mobile has identified 8,000 business process models by analysing a dataset of a dozen million key-value based event logs, which reflects the practice of 31 branches all over China. It provides valuable reference for future business regulation, strategic decision making, and operational optimization.

By analysing the types of logs generated during the system operation, we collect the following four types of operational data in practice.

1. Big data services component model;
2. Big data component configuration and parameters;
3. Time-series data generated by monitoring system clusters:
   (a) CPU: system usage rate, user usage rate;
   (b) Network: number of input bytes, the number of output bytes
   (c) Hard disk: write bytes, read the number of bytes
4. Spark task scheduling data represented as a directed acyclic graph

Data collection of following components: Map/Reduce, Spark, Cassandra, HDFS storage module take distributed the job for the smallest division unit, the collected data is pre-processed and stored in the unstructured database MongoDB. The runtime data management system provides the user with a log search function similar to Splunk. The user can write a certain query on the log data retrieval, the current query can respond to the following request: Query logs for a specific time range; Query logs that contains some keyword; Query logs of a given big data component; Query logs of a particular node in the cluster; and composition of these queries.

5.2 Log Pre-processing

All the pre-processing work on the original log, including log collection, template extraction and log matching three parts. This paper first uses the generic log framework Log4j to collect the logs generated by the user Spark cluster. One does not need to configure the additional log collection tool for the user cluster, but only needs to modify the configuration file of Log4j. For Spark clusters deployed on Yarn, one can also use Yarn's log aggregation tool for log collection. After getting the log, one need to convert the log into structured data that can be understood by the machine. We use the template base to do this. The template base is an extraction of the log output fragments in the system source code and can be matched with the actual log, which is interpreted as a regular expression that matches the log.

5.3 Log Feature Construction

Based on the understanding of the internal mechanism of the Spark system, we extracts the log features for the Spark system: the data block RDD feature and the task unit Task, and the feature extraction is combined with the log matching process. The RDD feature is used to describe the characteristics of the data blocks in the job execution process and to discover the abnormal performance of the system from the point of view of the data flow. The Task feature is used to describe the characteristics of the subtask in the job execution process, and the abnormal performance of the system is found from the perspective of the task flow. At the same time, in order to improve the performance and meet the requirements of log processing and feature extraction under big data scale, this paper can realize distributed extraction of two kinds of features.

Today, the majority of health IT projects involves clinical business processes. In the past two decades, requirements on such projects have changed gradually, it started with command-based user-system interaction mode, evolve into single process driven mode, to today's multi-process interweaved mode. Earlier electronic patient records systems help physicians edit their clinical documents has turned into a platform supporting multiple business processes, including documenting clinical records, generating insurance claims, respond to clinical quality monitoring. As an example, Healthcare is inherently event-based. Clinical data can be treated as logs for the corresponding clinical events reflecting interactions of a care provider with a patient, e.g., a symptom being observed, a medication being taken, an X-ray image being obtained, an order being issued, a care procedure being executed, a patient being discharged, just to name but a few. Many may argue that we have lots of other perspectives to view it, but the data under discussion is always associated with an event of some sort. If we can collect sufficient context information for these events, making decisions on what clinical service to deliver, and how to deliver it in an appropriate way will be made easier.

6 Findings from Real-World Cases

In this section, we summarise some experience on service requirements elicitation.

6.1 Identify Use Cases of True Value

We have witnessed many organizations thrown themselves into big data projects with great enthusiasm - collecting information on everything and mining on the go. Some were interesting – such as mining electronic medical records for diagnosis patterns, others were less interesting - such as analysing the daily encounter data and find that there are more patients visits on Monday morning, and there are constant complains about long wait time and patient not being admitted soon enough. But so what? The issue is that there are not enough doctors to see all the patients, which is obvious and already known without statistical analysis, we cannot do much to change the situation only by data analysis in isolation, the insight is not providing any positive change.

6.2 Matching Use Cases with Available Datasets

We have been working with a micro-chips manufacturer on big data projects. At the beginning, three possible use cases are identified, including: re-inspection of problematic mother boards falsely identified during solder paste inspection; optimization of solder paste inspection parameters; re-inspection of problematic mother boards falsely identified during automatic optical inspection of chip images. The problems we have encountered in this case is that we only have access to data set of abnormal cases, and missing samples of normal cases. Thus, the classification model is biased due to the lacking of balanced data set for all possible cases.

6.3   Identify Models, Algorithms and Technical Service Solutions

Once the above two steps are identified, we set out to explore the performance of the various available machine learning algorithms, such as Logic Regression, Random Forest, Naïve Bayesian, comparing the correctness of algorithms using Receiver Operating Characteristic Curve, the best model and algorithm are selected based on the specific features of data and the expected classification results. Once a model is selected, we then run experiment for the actual classification experiments.

7   Conclusion

In the big data era, understand service requirements face both challenges and opportunities. On the one hand, the software service engineering should focus on the needs of big data processing, to study how to develop software services that support all aspects of big data processing, and form a software service platform for big data - integrated design and development for big data lifecycle supports. On the other hand, the software system and the project implementation process will involve a number of big data characteristics of the services running status data, it is necessary for these multi-dimensional data to be studied using correlation mining and machine learning, data-driven development and operation based on rules. The formation of a big data service engineering methodology to guide the development of big data application and the big data application monitoring and evolution tool.

Big data application system is a "kaleidoscope", covering data collection and extraction, storage, calculation, analysis, visualization and other big data life cycle from multiple technical aspects, and a variety of solutions are involved, involving a variety of systems components, which makes the big data application system construction rather challenging. Turing Award winner Michael Stonebraker proposed the idea of "one size does not fit all" [26], arguing that big data infrastructure should be tailored and optimized for specific areas and issues. However, this will inevitably lead to fragmentation of big data ecosystem, while the Internet for consumers are transforming into the Internet for industry, the developers are changing from "technology geek" into the domain experts, which further exposed the difficulties in the infrastructure selection, configuration, maintenance and management in the big data application system.

This paper studies the engineering methodology for big data lifecycle services, through the big data system development and operation of the common model abstract, This paper puts forward the framework of an integrated services development and operation platform, which includes the development of integrated design and development environment, support high-level, domain-oriented requirements description framework, user-friendly programmability, and can identify business process model from event data. Developed a big data application system operation analysis tool, through the effective processing, analysis of software running life cycle generated in the running data, such as: log, system configuration, deployment scripts, performance indicators, extract useful information from, to optimize Decision-making, to help software developers to data-driven way to run big data application software optimization.

Acknowledgement. Partial financial support by National Science and Technology Support Program (No. 2015BAH14F02) and the National Natural Science Foundation of China (No. 61432020) are acknowledged.

References

1. Alves de Medeiros, A., van der Aalst, W.M., Weijters, A.: Quantifying process equivalence based on observed behavior. Data Knowl. Eng. **64**, 55–74 (2008)
2. van der Aalst, W.M., et al.: Process mining manifesto. In: Daniel, F., Barkaoui, K., Dustdar, S. (eds.) BPM 2011. LNBIP, vol. 99, pp. 169–194. Springer, Heidelberg (2012). https://doi.org/10.1007/978-3-642-28108-2_19
3. Beatty, J., Wiegers, K.: Forward thinking for tomorrow's projects requirements for business analytics. Seilevel Whitepaper (2015)
4. Bretthauer, M., Aabakken, L., Dekker, E., et al.: Reporting systems in gastrointestinal endoscopy: requirements and standards facilitating quality improvement: European society of gastrointestinal endoscopy position statement. United European Gastroenterol. J. (2016). https://doi.org/10.1177/2050640616629079
5. Chen, H., Chiang, R.H.L., Storey, V.C.: Business intelligence and analytics: from big data to big impact. MIS Q. **36**(4), 1165–1188 (2012)
6. Chung, L., et al.: NonFunctional Requirements in Software Engineering. Springer, New York (2012). https://doi.org/10.1007/978-1-4615-5269-7
7. Computing Community Consortium, Computing Research Association. Challenges and Opportunities with Big Data: A community white paper developed by leading researchers across the United States. White Paper, February 2012
8. Cysneiros, L.M.: Requirements engineering in health care domain. In: Proceedings of the IEEE Joint 10th International Requirements Engineering Conference, pp. 760–773, September 2002
9. Deutch, D., Milo, T.: A quest for beauty and wealth (or, business processes for database researchers). In: Proceedings of the Thirtieth ACM Sigmod-Sigact-Sigart Symposium on Principles of Database Systems, pp. 1–12 (2011)
10. David, R., Dong, F., Braun, Y., et al.: MyHealthAvatar survey: scenario based user needs and requirements. In: 2014 6th International Advanced Research Workshop on Silico Oncology and Cancer Investigation (IARWISOCI), pp. 1–5. IEEE (2014)
11. Dalrymple, P.W., Rogers, M., An, Y.: Effect of early requirements analysis and participative design on staff in an urban health clinic: civic engagement through collaboration. In: iConference 2009, Chapel Hill, NC (2009)
12. Fabian, B., Ermakova, T., Junghanns, P.: Collaborative and secure sharing of healthcare data in multi-clouds. Inf. Syst. **48**, 132–150 (2015)
13. Ghasemi, M., Amyot, D.: Process mining in healthcare: a systematised literature review. IJEH **9**(1), 60–88 (2016)
14. Rodrigues, J.P.C., de la Torre, I., Fernández, G., López-Coronado, M.: Analysis of the security and privacy requirements of cloud- based electronic health records systems. J. Med. Internet Res. **15**(8), e186 (2013)

15. Grigori, D., Corrales, J.C., Bouzeghoub, M., Gater, A.: Ranking BPEL processes for service discovery. IEEE Trans. Serv. Comput. **3**, 178–192 (2010)
16. Hua, L., Gong, Y.: Usability evaluation of a voluntary patient safety reporting system: understanding the difference between predicted and observed time values by retrospective think-aloud protocols. In: Kurosu, M. (ed.) HCI 2013. LNCS, vol. 8005, pp. 94–100. Springer, Heidelberg (2013). https://doi.org/10.1007/978-3-642-39262-7_11
17. Hu, H., Wen, Y., Chua, T.S., et al.: Toward scalable systems for data analytics: a technology tutorial. IEEE Access **2**, 652–687 (2014)
18. IBM: Data Driven Healthcare Organizations Use Data analytics for Big Gains (2013)
19. Kushniruk, A.: Evaluation in the design of health information systems: application of approaches emerging from usability engineering. Comput. Biol. Med. **32**(3), 141–149 (2002)
20. Kambatla, K., Kollias, G., Kumar, V., et al.: Trends in data analytics. J. Parallel Distrib. Comput. **74**(7), 2561–2573 (2014)
21. Liu, L., Feng, L., Cao, Z., Li, J.: Requirements engineering for health data analytics: challenges and possible directions. In: RE 2016, pp. 266–275 (2016)
22. Liu, L., Zhou, Q., Liu, J., Cao, Z.: Requirements cybernetics: elicitation based on user behavioral data. J. Syst. Softw. **124**, 187–194 (2017)
23. Llewellynn, T., Koller, S., Goumas, G., Leitner, P., Dasika, G., Wang, L., Tutschku, K., Fernández-Carrobles, M., Deniz, O., Fricker, S., Storkey, A., Pazos, N., Velikic, G., Leufgen, K., Dahyot, R.: BONSEYES: platform for open development of systems of artificial intelligence. In: Conference Computing Frontiers, pp. 299–304 (2017). Invited paper
24. Middleton, B., Bloomrosen, M., Dente, M.A., et al.: Enhancing patient safety and quality of care by improving the usability of electronic health record systems: recommendations from AMIA. J. Am. Med. Inform. Assoc. **20**(e1), e2–e8 (2013)
25. Raghupathi, W., Raghupathi, V.: Data analytics in healthcare: promise and potential. Health Inf. Sci. Syst. **2**(1), 3 (2014)
26. Stonebraker, M., et al.: The 8 requirements of real-time stream processing. ACM SIGMOD Rec. **34**(4), 42–47 (2005)
27. Teixeira, L., Ferreira, C., Santos, B.S.: User-centered requirements engineering in health information systems: a study in the hemophilia field. Comput. Methods Programs Biomed. **106**(3), 160–174 (2012)
28. Weidlich, M., Mendling, J., Weske, M.: Efficient consistency measurement based on behavioral profiles of process models. IEEE Trans. Softw. Eng. **37**, 410–429 (2011)
29. Yu, E.S.K.: Towards modelling and reasoning support for early-phase requirements engineering. In: Proceedings of the Third IEEE International Symposium on Requirements Engineering, pp. 226–235, 6–10 Jan 1997

An Empirical Study of the Software Development Process, Including Its Requirements Engineering, at Very Large Organization: How to Use Data Mining in Such a Study

Colin M. Werner[(⊠)] and Daniel M. Berry

Cheriton School of Computer Science, University of Waterloo,
Waterloo, ON N2L 3G1, Canada
colinwerner@gmail.com, dberry@uwaterloo.ca

Abstract. Very Large Organization (VLO) develops and manufacturers hardware and software products, with each product being developed in its own project. Each project, from its inception, maintains a database that contains a wealth of data pertaining to its software development lifecycle. To empirically study VLO's software development process, the authors mined the data from seven consecutive VLO projects to determine whether the data exhibit any anomalies and whether these anomalies can help assess a project's level of success. Some anomalies provide evidence of what VLO does well, while other anomalies highlight possible areas of improvement. Through the anomalies in the mined data, the organization can direct additional focus and research to specific areas of the development process, particularly its requirements engineering, to improve the likelihood of success for future projects.

While describing the results of the empirical study, the paper also shows how such a study can be conducted even when the mined data are not very detailed.

Keywords: Code repositories · Industry · Project management
Prototyping · Requirements engineering · Software engineering
Empirical case study

1 Introduction

Very Large Organization (VLO) is a mature organization that has released several products. Some of the products were deemed by the market to be successful, while others were deemed less successful. The authors were interested in determining the causes of success and of a lack of success. Fortunately, VLO, being a serious engineering firm, keeps a lot of data about each product, including, and in particular, its software development project. For each project, it keeps data from the project's inception, its requirements engineering (RE), its design, its implementation, its acceptance, through to its deployment, and beyond. These data have the potential to be mined to perhaps reveal key indicators of success and of its lack, a practice that is becoming more and more mainstream [1].

© Springer Nature Singapore Pte Ltd. 2018
M. Kamalrudin et al. (Eds.): APRES 2017, CCIS 809, pp. 15–25, 2018.
https://doi.org/10.1007/978-981-10-7796-8_2

The purpose of the research reported in this paper was to explore whether these data could be mined in order to determine causes of success and causes of lack of success. The research started with mining the data of whole projects in order to not make any assumptions as to which steps of the process were critical, i.e., to let the data take us where they do. The mined data were very telling. Included in this paper are some of the key data points and conclusions drawn from the mined data, as well as advice on how to conduct such a data mining study when the data are not very detailed.

This paper is derived from the master's thesis of the first author [2]. Details, in particular, the actual data and its full analysis, that were left out of this paper in order to meet its page limit can be found in the thesis.

In the rest of this paper, Sect. 2 describes the typical product lifeline; Sect. 3 defines the mined data; Sect. 4 analyzes the data and draws conclusions; Sect. 5 offers some possible solutions to the observed problems; Sect. 6 summarizes the answers to the research questions raised in Sect. 4; Sect. 7 discusses threats and limitations of the conclusions; and Sect. 8 concludes the paper.

2   Product Description

VLO produces hardware-and-software products, each of which includes hardware, an embedded system, and a set of applications. Each product released by VLO has an associated development project, whereby multiple products may be developed in the same project. Generally speaking, when VLO releases a new product, the product consists of a new hardware design-and-construction accompanied by its own new embedded system and an applications layer. The software release model used for the majority of releases is based on an iterative waterfall model, in which each subsequent project is built directly on top of its previous project.

Many consumers worldwide use VLO products. However, these consumers do not buy directly from VLO. Instead, VLO sells its products to customers, and these customers resell the products to the consumer. Each development project to develop at least one product has a set of customers, who are the ones that determine whether a delivered product is accepted. Each project's database logs a variety of data about each acceptance: its date, the name of its accepting customer, and a variety of other details pertaining to the various hardware platforms supported and software versions produced.

The initial phase of a project is to create the vision of the project's product. The vision roughly defines the hardware and software of the product along with some key factors differentiating it from those of other products. Once the product vision has been completed, the requirements phase begins.

The requirements phase at VLO starts with the product marketing team, who are deemed to have substantial market knowledge regarding the product and interface directly with the customers. The product marketing team describes various aspects of the product in several market requirement documents, which form the basis for a market-viewpoint specification of the product's requirements. The project's development team reviews this requirements specification and negotiates with the product marketing team to finalize a set of requirements that will be implemented. This set of requirements is encapsulated in a project requirements document.

Once the product's requirements are believed to be understood, the development phase begins. During the development phase, if a substantial or unrealized change is required to the product, a change request (CR) must be created and sent through the necessary approval process. The intention of the CR process is to minimize requirements creep; however, a substantial number of CRs for a product could indicate problems in the RE process and could merit further investigation.

As a project is nearing completion, a near final milestone is for its customer to provide acceptance of the product. The acceptance does not mean that the development of the product is complete, as the acceptance may include conditions for small tweaks to the product. However, these conditions are usually small enough to consider the acceptance as the final clearance from the customer that the product's requirements have been met.

3 Data Compilation

Without industrial data, research like that described herein would lack external validity. Therefore, we were fortunate that VLO granted to the authors access to a number of tools in order to mine the data pertaining to each project. All of the data mining occurred after the release of all the products. Thus the mining was observational and nonintrusive. Due to the confidential nature of the products and projects, and for the protection of VLO, each datum was anonymized. At the time the data were mined, each datum was associated with one of seven consecutive projects. Each dataset consisted of a series of data from source-control repositories, CR reports, customer acceptances, employee opinions, and any other pertinent project information that was uncovered during the data mining.

Data were gathered until the authors felt that they could not learn anything new from additional data, i.e., until *saturation* was achieved. Clearly, recognition of saturation is highly subjective, but there is no other way to know when to stop mining data.

3.1 Project Lifelines

In order to form the dataset for a project, a project lifeline was created. The lifeline for a project simply records the duration of the project's development lifecycle, from beginning to end. The lifeline formed the basis for the rest of dataset, as the project lifeline created a natural axis on which to map the remaining data. A project's lifeline did not have a fixed length. As more data were discovered, the lifeline could be extended in order to include the additional data. Thus, the project lifeline became an implicit portion of the dataset.

3.2 Source-Control Repository

The source-control repository provided the largest set of data. Each project has its own branch in the source-control repository, allowing simple scripts to collect the data. A source-control commit is a single source commit by a single developer to the source-control repository. These data are simply counted as each source-control commit occurred, so there is no advance notice of outstanding changes to be committed. A source-control commit may consist of a list of requested items, each of which is a feature request, a CR, a software bug fix, or a non-functional change such as an optimization or a change to a document. Therefore, the actions a developer may take for a single source-control commit can be any combination of (1) editing an existing file, (2) deleting an existing file, and (3) adding a new file to the source-control repository.

This paper does not classify the source-control commits based on content; for simplicity, each and every source-control commit is considered to be of equal value. This simplification may not be a fair evaluation and certainly deserves further attention [3]; however, the definition fits the purpose of this paper. As is typical with most source-control repositories, the data consisted of a series of source-control commits in each particular project branch. However, to ensure VLO's privacy, only the date of submission was retained during the data mining. The date of submission was sufficient information in order to keep track of the number of source-control commits in any project's lifeline.

3.3 CRs

At VLO, a process exists that must be followed whenever a new requirement or change in an existing requirement is desired, usually due to a customer's request. When a change is required, a CR must be submitted. A CR includes details of what is desired, why the change is required, and by when the change is expected. Normally, submission of a CR blocks its product's release. Once a CR has been submitted, the CR is first evaluated by a team of marketing experts to determine if the CR is worth pursuing. Next, the teams that would be involved in implementing the change must provide an impact analysis of the change. The analysis includes estimates for development, testing, localization, certification, or any other areas that may be affected by the change. Normally, it is very difficult to compile a complete list of all the teams that may be affected by a particular change. Therefore, any particular CR may include an incomplete list of estimates. This deficiency is itself a problem, as other work that was not in the original impact analysis is often discovered and consequently delays the completion of a CR. After the implementation information is gathered, the CR is forwarded to the CR committee, which ultimately decides whether to approve or reject the CR. The CR data collected for this paper describes only the approved CRs that were implemented for each product and not the rejected CRs. Moreover, the data about a CR do not include any details about the size, nature, or complexity of the change requested in the CR. So all we know about any CR is that it was approved and that its size, nature, and complexity must have been such that the CR was approved.

3.4 Customer Acceptances

VLO maintains a customer database which contains a variety of information related to each customer, including the date each product was accepted by the customer. For the purpose of this paper, this date shall be considered the date the product was fully accepted by the customer, even if the acceptance was conditional for any number of reasons. The acceptance dates for each product were mined from this database and added to the dataset for the product's project.

3.5 Hardware

Every project did feature some new hardware. As part of the dataset, the number of hardware platforms per project was recorded. However, each hardware platform could also be classified into two different categories: revolutionary or evolutionary. Evolutionary hardware is typically providing an update to the hardware from a previous product. On the other hand, revolutionary hardware is ground breaking and carries with it a more substantial amount of novel technical innovation than does evolutionary hardware.

On occasion, the software developed for a new project could also be released on hardware from previous projects, also known as in-market hardware. Whether a project release included in-market hardware was recorded and added to the dataset.

3.6 Data Summary

The resulting project dataset includes from each of the seven projects

1. lifeline,
2. number of source-control commits,
3. number of approved CRs,
4. number of customer acceptances,
5. number of hardware platforms,
6. whether the project targets in-market hardware, and
7. whether the project includes revolutionary hardware.

4 Data Analysis

Some of the research questions (RQs) intended to be addressed by the work described in this paper are:

RQ1: Do the VLO project data say anything about the success or failure for any product?

RQ2: Do the VLO project data say anything about the *reasons* for success or failure?

RQ3: Are there any VLO project data that can serve as predictors of a product project's outcome [4, 5]?

The thesis [2] poses different, project-specific research questions, which are not answered here, because to do so would require more pages than are available. The interested reader is encouraged to download and read the thesis.

To answer these RQs, each project is compared with every other project. In addition, each project is compared with an ideal, but non-existent golden[1] project. The

---

[1] In empirical work, the *golden data* are the data to which each subject's data are compared to evaluate the subject's data. The researchers try to make the golden data completely correct, but know that they may not be.

golden project does not have any real data associated with it. Instead, the golden project is described by made-up data that represent the way we hope that every project would proceed, knowing full well that no project ever proceeds that way. The purpose of the golden project is to provide criteria that can easily be compared with any real project to provide answers to our research questions. The golden project

1. has a perfect, i.e., complete and consistent, requirements specification, but if not, the CRs are minor,
2. has all of its source code committed prior to any customer acceptances,
3. has all of its source code committed in the first half of the project,
4. has no CRs, but if a CR is required it should be resolved in the first half of the project,
5. has only one hardware platform,
6. has no in-market hardware platform, if the project involves a revolutionary hardware platform, and
7. has at most one revolutionary hardware platform.

Yes, these criteria *do* overlap.

The data about a project that are needed to evaluate how close the project is to the golden project are measures that allow the project to be compared to the golden project. These project data are, respectively,

1. the percentage of all code commits for the project that are done prior to the project's first customer acceptance.
2. the percentage of all code commits for the project that are done during the first half of the project,
3. the percentage of all CRs for the project that are resolved during the first half of the project,
4. the number of hardware platforms the project targets,
5. whether the project targets at least one revolutionary hardware platform,
6. whether the project targets at least one in-market hardware platform,

Note that the fifth criterion is decided by the fifth *and* sixth datum combined. Table 1 shows the values of the required data for each of the projects.

Table 1. Key data summary

	%-age code committed at first acceptance	%-age code committed at half way	%-age CRs resolved at half way	Number of hardware platforms	In-market hardware	Revolutionary hardware
Project 1	72.45	97.8	94.12	7	Yes	No
Project 2	88.15	95.4	74.19	4	No	No
Project 3	87.92	96.08	81.91	12	Yes	No
Project 4	72.05	94.53	90.23	2	No	No
Project 5	65.79	76.91	67.62	4	No	No
Project 6	67.88	78.88	71.62	2	No	Yes
Project 7	87.47	82.54	93.88	1	No	No

Comparing each project's data to the golden project's criteria reveals that no single project is quite a golden project, which was expected. For any project, the reason that the project fails to be a golden project depends on the project's circumstances and on the specific project data that deviate from the golden project criteria. In fact, a project with a single deviation[2] is likely to have a completely normal project lifeline. Charette points out that a failing project rarely fails for just one or two reasons [6]. Each of Projects 2, 4, and 7 has a single large deviation. However, none of them represents an extremity. In fact, each of these projects was typical for VLO and proves that VLO can successfully create incremental products. Ruhe *et al.* claim that a company's ability to create incremental products is a primary factor in the company's ability to produce large successful software products [7].

Each of the four remaining projects has multiple deviations and is far more interesting. Each of Projects 1 and 3, is one of the only two projects to target in-market hardware, thus explaining why these two projects had the most hardware platforms. The large number of hardware platforms explains each project's other deviations. In a typical VLO project targeting a new hardware platform, the new hardware platform would be released first. Only later would the versions running on in-market hardware platforms be released, thus explaining why the project's customer acceptances are scattered throughout the project's lifeline. The additional hardware platforms cause the project lifeline to be extended to cover the later in-market hardware platform releases; whereas a project without an in-market hardware platform release would be completed much sooner.

The two remaining projects, Projects 5 and 6 had by far the lowest data for the first three criteria. Closer examination shows that Project 5 had an additional hardware platform added approximately half way through its lifeline. As with Projects 1 and 3, the additional hardware platform extended the project's lifeline and caused other important data points to deviate even more. The added hardware platform can explain the deviations, but only if the originally planned hardware platforms were completed in a typical matter. Separating the statistics based on hardware platforms could be a worthwhile exercise but is outside the scope of this paper.

Project 6 is the most interesting, as it is the only project that was released on a revolutionary hardware platform. While the release on a revolutionary hardware platform can easily explain the deviations, it is more useful to use the data as indicators of *how well* VLO performed in the project. These indicators can be later used to help VLO perform better whenever it is implementing a revolutionary hardware platform and to bring VLO to the point that it is producing revolutionary hardware platforms on a routine basis.

In particular, when an organization is creating a product with a revolutionarily new hardware platform, the organization must perform adequate research, i.e., RE, prior to committing the revolutionarily new hardware platform to the product. The amount of research that VLO undertook before making the decision to include the revolutionary hardware platform in Project 6 is unknown. However, there is evidence that indicates that the prior research was not enough. There exists no strict criterion allowing a conclusion that enough research was performed. However, the poor outcome of Project 6 indicates that the technology was not thoroughly researched. That being said, there has been

---

[2] In the rest of this paper "deviation" means "deviation from the golden project criteria".

research on prototyping methods that can help to adequately and correctly identify requirements [8–12]. Typically, the point of prototyping is to allow starting early. DeMarco [13] indicates that all late projects have one thing in common: each started late[3].

If a project is late, there is a good chance that the original effort estimates were inaccurate [14–16], which in turn, indicates that its software requirements were not well understood [17].

That doing thorough RE proved to be a factor in the success of a project was not surprising. There are other studies that have observed the same [e.g., 17, 18].

5   Possible Ways to Avoid Deviations

Whenever a project's requirements call for a revolutionary hardware platform, in addition to project's doing adequate research and prototyping, the project should minimize other new aspects of the product requirements. Minimizing other new aspects allows the project to focus on the revolutionary hardware platform and gives the project the best chance of success. Remember, it is very likely that a revolutionary hardware platform will create a number of dependent requirements. While these dependencies cannot be avoided, they create the necessity, and therefore, an additional motivation, to perform effective and efficient requirements analysis and management. According to Blyth et al. [19], the most crucial aspect of software engineering is the gathering of requirements. Much akin to prototyping, there are multiple methods that can be used in order to increase the effectiveness of the requirements specification, such as those proposed by Liou et al. and by Bowles [20, 21]. Finally, if a requirement is considered revolutionary, then perhaps VLO should consider following a slightly different development model, as Molokken-Ostvald et al. suggest [22].

The first author's thesis has a whole chapter devoted to a discussion of possible solutions [2].

6   Answering the Research Questions

The research questions driving the data mining study reported in this paper are:

RQ1:   Do the VLO project data say anything about the success or failure for any product?

RQ2:   Do the VLO project data say anything about the *reasons* for success or failure?

RQ3:   Are there any VLO project data that can serve as predictors of a product project's outcome?

---

[3] Lest the reader think that DeMarco's point is only a tautology, please note that DeMarco's observation is that in the typical late project he has known, the project was started well after the date that it should have been started in order to be able to guarantee finishing by the required deadline, everyone on the project knew that the project was starting late, and all on the project agreed to start the project anyway despite the certainty that the project had no chance to finish on time.

During the data mining, we were able to determine that

RQ1:   the VLO project data do allow us to judge, by the absence or presence of project-and-VLO-specific secondary effects, the success or failure of any product,

RQ2:   the VLO project data do allow deducing some of the reasons for any success or failure, and

RQ3:   the most important VLO project data that can serve as predictors of a product project's outcome are the number and severity of the deviations from the golden project

7   Threats and Limitations

The biggest threats to the validity of the conclusions drawn from the data are the various assumptions and simplifications that were made to be able to conduct the analysis with the data that could be gathered. At each place such an assumption or simplification was made, it was described. On the other hand, since the project data were mined well after the fact, there is no chance (1) that these data could have been biased by a desire to support any particular hypothesis and (2) that the mining and the analysis could have affected the outcomes of the projects. Finally, as with any other case study, the results are about the particular case and cannot be generalized to other situations. However, multiple case studies on similar contexts coming to similar conclusions begins to indicate possible truths. So, we encourage others to do similar data mining studies on other software development projects.

8   Conclusion

Very Large Organization (VLO) clearly has the ability to release successful products. However, not all of the products are deemed by the market to be successful. The authors attempted to discover whether any predictors of success could be revealed through mining the available data from some of VLO's development projects. The data revealed a number interesting points, which can be used in predicting the likelihood of success for future products. In particular, there are clear indications that adequate prior research, prototyping, and RE are necessary to developing a successful product. There is a lot of literature, cited in this paper, that agrees with this finding. The authors have shown also that data mining can be used to reveal the causes of success and of a lack of success of projects in practical environments.

Acknowledgment. Daniel Berry's work was supported in part by a Canadian NSERC grant NSERC-RGPIN227055-15.

References

1. Hassan, A.E.: The road ahead for mining software repositories. In: Frontiers of Software Maintenance (FOSM), pp. 48–57 (2008)
2. Werner, C.M.: A case study of a very large organization. Master's thesis, University of Waterloo, Waterloo (2012)
3. Agrawal, K., Aschauer, M., Thonhofer, T., Bala, S., Rogge-Solti, A., Tomsich, N.: Resource classification from version control system logs. In: IEEE 20th International Enterprise Distributed Object Computing Workshop (EDOCW), pp. 1–10 (2016)
4. Graves, T.L., Karr, A.F., Marron, J.S., Siy, H.: Predicting fault incidence using software change history. IEEE Trans. Software Eng. **26**(7), 653–661 (2000)
5. Engler, D., Chen, D.Y., Hallem, S., Chou, A., Chelf, B.: Bugs as deviant behavior: a general approach to inferring errors in systems code. In: 18th ACM Symposium on Operating Systems Principles (SOSP), pp. 57–72 (2001)
6. Charette, R.N.: Why software fails [software failure]. IEEE Spectr. **42**(9), 42–49 (2005)
7. Ruhe, G., Greer, D.: Quantitative studies in software release planning under risk and resource constraints. In: International Symposium on Empirical Software Engineering (IS-ESE), pp. 262–270 (2003)
8. Hooper, J.W., Hsia, P.: Scenario-based prototyping for requirements identification. SIG-SOFT Softw. Eng. Notes **7**(5), 88–93 (1982)
9. Davis, A.M.: Operational prototyping: a new development approach. IEEE Softw. **9**(5), 70–78 (1992)
10. Li, P.L., Kivett, R., Zhan, Z., Jeon, S.-e., Nagappan, N., Murphy, B., Ko, A.J.: Characterizing the differences between pre- and post- release versions of software. In: 33rd International Conference on Software Engineering (ICSE), pp. 716–725 (2011)
11. Coldrick, S., Lawson, C.P., Ivey, P.C., Lockwood, C.: A decision framework for R&D project selection. In: IEEE International Engineering Management Conference (IEMC), vol. 1, pp. 413–418 (2002)
12. Bowers, J., Pycock, J.: Talking through design: requirements and resistance in cooperative prototyping. In: SIGCHI Conference on Human Factors in Computing Systems (CHI), pp. 299–305 (1994)
13. DeMarco, T.: All late projects are the same. IEEE Softw. **28**(6), 104 (2011)
14. Ferens, D.V.: The conundrum of software estimation models. IEEE Aerosp. Electron. Syst. Mag. **14**(3), 23–29 (1999)
15. Grimstad, S.: Understanding of estimation accuracy in software development projects. In: 11th IEEE International Software Metrics Symposium (METRICS), pp. 2–42 (2005)
16. Moloekken-Oestvold, K., Joergensen, M., Tanilkan, S.S., Gallis, H., Lien, A.C., Hove, S. W.: A survey on software estimation in the norwegian industry. In: International Symposium on Software Metrics, pp. 208–219 (2004)
17. Ellis, K., Berry, D.M.: Quantifying the impact of requirements definition and management process maturity on project outcome in large business application development. Requirements Eng. J. **18**(3), 223–249 (2013)
18. Damian, D., Chisan, J., Vaidyanathasamy, L., Pal, Y.: Requirements engineering and downstream software development: findings from a case study. Empirical Softw. Eng. **10**(3), 255–283 (2005)
19. Blyth, A.J.C., Chudge, J., Dobson, J.E., Strens, M.R.: A framework for modelling evolving requirements. In: 17th Annual International Computer Software and Applications Conference (COMPSAC), pp. 83–89 (1993)

20. Liou, Y.I., Chen, M.: Integrating group support systems, joint application development, and computer-aided software engineering for requirements specification. In: 26th Hawaii International Conference on System Sciences (HICSS), vol. 3, pp. 4–12 (1993)
21. Bowles, J.B.: Better software reliability by getting the requirements right. In: Annual Reliability and Maintainability Symposium (RAMS), pp. 110–115 (2006)
22. Moloekken-Oestvold, K., Joergensen, M.: A comparison of software project overruns — flexible versus sequential development models. IEEE Trans. Software Eng. **31**(9), 754–766 (2005)

Cyber Security

Social Engineering Based Security Requirements Elicitation Model for Advanced Persistent Threats

Seung-Jun Kim[1(✉)] and Seok-Won Lee[2(✉)]

[1] Department of Computer Engineering, Ajou University, Suwon, Korea
dregonc@ajou.ac.kr
[2] Department of Software and Computer Engineering,
Ajou University, Suwon, Korea
leesw@ajou.ac.kr

Abstract. APT attacks are increasing every year, and these APT attacks begin with social engineering attacks. In order to be effective in blocking APT attacks, blocking social engineering attacks make it possible to prevent APT attacks in advance. In this study, we define human factors which greatly influence social engineering attacks, and make it possible to obtain appropriate security requirements by modeling the relationships among human vulnerability, social engineering attacks and security requirements.

Keywords: Social engineering attack · Advanced Persistent Threat
Security requirement · Human factor · Ontology

1 Introduction

Cyber security threats on socio-technical systems are increasing every year. Hence, governments and enterprises are putting much effort and money into fighting against cyber security threats. However, many vulnerable points in security are being discovered and because security threats are becoming more intelligent as well as advanced it is becoming harder to be effective in fighting against cyber security threats. Among the many cyber threats, APT (Advanced Persistent Threat), in particular, is one of the threats that are becoming a bigger issue. NIST defined APT as follows. "An adversary that possesses sophisticated levels of expertise and significant resources which allow it to create opportunities to achieve its objectives by using multiple attack vectors. [12]" According to a survey carried out by ARBOR Co., APT threats on EGE (Enterprise, Government and Education) have increased from 5% in the year 2015 to 28% in the year 2016 and has ranked 5th among the top most threats [1]. However, as seen in Table 1, APT is listed as EGE's number one concern as a cyber-threat. While it is not one of the most threats used, the reason why there is much interest and concern about it is because along with the increase in the frequency of occurrences of APTs the cost for damage repair has grown to be astronomically greater than the other threats.

According to a survey conducted in the year 2012 by Ponemon Institute, the cost for repairing the damages caused by APT attacks exceeded 5.5 million dollars per attack [2].

© Springer Nature Singapore Pte Ltd. 2018
M. Kamalrudin et al. (Eds.): APRES 2017, CCIS 809, pp. 29–40, 2018.
https://doi.org/10.1007/978-981-10-7796-8_3

Table 1. Rank of EGE concerns [1]

EGE Concerns	
1. Advanced persistent threat (APT) on corporate network	61%
2. Internet connectivity congestion due to DDoS Attack	51%
3. Malicious insider	47%
4. Accidental data loss	43%

However, because APT occurs in secret for a long period of time, the subject that is under attack by APT will not realize that it is being attacked, and when the victim notices the attack, by that time there is an already a massive amount of damage that has been done. Therefore, while extensive research is being carried out to effectively block APT, most of the research is being carried out on tracking down and analyzing logs which are seemingly under an APT attack [13–15]. However, considering the fact that, human factors contribute to 95% of the total security accidents [4], and that in an APT lifecycle, APT attacks begin with social engineering attacks, if social engineering attacks which contain many human factors are blocked in its early stages, APT attacks can be effectively prevented. However, the definition of human factors is not clear, and the correlation between human factors and social engineering attacks is unclear.

To deal with this, research is needed in order to find human factors and analyze social engineering attacks related to these human factors so that we can deduct the appropriate security requirements that will help reduce threats of social engineering attacks. In this study, first we analyze the various human factors and define the human factors that are related to social engineering attacks. Second, we predict what the vulnerable social engineering attacks are through human factors and attack vectors, and propose an ontological model to deduct the security requirements that will decrease social engineering attacks.

This study is composed of the following sections. In Sect. 2, we explain the background of this research and in Sect. 3, we define human factors and propose a model to be used to deduct the security requirements. Next, in Sect. 4, we carry out a case study to verify this through a scenario and in Sect. 5 we conclude this study.

2 Background

In this section, we briefly discuss the background and related works. Firstly, we explain the Advanced Persistent Threat. Secondly, we present Social Engineering Attack and Social engineering ontology. And finally, we explain the Human factor.

2.1 Advanced Persistent Threat

Advanced Persistent Threat (APT) is not a hacking skill or technique. It is a set of computer hacking processes or attack type. APT is the evolution of the Target Attack in the past. Therefore APT aims at particular data or damage of the target more specifically than a specific target. It is occurs very steadily and is continuous. The characteristics of the APT are described below according to the alphabet.

Advanced. 'Advanced' can be interpreted as the technical range or technical grade used in the organization that carries out an APT. Whereas in the past, security threats were limited to a virus, worm or malware, APT uses a broad range of techniques to carry out its specific purpose. For example, in order to understand a company's internal security system, it uses a social engineering technique to attract the person in charge of the company's security and analyzes the Microsoft's Windows operating system to detect the Zero-day vulnerable point to abuse it. In this way, APT is a threat which gathers a wide range of various techniques to carry out its specific purpose.

Persistent. Persistent can be seen as the attitude of the organization while it deals with the object of attack. APT continues to attack the object using various types of new techniques until it achieves its purpose. For example, an attacker attacks the target object continuously through the Command & Control Server (C & C).

Threat. This is a cause or action that brings loss to assets, and anything that damages security is defined as a threat. This threat can be in the form of IT or can be a social engineering attack carried out by a person.

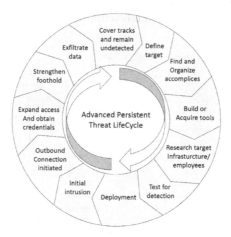

Fig. 1. Advanced Persistent Threat Lifecycle (https://www.secureworks.com/blog/advanced-persistent-threats-apt-a)

Figure 1 displays the lifecycle of an APT. While not all APT attacks follow this lifecycle, they generally maintain a similar cycle, and the onset of a full-scale APT attack begins with the success of the social engineering attack in the early stages. Therefore, if the social engineering attack is blocked, the APT can be effectively prevented in the early stages of the APT. However, most existing studies or solutions consist of analyzing internet packets that are suspected to be APTs [13–15], or propose solutions using integrated security by combining various security technology such as antivirus programs, firewalls, IPS (Intrusion Prevention System) and etc[1].

---

[1] http://global.ahnlab.com/site/product/productSubDetail.do?prodSeq=15231.

2.2   Social Engineering Attack and Ontological Model

Social engineering attack is a non-technical attack, which is carried out by breaking the normal security process by using the trust relationship between people in order to deceive the subject. In this kind of social engineering attack it is hard for the victim to become aware of the attack and therefore, it is harder to prevent. Also, because of its non-technical nature a variety of definitions exist and it is difficult to make a quantitative measurement of the attack. Therefore, many have conducted research in order to define social engineering attacks. [5] Harley, [6] Laribe, [7] Tetri and Vuorinen have tried to define social engineering attacks by studying the taxonomy of social engineering attacks. However, taxonomy was not enough to define the meaning of social engineering attack. Further studies have combined these studies and [8] Francois et al. have defined social engineering attacks using ontological models. By expressing social engineering attacks using an ontological model, (1) it has become possible to establish the relationship between the taxonomy classes which was not sufficiently complete when taxonomy was used to define social engineering and social engineering attacks and (2) it has laid a foundation for ontology of social engineering attacks. Figure 2 is a social engineering attack ontological model by Francois M. et al. In this model, attack vectors are defined and represent each relationship.

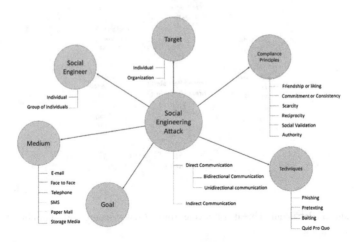

Fig. 2.   An Ontological Model of a Social Engineering Attack [3]

2.3   Human Factor

There is a great amount of security software including firewalls, intrusion detections systems, antivirus solutions and etc. However, these are designed only to carry out specific functions and only help protect the system, and there is no guarantee that the system's security is 100% safe[2]. When these software types are designed and developed human mistakes are included in it and because the main users of the system are

---

[2] https://securelist.com/the-human-factor-and-information-security/36067/.

people, we can say that human factors are part of the system we use. Also, human factors are related to more than 95% of the security accidents, and it is seen as a very vulnerable factor. Therefore, human factors are factors that must be dealt with in security. However, there is no clear definition on what human factor means and its constituents are not yet defined. Also, there is lack of research on what kind of human factors create what type of vulnerable points in security. The term, 'human factor', is also used interchangeably with the terms 'human elements' or 'human vulnerability.'

Among studies attempting to find human factors that affect security, A. J. Widdowson and P. B. Goodliff et al., defined the human factor and proposed the CHEAT (Cyber Human Error Assessment Tool) model [4]. CHEAT has five high-level categories; People, History, Technology, Environment, and Organization. And categories have total fifty seven human factor indicators.

3 Proposed Idea

In this chapter, we define the various human factors which are vulnerable within cyber security, and propose an ontological model which demonstrate the relationships among social engineering attacks, security requirements and the vulnerable areas that are brought about through human factors.

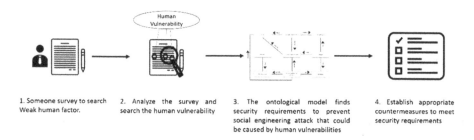

1. Someone survey to search Weak human factor.

2. Analyze the survey and search the human vulnerability

3. The ontological model finds security requirements to prevent social engineering attack that could be caused by human vulnerabilities

4. Establish appropriate countermeasures to meet security requirements

Fig. 3. Proposed Concept

Figure 3 shows the overall concept that is proposed. (1) The subject fills out a survey which measures human factors. (2) The security specialist analyzes the survey to analyze which human factor is vulnerable and detects human vulnerability. (3) It is detected using the ontological model which suggests the relationships among human vulnerability, social engineering and security requirements. (4) Establish appropriate countermeasures to meet security requirements.

3.1 Defining Human Factor and Elements

First of all, we do not use the terms 'human factor' and 'human vulnerability' interchangeably, but define it as two individual categories. Human factor is defined as all factors that all humans possess which have not yet been detected and analyzed. Human vulnerabilities are human factors which have been considered vulnerable through analysis.

Human factors can include an individual's character or habit as well as the culture of an enterprise or its security policy and technology that is used [4]. As seen in Table 2, our study defined human factors related to social engineering attacks using 'Resources Required' and 'Example, attacker skills or knowledge required' which is stated in CAPEC (Common Attack Pattern Enumeration and Classification). We can see that Jone lacks in carelessness through the fact that he opened the link included in the e-mail without questioning it (Table 3).

Table 2. CAPEC 163: spear phishing

Examples
John gets an official looking **e-mail** from his bank stating that his or her account has been temporarily locked due to suspected unauthorized activity that happened in the area different that where he lives (details might be provided by the spear phishers) and that **John needs to click on the link included in the e-mail to log in to his bank account in order to unlock it.** The link in the e-mail looks very similar to that of his bank and once the link is clicked, the log in page is the exact replica. John supplies his login credentials after which he is notified that his account has now been unlocked and that everything is fine. An adversary has just collected John's online banking information which can now be used by him or her to log into John's bank account and transfer John's money to a bank account of the adversary's choice
Attacker Skills or Knowledge Required
Spear phishing attacks require specific knowledge of the victims being targeted, such as which bank is being used by the victims, or websites they commonly log into (Google, Facebook, etc.)
Resources Required
An adversary must have the ability communicate their phishing scheme to the victims (**via email, instance message, etc**.), as well as a website or other platform for victims to enter personal information into

People. This is considered the most important factor among human factors. Each factor exhibits the person's character and tendency which can affect security. For example, a highly curious person is vulnerable to attacks that stimulate curiosity. The possibility of a person with much curiosity opening a letter or e-mail from an uncertain addressee is very high. Each factor is not independent of each other but in relation to other factors. A person who has many feelings towards others and low morality will have a higher possibility to disclose a secret to another person who is an acquaintance. Also, it is possible to combine factors from different classes, and in this case, curiosity and the e-mail, which acts as the medium, are examples of that. A highly curious person, compared to someone who is not, is more likely to open an e-mail without questioning it even if there is uncertainty of who the sender is.

Organization. The amount of interest the organization has on security as well as how much the organization invests in security highly affects the overall security standard of the organization. The organization's systematic security policy will control the people element from being exposed to danger. For example, having a policy which says "all unregistered devices must not be connected to the company's internal devices" will lower the security problems that could occur due to people's laziness. Also, if the

Table 3. Human Factor

Class	Element
People	Negligence
	Carelessness
	Curiosity
	Morality
	Vacillation
	Feeling
	Laziness
Organization	Security manager
	Secret management
	Access control
	Security education
Medium	E-mail
	Face to Face
	Social Media
	SMS
	Paper mail
	Storage media
	Web-page

supervisor's authority infringes upon the security manager's authority, the possibility of vulnerability in security increases. Therefore, organization factors are very important in terms of security management and are in need of continuous attention.

Medium. Medium, which include letters, e-mail, telephones calls or face-to-face meetings and etc., is the method or device that is used for work or communication in a normal daily life. However, it can be used as a channel when attacking human factors as the vulnerable points in the medium's security can be targeted for an attack or the medium itself can be used as an instrument to attack people's vulnerable areas.

3.2 Security Requirement for Social Engineering Related Human Factor

Bongjae Kim's research [9] has investigated various security requirement modeling techniques to obtain security requirements and out of that, using [10] the Common Criteria General Model and [11] the Problem Domain Ontology of Lee et al., we defined the relationship between the attack vectors including vulnerability and security requirements through the ontological model. Building on this foundation, we used the attack vectors of the social engineering attack ontological model defined in [3] Mouton et al., to define the relationship between human vulnerability and social engineering attack vectors through the ontological model.

Table 4 displays the social engineering attack vectors. For social engineering attack vectors, we referred to part of the attack vector defined in the social engineering attack ontological model according to Mouton et al. [3]. Figure 4 shows the relationships

Table 4. Social engineering attack vector

Attack vector	Description	Type
Goal	That which is to be obtained through the attack	Financial Gain
		Unauthorised Access
		Service Disruption
Target	The subject under attack	Individual Organization
Attacker	The subject that carries out the attack	Individual
		Group of Individuals
Medium	The medium used to carry out the attack	E-mail
		Face to Face
		Telephone
		SMS
		Paper Mail
		Storage Media
		Webpage
		Pamphlets
		Social media

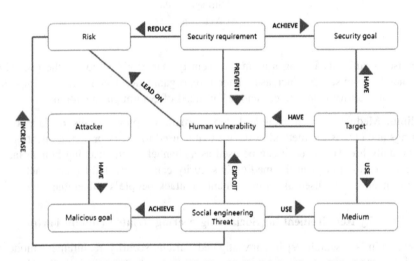

Fig. 4. Social Engineering with Human Factor Ontological Model

among human factors, attack vectors and security requirements using an ontological model. The target has a security goal and in order to obtain the security goal it needs an appropriate security requirement. The counteragent of a security goal is a malicious goal and this is what a social engineering threat aims to achieve. Human vulnerability is the factor that must be protected by social requirement as well as the factor which is threatened by social engineering threats. Social engineering attack mechanisms are extrapolated and identified by ontology through the relationship between the attack vectors. Hence, human vulnerability and counter-measures of social engineering attack techniques are taken into consideration when searching for the appropriate security requirements. Here the social engineering attack mechanisms and security requirements are extrapolated and the CAPEC (Common Attack Pattern Enumeration and Classification) is used to detect it.

4   Case Study

To represent the applicability of the proposed approach, a case study using scenario was conducted. The following is a real life case scenario of a successful social engineering attack where a Korean company lost 21 million dollars. Based on this case scenario, we analyzed the human factor in advance and identified the human vulnerability and verified whether the appropriate security requirements and security policies can be applied.

Scenario[3] An employees of A company received an e-mail from B company which was a subsidiary company of the company that it was trading with. The e-mail address was spelt different from before where one of the letters had been changed from 'q' to 'p'. The e-mail noted that the account number for receiving the payment of the traded goods had been changed. The corresponding employee phoned the number written on the email instead of the number that he/she always called and after sending and receiving documents to verify the change that was made, without much doubt the employee transferred the money to the new account number.

Apply the proposed Approach. In the past, this employee had been caught using an USB storage that was not authorized. Also, by using his personal e-mail account and company e-mail account interchangeably, he did not use the company's e-mail system. Through this we see that he has a high amount of negligence and carelessness. Also, in this scenario, the employee has not verified the sender and therefore, opened an e-mail that should not have been opened. If there was a malignant code in the email, there was a high possibility of this resulting in an APT attack. In order to comply with the company's regulation on carrying out a double check when the payment account details change, the employee called the phone number on the e-mail, but this was not the correct number. Also, there was no regulation stating that his/her supervisor needed to verify any changes made to the payment account details. Table 5 analyzes the scenario to analyze the attack vectors. It was unclear who the attacker was in the scenario. The target was the accountant in the company. The attacker had set two malignant goals to obtain financial benefits from the target. The first goal was that the target would check his email and at the same time not question the contents of the e-mail. For this goal, the attacker collected many e-mails in advance, and investigated the layout and wording and etc., in the e-mail to lower suspicion. Secondly, in order to make the target believe

---

[3] http://biz.chosun.com/site/data/html_dir/2016/04/29/2016042900679.html?Dep0=twitter.

Table 5. Attack Vector Related Case Study

Attack vector	Element
Attacker	Unknown
Target	Accountant employee
Malicious goal	1. Open the e-mail without doubt 2. Call the Attacker
Medium	E-mail, Telephone
Vulnerability	1. Curiosity 2. Negligence 3. Carelessness 4. Security policy: Divide the E-mail account between private and work It must be confirmed by an advanced person, when a payment account is changed

the e-mail contents, the attacker carried out a telephone conversation to make the target believe the e-mail contents. The mediums used were e-mail and telephone.

Using the ontological model, we found that social engineering attacks most vulnerable due to human vulnerability and attack vectors were most likely to be 'spear phishing' or 'baiting'. We searched for security requirements that will block the following social engineering attacks, and the counter-measures or security policies that will satisfy these requirements. Table 6 lists the security requirements and countermeasures analyzed based on employee A's human factor and attack vector.

The analyzed security requirements correspond to the vulnerabilities as seen in Fig. 5, and through that we can see that these reduce vulnerabilities.

Table 6. Security requirement and countermeasure in scenario

Security requirement	Countermeasure or security policy
• If the source is unclear, access should not be allowed	• Manage the list of authorized email sender
• It should not be randomly accessed place (outdoor or website) where unauthorized or unclear	• Unknown external link must be accessed after being investigated. These investigations can be delegated, e.g., to the IT security team
• Data or information (including document or e-mail) to be delivered can only be received by an interested and authorized people	• Manage the list of people of project • Use the organization's mail system
• Data or information should not be modified without approval	• Changes to important content should be subject to a second approval

Vulnerabilities of scenario   Security Requirement

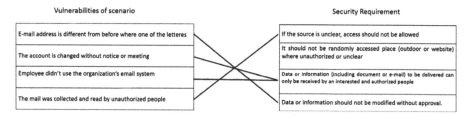

Fig. 5. Relationships between the Vulnerabilities and the elicited Security Requirements

5   Conclusion

APT attacks are increasing each year, and as much as social engineering attacks are used in the early stages of APTs, social engineering attacks need to be blocked in advance in order for APT attacks to be prevented. Social engineering attacks are highly influenced by human factors, and therefore, if we administer the appropriate security requirements by analyzing the vulnerable points of human factors we can effectively block social engineering attacks. In this study, we defined human factors that are in connection with social engineering attacks and modeled the relationships among human vulnerability, social engineering and security requirements. Through this, we can identify human vulnerability and determine and administer the appropriate security requirements before social engineering attacks are carried out so that APT attacks can be blocked. This research makes the following contributions. Despite the increasing sophistication and complexity of cyber-attack techniques, the countermeasures were focused on the technical side. But human are the most vulnerable part of security and are vulnerable to social engineering attack. Through this research, we could confirm the relationship and influence between social engineering and security, and showed the danger of social engineering.

However, all the various types of human factors were not dealt with in this study, and an index to detect and measure human factors quantitatively was not provided. Also, the fact that social engineering attacks are technical along with the fact that physical vulnerabilities are also related to it was not taken into consideration. Further research is required to define the various human factors along with criteria that can be used to measure the factors. And we also seek to develop an application that will automate this.

Acknowledgement. This research was supported by Basic Science Research Program through the National Research Foundation of Korea (NRF) funded by the Ministry of Education (NRF-2017R1D1A1B03034279).

This research was supported by the MIST(Ministry of Science and ICT), Korea, under the National Program for Excellence in SW supervised by the IITP (Institute for Information & communications Technology Promotion) (20150009080031001).

References

1. Darren, A., Paul, B., Chui, C.F., Gary S.: WorldWide infrastructure security report, Arbor networks special report vol. XII (2017)
2. Ponemon Institute: 2011 Cost of Data Breach Study, US (2012)
3. Mouton, F., Leenen, L., Malan, M.M., Venter, H.S.: Towards an ontological model defining the social engineering domain. In: Kimppa, K., Whitehouse, D., Kuusela, T., Phahlamohlaka, J. (eds.) HCC 2014. IAICT, vol. 431, pp. 266–279. Springer, Heidelberg (2014). https://doi.org/10.1007/978-3-662-44208-1_22
4. Widdowson, A.J., Goodliff, P.B.: CHEAT, an approach to incorporating human factors in cyber security assessments. In: System Safety and Cyber-Security Conference (2015)
5. Harley, D.: Re-floating the titanic: Dealing with social engineering attacks. In: European Institute for Computer Antivirus Research (1998)
6. Laribee, L.: Development of methodical social engineering taxonomy project. Msc, Naval Postgraduate School, Monterey, California, June 2006
7. Tetri, P., Vuorinen, J.: Dissecting social engineering. Behav. Inform. Technol. **32**(10), 1014–1023 (2013)
8. Mouton, F., Leenen, L., Malan, M.M., Venter, H.S.: Towards an ontological model defining the social engineering domain. In: 11th Human Choice and Computers International Conference, Turku, Finland, July 2014, pp. 266–279 (2014)
9. Kim, B.J., Lee, S.W.: Analytical study of cognitive layered approach for understanding security requirements using problem domain ontology. In: 23rd Asia-Pacific Software Engineering Conference (APSEC), pp. 1530–1362 (2016)
10. Common Criteria, Part 1: Introduction and general model in Common Criteria for Information Technology Security Evaluation, Common Criteria, pp. 38–44 (2012)
11. Lee, S.-W., Gandhi, R., Muthuranjan, D., Yavagal, D., Gail-Joon, A.: Building problem domain ontology from security requirements in regulatory documents. In: Workshop on Software Engineering for Secure Systems, New York (2006)
12. NIST: Managing Information Security Risk: Organisation, Mission, and Information System View. National Institute of Standards and Technology, March 2011
13. Beth, E.B., McRee, R., O'Connor, T.J.: Assessing outbound Traffic to Uncover Advanced Persistent Threat. SANS Technology Institute (2011)
14. Marchetti, M., et al.: Analysis of high volumes of network traffic for Advanced Persistent Threat detection. Comput. Netw. **109**, 127–141 (2016)
15. Niu, W., et al.: Identifying APT Malware Domain Based on Mobile DNS Logging. In: Mathematical Problems in Engineering, vol. 2017 (2017)

Eliciting Requirements for Improving Users' Behavior Using Transparency

Haruhiko Kaiya[1(✉)], Nobukazu Yoshioka[2], Hironori Washizaki[3],
Takao Okubo[4], Atsuo Hazeyama[5], Shinpei Ogata[6],
and Takafumi Tanaka[7]

[1] Faculty of Science, Kanagawa University, Hiratsuka 259-1293, Japan
kaiya@kanagawa-u.ac.jp
[2] National Institue of Informatics (NII), Tokyo 101-8430, Japan
[3] Waseda University, Tokyo 169-8555, Japan
[4] Institute of Information Security (IISEC), Yokohama 221-0835, Japan
[5] Tokyo Gakugei University, Tokyo 184-8501, Japan
[6] Shinshu University, Nagano 380-0928, Japan
[7] Tokyo University of Agriculture and Technology, Tokyo 183-0057, Japan

Abstract. A software system is developed for satisfying requirements of
stakeholders. Each requirement will be never satisfied without the collaboration
of several components such as the system, devices and people interacting with
them, i.e. users. However, a user does not or cannot always behave toward the
other components according to their expectations. For example, a user sometimes makes mistake or even misuse of the system. The system thus has to
encourage users to behave according to such expectations as well as possible. In
this paper, we propose a method for eliciting software requirements that will
improve users' behavior with respect to the expectations. We rely on transparency, i.e. the open flow of information amongst stakeholders because no one
can directly manipulate users but transparency has an influence on users'
behavior. We expect users will voluntarily behave better than ever when the
system provides suitable information flows. We represent our method by using
KAOS goal modeling notation, and show examples how it works.

Keywords: Requirements elicitation · Transparency · Quality requirements
Goal model · KAOS · Expectation violation

1 Introduction

Almost all systems today are operated under the collaboration of many components
such as the software system, hardware devices including sensors and actuators, external
systems, human and so on. Because the components except human are artifacts, such
artificial components can be carefully developed or chosen. For the human components, developers have the assumption or expectation that he/she will behave properly
during the system operation. The requirements specification for a system contains such
expectation, and all stakeholders believe or pray the expectation is met. However, no
one can completely guarantee that human meets such expectation because no one has

© Springer Nature Singapore Pte Ltd. 2018
M. Kamalrudin et al. (Eds.): APRES 2017, CCIS 809, pp. 41–56, 2018.
https://doi.org/10.1007/978-981-10-7796-8_4

means to directly control human activities. Therefore, we thus have to improve the functionalities of artificial components in the system so that human can meet the expectation as much as possible.

In this paper, we propose and exemplify a method for eliciting software requirements corresponding to such functionalities. To control human components indirectly, we focus on a concept *transparency*, i.e. "the open flow of information" [8] because transparency has an influence on the human behavior. When the suitable information is provided to a user, the user can behave more properly than ever. For example at a self-checkout in a supermarket, the frequency of shoplifting will decrease when the self-checkout system always supervises users and the system lets users know its activities. For the online booking system of the hotel rooms, the system never always stir us up such as "a few rooms only remain!" when we know the actual vacancy via some reliable source and the system knows such our behavior.

We use KAOS goal modeling notation in this research because the expectation assigned to users is clearly represented in KAOS. We use the processes of self-adapting systems such as monitoring, detecting, deciding and acting for constructing goals that make users behave more properly than ever. Note that the breakdown of hardware components is out of scope in this paper.

The rest of this paper is organized as follows. In the next section, we briefly review related works to clarify the differences between them and our work. In the section, we also explain KAOS goal modeling notation because we use the notation in this research. Section 3 explains the method for eliciting requirements for avoiding or mitigating expectation violation. We first categorize the reasons why a user violates expectations to him/her. We then present the steps to construct goal models to avoid such violation. In Sect. 4, we show illustrative examples where our method is applied so as to show the method works. Finally, we summarize our current results and show our future issues.

2 Related Work

2.1 Quality Requirements and Human Error Understanding

In an article [1], functional and quality requirements are explained very simply as follows: "Functional requirements specify what a system does, quality requirements describe how well those functions are accomplished." We have already have several standards such as ISO 9126 and ISO 25010 and catalogs of quality requirements such as NFR framework [4] or FURPS [7]. Quality characteristics such as security and usability are usually used as goals or soft-goals of a system in many goal-oriented modeling languages. According to the simple definition in the article [1], using quality characteristics as goals is very natural because goals here are not those of stakeholders but those of the system. However, we have to deeply understand the goal of stakeholders especially users when we focus on why expectations assigned to users are violated. In the context of problem frames [13], we think quality characteristics are just solutions for resolving the problems of people. Analyzing expectation violation requires concepts in problems beyond the concept of solutions such as security or usability.

Understanding human errors enables us to understand why expectations to users are violated. In a book [5], human error is regarded as a symptom of a problem in a system instead of a cause of system failure. According to the book, human performance can go wrong due to some causes such as cognitive fixation, stress, fatigue and buggy or inert knowledge. We may focus on such causes to avoid or mitigate expectation violation.

2.2 Transparency

Transparency is defined as "the open flow of information" [8]. The receivers of the information use their decision making [12]. We believe suitable information will improve such decision making. In this sense, we may use a term "feedback information" instead of transparency. If a system gives more transparency than ever to its users, there are three possibilities. First, users can understand the behavior of the system better than ever, and they can behave to the system more proper than ever. Second, users can understand the behavior better than ever, and they can make a misuse of the system on the basis of their malicious and selfish intention. Third, users cannot process too vast information, and they are confused and make a mistake. Because the demand for transparency has been increasing [16], we have to encourage the first possibility above during system development. We also have to avoid or to mitigate other possibilities as much as possible.

In requirements engineering field, we found several researches related to transparency. In an article [6], transparency is regarded as one of non-functionalities, and it is embedded in NFR framework. Relationships between transparency and other non-functionalities are clarified in the extended NFR framework. Hosseini et al. clarified the concept of transparency from the viewpoint of four facets: stakeholders, usefulness, information, quality, and meaningfulness [10, 12]. Transparency can be modelled as information flows and transformations [9]. Furthermore, a modelling language for transparency requirements has been proposed [11]. Although the reference model [12] contains a concept "intention", the reasons why users need transparency are not clearly modeled. In the same way of other quality characteristics mentioned in Sect. 2.1, most researches focus on the solution side.

2.3 Use Cases for Security, Hazard Analysis and Embedded System Analysis

Using use case models are used for analyzing security requirements. In abuse cases [17], misuse cases [23], attack functions of malicious users (attackers) are suspected and analyzed. Countermeasures are then added against such attacks. In MASG [19], assets and security goals such as confidentiality, integrity and availability are combined to misuse cases. Analysts can find attacks and countermeasures easier than ever with the help of such additional elements. However, it is not easy to introduce suitable assets without the intention why attackers want to attack. Such intention is out of scope in MASG. In addition, these techniques do not focus on other types of expectation violation caused by usability or efficiency because they are specialized for security analysis.

Hazard and Operability (HAZOP) [2] and Failure Mode and Effect Analysis (FMEA) [20] are typical techniques for safety risk analysis, and they are already used in software requirements analysis. In HAZOP, guidewords such as "no" and "larger" help analysts to find potential deviations in a system. FMEA helps analysts to identify and eliminate system deviations using a matrix of causes and effects. Because these techniques basically focus on mechanical components, such components have no intention. The techniques are thus not suitable for analyzing expectations assigned to human.

In embedded system area, researches about unexpected phenomena and obstacle analysis have been studied a lot. For example, an analysis method using information flow diagram (IFD) was proposed [14]. In the method, processes, devices in an embedded system and information flows among them are modeled. Because causal relationships about each failure can be traced in the model, non-expert engineers can systematically analyze obstacles in the system. A method called Embedded Systems Improvement Method (ESIM) was also proposed [18]. In ESIM, unexpected phenomena are found by using guide words, and device failures are extracted using the phenomena. In addition, a matrix between states and events are used for analyzing unexpected phenomena comprehensively. These two methods were combined together [15, 22].

Researches above mainly focus on comprehensiveness of finding problems because only one missing obstacle can destroy the whole system. However, they do not focus on the intention of the causes because they mainly assume the causes are system components or hardware components. In this research, we focus on the expectations that are assigned to human agents.

2.4 KAOS and Its Obstacle Analysis

KAOS [25] is one of famous goal modeling languages although it contains other types of models such as an object model, an operational model and so on. Because we only use a goal model in KAOS, we briefly explain the goal model. In a KAOS goal model, goals are simply decomposed into sub-goals hierarchically. Both and-type and or-type decompositions are used in KAOS. When a decomposed goal can be achieved by only one agent, we may stop decomposing the goal. An agent has the responsibility to achieve several goals and there are following two types of agents in KAOS.

- Environmental agent: Examples of this agent are human, mechanical machines, hardware devices or other computer systems.
- Software agent: The software system to be developed consists of software agents. Therefore, goals assigned to software agents are just requirements for the system to be developed.

Each leaf goal in a goal model is distinguished and named according to the assigned agents as follows.

- Requirement: A goal achieved by a software agent is called a requirement. A requirement is almost the same as a specification in problem frames [13].
- Expectation: A goal achieved by an environmental agent is called an expectation. Because environmental agents are not fully controlled, we just expect the goal will be achieved.

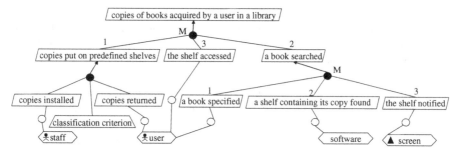

Fig. 1. An example of KAOS goal model: finding a copy of a book in a library

- Domain property: A goal which is naturally achieved under the given environment is called a domain property. Its examples are laws, regulations, customs and physical and natural laws. In this case, no agent is specified.

Although KAOS goal model contains other model elements such as conflict marking, we do not use them. There are two typical goal decomposition patterns in KAOS as follows.

- Milestone driven decomposition: When a goal is decomposed into several sub-goals and a sub-goal requires a condition satisfied by another sub-goal, a dependency exists between these two sub-goals. This type of decomposition is called milestone driven decomposition. In many cases, sub-goals in milestone driven decomposition correspond to subroutines or sub-steps of a decomposed goal.
- Case driven decomposition: A goal can be refined differently when cases are different with each other. Case driven decomposition naturally represents this kind of refinement.

For the sake of our method, we extend KAOS to the following two points.

- An environmental agent who is human and another environmental agent are distinguished explicitly. We are interested in how to encourage human agents such as users to behave property, but breakdown of machines is out of scope of our method. We thus introduce an icon which is used for the distinction above.
- In a milestone driven decomposition, the sequence numbers are explicitly given to the sub-goals. Such numbers may be duplicated if no-conditional dependency between several goals exists. We want to know a goal can be achieved without any conditions or not. This is the reason why we apply this extension.

Figure 1 shows an example of an extended KAOS goal model. In this model, we focus on a supporting system for a user to find a copy of books in an open-access library. In the library, users can freely pick up and return copies of books from/to shelves. The top goal of the model is "copies of books acquired by a user in a library", which is represented in a parallelogram. We decomposed the top goal into three sub-goals as shown in the figure. First, the copies should be installed in shelves.

Second, the user try to identify a shelf where a copy of a book he/she wants to read located. The search function is used here. Finally, the user goes to the front of the shelf, and get the copy. Because the first decomposition is the typical milestone driven decomposition, labels such as "M", "1", "2" and "3" are attached according to our extension. In this model, six leaf goals exists, and only one of them is achieved by an agent "software". Other goals are achieved by environmental agents, or become domain properties. Domain property is represented in a trapezoid, and one of its instance exists in this model. An agent is represented in hexagon. When an agent is human, a stickman-icon is put to the agent according to our extension. When an environmental agent is not human, black triangle icon is also put to the agent.

As shown in the example in Fig. 1, we can identify the amount of responsibility of human agents is large when a goal is achieved. By using KAOS, the degree of human responsibility can be easily grasped as shown in this example. Another famous goal oriented notation is i* [27], and almost the same contents can be represented in i*. However, we cannot easily grasp such a degree by using i* because i* contains other viewpoints such as dependencies between agents, negative and positive contribution relationships among goal and other types of intentions.

KAOS has its own obstacle analysis method [26]. In this method, an obstacle of a goal g is systematically generated as its negation, i.e. $\neg g$. Countermeasures are then added to a goal model so that the obstacle is not satisfied. Although the idea is systematic, human intention is not focused. Therefore, it is not suitable for analyzing obstacles of expectations.

3 Method for Avoiding or Mitigating Expectation Violation

We focus on each expectation, and assume the expectation is violated on the basis of some intention of some users. We predefined the reasons of such violation, and expand a goal corresponding to the expectation according to each reason. We first explain the types of such reasons, and then show steps to expand the goal.

3.1 Reasons of Violating Expectations

When an expectation is assigned to a user, following two cases can be considered.

- proper achievement: an expectation is fulfilled properly.
- improper achievement: an expectation is not fulfilled due to some intention of some users, i.e. the violation of the expectation. A user assigned to the expectation is usually the person who violates the expectation. In addition, the other users set some traps in the system, and an expectation is violated.

We have to explore the reason(s) for the latter case to avoid or mitigate such violation.

We assume following types of user's intention will raise up expectation violation above. Each type enables us to find different ways of countermeasures to each type.

We thus call such types *violation reasons* or reasons of violating expectations. For each reason, typical patterns of a goal structure can be defined as countermeasures in advance.

We also explain such pattern together.

- **malicious:** When a user has malicious intention, he/she is an attacker. An attacker normally does not achieve expectations assigned to him/her. We call such situation *malicious violation*. Security functions can mitigate such violation. Especially with respect to transparency, some surveillance functions are effective. In addition, warning functions which makes attackers know they are surveilled are also effective.
- **unskilled:** Because a user is unskilled, an expectation does not sometimes achieved. We call such situation *unskilled violation*. Some usability functions usually can mitigate such violation. Before applying such usability functions, the system should identify whether the user really unskilled or not. Transparency from a user to the system is important.
- **careless:** Even if a user is skillful, he/she is sometimes careless to violate expectations. We call such situation *careless violation*. Some usability functions can also mitigate or avoid such violation.
- **hotheaded:** When a user hurries and becomes hotheaded, he/she cannot achieve expectations to him/her. We call such situation *hotheaded violation*. Because countermeasures to unskilled or careless violation sometimes promote such hothead, the system has to carefully observe the behavior of the user for providing suitable countermeasures. Functions related to time efficiency usually contribute to mitigate hotheaded violation. For example, macros or commands like UNIX shells satisfy hotheaded users because they are normally efficient.
- **cheated:** A user him/herself causes violation types above, and expectations to him/her are not fulfilled. However, another user of a system makes mistakes or misuses, and the user happens to violate expectations to him/her after all. For example, CSRF (Cross Site Request Forgery) is a typical case because an attacker sets some trap in advance and the trap catches some proper user. We also focus on this type of violation, and called *cheated violation*. To mitigate or avoid this violation, a user has to know whether a trap is set or not. Using independent, external and reliable systems together is one of the ways to do so.

3.2 Steps

According to the following steps, expectation violation is mitigated or avoided. An input of these steps is a KAOS goal model. Basically, a requirement analyst performs the steps.

1. Describe or acquire a KAOS goal model.
2. For each expectation, assume it is not fulfilled. We thus expand an expectation on the basis of violation types above as shown in Fig. 2. As shown in the right hand side of the figure, an expectation is at most decomposed into five sub-goals corresponding to violation types and one sub-goal labeled "proper" where the

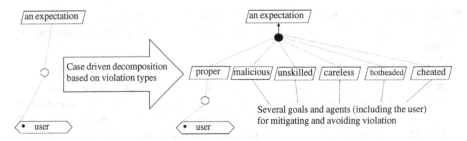

Fig. 2. Expanding each expectation based on violation types

expectation is properly fulfilled. If we do not have to take some violation types into account, sub-goals corresponding to the types may be omitted.

3. For each sub-goal expect proper one, it is also decomposed into countermeasures for avoiding or mitigating its violation type. In self-adaptive systems [21], processes such as monitoring, detecting, deciding and acting play important roles. The idea of self-adaptive systems has been used in software engineering field [3]. On the basis of idea of self-adaptive systems, we introduce the following goals as countermeasures.

 – A user shows some symptoms of deviation from its expectation.
 – Some devices identify such symptoms.
 – The system decides some information flows that can let the user know the deviation.
 – The system also decides other users or organizations who can be deterrents to the deviation, and information flows for them.
 – The system sends information flows to the user him/herself and other users or organization if necessary.

During this step, new agents such as devices or outside organizations can be introduced. Because knowledge about monitoring and acting devices is required, we need the collaboration with engineers of such devices.

The goal decompositions for each sub-goal here may be depicted separately if the model is too complex to be read. In the next section, such decompositions are depicted separately.

4   Illustrative Examples

In this section, we exemplified application of our method to show the method works.

4.1   A Library System

We first apply our method to a library example shown in Sect. 2.4. In the example, a user in a library try to find copies of books. As shown in Fig. 1, three expectations "copies returned", "the shelf accessed" and "a book specified" is assigned to a user. We focus on the first expectation here because user's intention largely affects it.

If copies of books were not returned to their suitable shelves, users could not find copies they needed. However, some users make mistakes to return them. To avoid this problem, some libraries prepare a specific shelf or a box and users return copies to it so that the users do not have to return each copy to its suitable shelf. In an open-access library, the library cannot let all users to use such a shelf. Some user tries to return a copy to its shelf, and he/she sometimes makes mistake. An IC-tag based system is introduced to detect and avoid such mistakes as shown in Fig. 3. In this case, unskilled and careless violation may be handled in the same way as shown in the figure. This system works on the basis of the following three goals.

- "returned to an unsuitable shelf" by a user: This goal initiates the countermeasures to avoid unskilled or careless violation.
- "suitability checked" by a device and the system: By using IC tag embedded in a book and a scanner in a shelf, the system checks whether a copy was returned to a suitable shelf.
- "warning given": If the system decided the copy was returned to an unsuitable shelf, a device such as speaker gives warning to the user.

If the user does not have malicious intention, violation here can be avoided in this way.

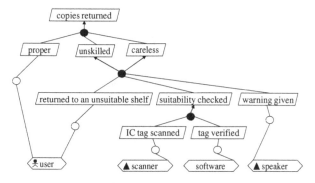

Fig. 3. copies returned: unskilled and careless violation

If a user has malicious intention and he/she wants to disturb the library operation, we have to install additional countermeasures. Figure 4 shows the consequence including such countermeasures. In this case, a history database of mistakes is added, and frequency of each user's mistakes have been recorded with the help of user ID (UID) scanner. According to the history, warning is chosen and told to the user. We may construct a blacklist and the library may shut users on the list out although such countermeasures are not contained in Fig. 4.

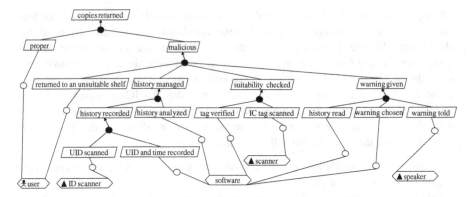

Fig. 4. copies returned: malicious violation

4.2 A Self-checkout System

A lot of supermarkets introduce self-checkout system because they want to reduce labor costs. In addition, customers of supermarkets usually finish their checkout faster than ever. However, several problems related to expectations of users remain. We systematically resolve such problems by using our requirements elicitation method.

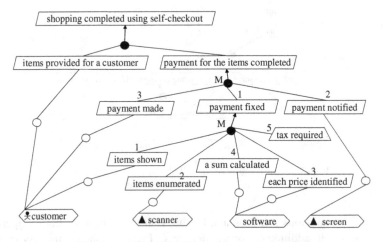

Fig. 5. An initial KAOS model of self-checkout

Figure 5 shows an initial KAOS model of self-checkout system. In this model, a customer is expected to achieve the following three expectations.

– "items provided for a customer": A customer sometimes leaves some items he/she bought behind at the checkout counter. When a clerk makes checkout, the clerk will caution the customer against the item left behind. However, the model in Fig. 5 simply represents the user achieves this expectation properly.

- "payment made": There are two possibility of violation about this expectation. If a customer is not familiar with self-checkout, he/she is confused and then cannot make payment properly[1]. Another possibility is related to the malicious intention of a supermarket manager. Even if the manager does not set the tax rate properly, most customers cannot usually identify it and the manager earns unlawful money. Although this case is too unrealistic, we have to always doubt and check the result of the system. At least, inciting messages at a hotel booking site mention in Introduction is usually doubtful.
- "items shown": To use a self-checkout system, the customer has to show all the items he/she wants to buy. However, some customer tries to shoplift some of items.

For each expectation, we examine its violation, and add new goals to mitigate or avoid such violation.

In Fig. 6, we focus on an expectation "items provided for a customer". The figure shows a careless violation about the expectation and additional goals for mitigating the violation. At least in this expectation, other kinds of violation "malicious", "unskilled" and "cheated" rarely happen. The customer can sometimes achieve the expectation properly without additional help. We thus decomposed the expectation into two sub-goals "proper" and "careless" at the first step. In the "proper" goal, we may simply assign the responsibility to achieve the goal to the customer. In the "careless" goal, we introduce two equipment agent "camera" and "speaker" to caution the customer against the item left behind. The software system has to achieve additional requirement "the items (left behand) identified" as shown in the figure. Four typical processes of self-adaptive systems mentioned in Sect. 3.2 help us to find this kind of additional requirement.

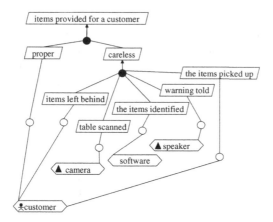

Fig. 6. Careless violation about "items provided for a customer" and its mitigation

---

[1] I had this experience at the small supermarket in Sweden.

In Fig. 7, we focus on an expectation "items shown" at the table of self-checkout. The figure shows a malicious violation about the expectation and additional goals for mitigating the violation. In this example, a customer and stock selves have been observed during his/her shopping. The self-checkout system then verifies whether all items picked up are shown. We may introduce some IC tags to avoid this violation in a different way.

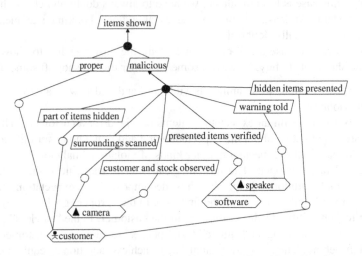

Fig. 7. Malicious violation about "item shown" and its mitigation

In Fig. 8, we focus on an expectation "payment made" at the table of self-checkout. The figure shows an unskilled violation about the expectation and additional goals for mitigating the violation. If you use a self-checkout system in a foreign country, you fall into this kind of situation. In this mitigation, a system has to identify its user is unskilled. In this case, the system can identify it because the user operate it in a wrong way or he/she pauses for a long time. The system then provides some guidance system such as a wizard UI. The user can mitigate his/her violation by following the wizard. If such wizard is always provided, hotheaded users may operate the system improperly. Identifying unskillfulness is thus important for mitigating violations.

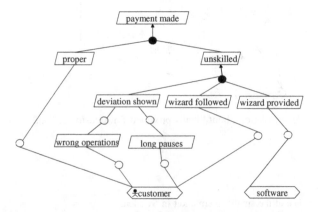

Fig. 8. Unskilled violation about "payment made" and its mitigation

In Fig. 9, we also focus on an expectation "items shown" at the table of self-checkout. The figure shows a cheated violation about the expectation and additional goals for mitigating the violation. In this case, a user him/herself tries to behave properly. However, the user cannot do it because of the malicious intention of another user. A manager of the shop with the self-checkout system maliciously setup the tax rate, and the user thus pay more money than the proper case. The user in this example found the tax rate seems to be strange, and he/she then verified the rate by using independent applications on a smartphone. If the user found he/she was cheated, the system reported it both the manager and the tax office. Transparency in this example is a strong deterrent to avoid the misuse of shop staffs.

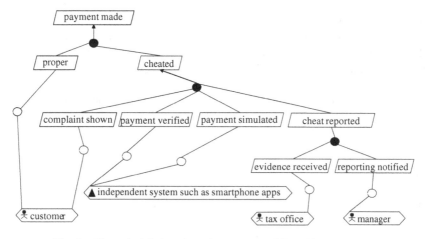

Fig. 9. Cheated violation about "payment made" and its mitigation

5 Conclusion

A system cannot achieve its goals when users do not or cannot properly achieve the expectations assigned to them. We call such improper achievement of expectations by the users as expectation violation. In this paper, we proposed and exemplified a requirements elicitation method for avoiding and mitigating expectation violation. By using the KAOS goal modeling notation, we can clarify expectations assigned to each user. We then decompose each expectation according to the predefined reasons why a user does not or cannot achieve it. To construct countermeasures for avoiding or mitigating such violation, we use processes of self-adapting systems such as monitoring, detecting, deciding and acting. Because no one have means to directly control users, we use transparency, i.e. the open flow of information. We expect transparency makes users try to achieve their expectations voluntarily.

We show several research issues for our future. First, security and usability mechanism are mainly used as countermeasures against expectation violation. When we focus on the solution space [13], security and usability are usually conflict with each other [24]. Such relationships are explicitly represented in NFR framework [4].

However, security and usability become alternative for resolving our problems, i.e. exception violation, as shown in our method and examples. Therefore, there is a possibility to construct another NFR framework within the problem space. Second, we currently predefined five types of reasons why users violate expectations on the basis of our experiences. We have to expand the reasons according to literatures in human-related disciplines. Human error handing is one of such disciplines. Third, although we have a guideline to add countermeasures based on the idea in self-adapting systems, it is too general to add such countermeasures systematically or automatically. We thus want to prepare concrete patterns to add such countermeasures. Fourth, we regard deviation of users are bad phenomena, and it should be mitigated or avoided in this paper. However, such deviation sometimes brings benefits for the users and suggest improvements for the system. We would like to focus on such viewpoint with the help of ideas of self-adaptive systems. Finally, we want to discuss the relationships between our work and testing methods. Testing methods especially user testing are also used for surfacing unexpected usage of a system. We believe their combination will improve the ability of avoiding and mitigating deviation of users.

Acknowledgement. This work was supported by JSPS KAKENHI Grant Number 15H02686, 16H02804, 15K00109, 17K00475 and 16K00196. The authors also thank to Prof. Takako Nakatani who suggested important related works.

References

1. Blaine, J.D., Cleland-Huang, J.: Software quality requirements: how to balance competing priorities. IEEE Softw. **25**(2), 22–24 (2008)
2. Imperial chemical industries: A guide to hazard and operability studies. Chemical Industry Safety and Health Council of the Chemical Industries Association (1977)
3. Cheng, B.H.C., et al.: Software engineering for self-adaptive systems: a research roadmap. In: Cheng, B.H.C., de Lemos, R., Giese, H., Inverardi, P., Magee, J. (eds.) Software Engineering for Self-Adaptive Systems. LNCS, vol. 5525, pp. 1–26. Springer, Heidelberg (2009). https://doi.org/10.1007/978-3-642-02161-9_1
4. Chung, L., Nixon, B.A., Yu, E., Mylopoulos, J.: Non-functional Requirements in Software Engineering. Springer Science & Business Media, Boston (2012). https://doi.org/10.1007/978-1-4615-5269-7
5. Dekker, S.: The Field Guide to Understanding Human Error. Ashgate Publishing, Ltd. (2014)
6. do Prado Leite, J.C.S., Cappelli, C.: Software transparency. Bus. Inform. Syst. Eng. **2**(3), 127–139 (2010)
7. Dromey, R.G.: A model for software product quality. IEEE Trans. Software Eng. **21**(2), 146–162 (1995)
8. Burkart, H., Holzner, L.: Transparency in Global Change: The Vanguard of the Open Society Burkart Holzner and Leslie Holzner. University of Pittsburgh Press Pittsburgh, PA (2006)
9. Hosseini, M., Shahri, A., Phalp, K., Ali, R.: Towards engineering transparency as a requirement in socio-technical systems. In: 23rd IEEE International Requirements Engineering Conference, RE 2015, Ottawa, ON, Canada, 24–28 August 2015, pp. 268–273 (2015)

10. Hosseini, M., Shahri, A., Phalp, K., Ali, R.: Foundations for transparency requirements engineering. In: Requirements Engineering: Foundation for Software Quality - 22nd International Working Conference, Proceedings, REFSQ 2016, Gothenburg, Sweden, 14–17 March 2016, pp. 225–231 (2016)
11. Hosseini, M., Shahri, A., Phalp, K., Ali, R.: A modelling language for transparency requirements in business information systems. In: Nurcan, S., Soffer, P., Bajec, M., Eder, J. (eds.) CAiSE 2016. LNCS, vol. 9694, pp. 239–254. Springer, Cham (2016). https://doi.org/10.1007/978-3-319-39696-5_15
12. Hosseini, M., Shahri, A., Phalp, K., Ali, R.: Four reference models for transparency requirements in information systems. Requirements Engineering, March 2017. https://doi.org/10.1007/s00766-017-0265-y
13. Jackson, M.: Problem Frames: Analysing and Structuring Software Development Problems. Addison-Wesley, New York (2001)
14. Kametani, H., Shinyashiki, Y., Mise, T., Hashimoto, M.A., Ubayashi, N., Katamine, K., Nakatani, T.: Information flow diagram and analysis method for unexpected obstacle specification of embedded software. In: Knowledge-Based Software Engineering, Proceedings of the Seventh Joint Conference on Knowledge-Based Software Engineering, JCKBSE 2006, 28–31 August 2006, Tallinn, Estonia, pp. 115–124 (2006)
15. Kametani, H., Shinyashiki, Y., Mise, T., Hashimoto, M.A., Ubayashi, N., Katamine, K., Nakatani, T.: A conceptual model for analysis method of extracting unexpected obstacles of embedded systems. In Knowledge-Based Software Engineering, Proceedings of the Eighth Joint Conference on Knowledge-Based Software Engineering, JCKBSE 2008, 25–28 August 2008, University of Piraeus, Piraeus, Greece, pp. 22–31 (2008)
16. Kemball-Cook, A.: Winning the trust of millennials. Global Coaching, p. 30 (2015)
17. McDermott, J.P., Fox, C.: Using abuse case models for security requirements analysis. In: 15th Annual Computer Security Applications Conference (ACSAC 1999), 6–10 December 1999, Scottsdale, AZ, USA, pp. 55–64 (1999)
18. Mise, T., Shinyashiki, Y., Nakatani, T., Ubayashi, N., Katamine, K., Hashimoto, M.: A method for extracting unexpected scenarios of embedded systems. In: Knowledge-Based Software Engineering, Proceedings of the Seventh Joint Conference on Knowledge-Based Software Engineering, JCKBSE 2006, 28–31 August 2006, Tallinn, Estonia, pp. 41–50 (2006)
19. Okubo, T., Taguchi, K., Kaiya, H., Yoshioka, N.: MASG: advanced misuse case analysis model with assets and security goals. JIP 22(3), 536–546 (2014)
20. Reifer, D.J.: Software failure modes and effects analysis. IEEE Trans. Reliab. 28(3), 247–249 (1979)
21. Salehie, M., Tahvildari, L.: Self-adaptive software: Landscape and research challenges. ACM Trans. Auton. Adapt. Systems (TAAS) 4(2), 14 (2009)
22. Shinyashiki, Y., Mise, T., Hashimoto, M., Katamine, K., Ubayashi, N., Nakatani, T.: Enhancing the ESIM (embedded systems improving method) by combining information flow diagram with analysis matrix for efficient analysis of unexpected obstacles in embedded software. In: 14th Asia-Pacific Software Engineering Conference (APSEC 2007), 5–7 December 2007, Nagoya, Japan, pp. 326–333 (2007)
23. Sindre, G., Opdahl, A.L.: Eliciting security requirements with misuse cases. Requir. Eng. 10(1), 34–44 (2005)
24. Tanabe, D., Uno, K., Akemine, K., Yoshikawa, T., Kaiya, H., Saeki, M.: Supporting requirements change management in goal oriented analysis. In: 16th IEEE International Requirements Engineering Conference, RE 2008, 8–12 September 2008, Barcelona, Catalunya, Spain, pp. 3–12 (2008)

25. van Lamsweerde, A.: Requirements Engineering: From System Goals to UML Models to Software Specifications. Wiley, Hoboken (2009)
26. van Lamsweerde, A., Letier, E.: Handling obstacles in goal-oriented requirements engineering. IEEE Trans. Software Eng. **26**(10), 978–1005 (2000)
27. Yu, E., Giorgini, P., Maiden, N., Mylopoulos, J.: Social Modeling for Requirements Engineering. The MIT Press, Cambridge (2010)

Comparative Requirements Analysis for the Feasibility of Blockchain for Secure Cloud

Irish Singh[1] and Seok-Won Lee[2(✉)]

[1] Department of Computer Engineering, Ajou University, Suwon, Korea
singhirish@ajou.ac.kr
[2] Department of Software and Computer Engineering, Ajou University,
Suwon, Korea
leesw@ajou.ac.kr

Abstract. Cloud users are striving for minimum provider interference in accessing services from cloud's shared pool of resources due to the dynamic and untrusted nature of cloud, and untrusted, vulnerable and greedy nature of Cloud Service Providers (CSPs). Service level agreements (SLA) are a critical aspect in maintaining security, trust and provisioning Quality of Service (QoS) in Cloud. The SLA consists of Service-level goals or the Functional and Non-Functional levels that are officially agreed by the customer and the providers. The SLA lifecycle is costly and time-consuming process. Using Blockchain technology's use-cases with Cloud can solve the trust and security requirements of cloud users as well as make SLAs transparent and open to cloud users for quick service provisioning. In order to analyze the feasibility of using Blockchain technology with Cloud, this paper, comparatively analyze the Security and trust requirements and Non-Functional requirements of Cloud and Blockchain to solve the security and trust requirements of cloud users in cloud. We also propose a secure and self-adaptive Blockchain based framework for cloud. Blockchain being the backbone of this framework, this framework exploits the feasible use cases of the Blockchain to enhance the trust requirement of the third party (Cloud Service provider) in Cloud and maintain trust and security in the Cloud by making data secure and SLA transparent and open to all Cloud users, aiding users to analyze and make spontaneous decisions for using Cloud services.

Keywords: Non-functional requirements · Security requirements
Comparative analysis · Cloud · Security · SLA · Blockchain

1 Introduction

Cloud was evolved to facilitate its customers/organizations by providing them with services through various deployment models such as Public, Private, Community, and Hybrid. But as the control is accessed by the Third party (Cloud Service Providers) the trust and security and uncertainty in Cloud is growing and the Cloud User/tenant personal control is much lower. Cloud users outsource their data and request services

© Springer Nature Singapore Pte Ltd. 2018
M. Kamalrudin et al. (Eds.): APRES 2017, CCIS 809, pp. 57–72, 2018.
https://doi.org/10.1007/978-981-10-7796-8_5

from the Cloud storage using the third-party providers such as Cloud Service Providers (CSP), Attribute Authority (AA), and Third-Party Auditor (TPA). These third parties are supposed to provide security functionalities in the cloud [1, 2]. The CSP and TPA are not completely trusted parties. They are viewed as greedy and vulnerable providers in the Cloud system. The information data of cloud users are acquired by the CSP and utilized for their own needs [5]. Verizon investigation report shows that in recent years many data breach incidents have been accounted [3]. CSPs dispose of the cloud users seldom used data to preserve space and derogate prices. Security and trust are the most critical issues in Cloud because of many reasons. Some of the reasons are firstly, the Cloud users/tenants are not completely aware to who is he/she dealing with. Secondly, Cloud users do not have transparency to their data, information of who accessing their data on Cloud, and how the data is moving inside Cloud. Thirdly, Cloud Users do not have recourse when things go wrong such as their data is lost, leaked or attacked. Blockchain is a novel technology that can alter how the users/organizations outsource data and acquire services from Cloud. Using Blockchain, cloud users can increase the trust and security when outsourcing data and acquiring services from Cloud.

The SLAs are a critical aspect in maintaining security, trust and provisioning Quality of Service (QoS) in Cloud. However, the SLA lifecycle is a costly and time taking process in provisioning services from cloud, because of several phases involved between SLA development and the SLA Termination. Secondly, frequent user interaction with the system during SLA Negotiation and Service Execution, might holds up progress for the success of Cloud Computing. Thirdly, established SLAs may fail to agree due to changing functional and non-functional requirements, components, hardware/software failure, and workload [6, 8]. Therefore, there is an emerging need for a transparent, trustworthy, self-adaptive and secure service execution in a heterogeneous, distributed and service oriented environment like Cloud. This environment can be achieved by using Blockchain technology use cases in Cloud. Blockchain based Cloud can make SLAs transparent and open to cloud users, improving the reliability, performance and quick service provisioning in cloud. In order to analyze whether Blockchain technology is feasible with Cloud, this paper comparatively analyzes the Security Requirements and Non-functional requirements of Cloud and Blockchain.

The rest of the paper is organized as follows: In Sect. 2 of this paper, we discuss some related works and discuss the concept of Blockchain and Cloud and it's Service Level Agreements (SLAs). Section 3 comparatively analyzes Blockchain and Cloud technologies with respect to Applications, Security Requirements supported by Blockchain, which are critical for Cloud Security and the Non-Functional requirements to analyze the feasibility of using the Blockchain use cases with Cloud. In Sect. 4, we propose the Blockchain based Cloud by utilizing the use-cases of Blockchain in Cloud. Section 5, presents our proposed Blockchain based Cloud Framework, showing how our framework can solve the existing security and trust issues in Cloud. Finally, in Sect. 6, we conclude the paper with some remarks on our proposed idea and possible future work for improvement.

2   Background and Related Works

In this section, we briefly discuss the related work. Firstly, we discuss the related work for achieving security capabilities in Cloud. Secondly, we present background study of Blockchain technology and Cloud. Next, we discuss about Service Level Agreement Lifecycle and its components in Cloud.

Almorsy et al. [7] have proposed a model driven security engineering approach using the system description model developed at design time and the system specification model developed at runtime to achieve security capabilities automatically at runtime for software applications. However, their approach is not suitable in cloud environments, where multiple applications need to implement similar security requirements because even one update to their model leads to updating all systems connected to it. Kertesz et al. [8] have presented a SLA-based service virtualization automatic service deployment architecture based on MAPE-K autonomic computing. However, their architecture still involves the costly SLA lifecycle. Rong et al. [6] provided a framework of security mechanism with the Cloud SLAs to cover security aspects in Cloud. Most of the existing works address provision of SLA guarantees to the consumer. In this paper, we use Blockchain for maintaining transparency of the cloud SLAs, policies and cloud users' data stored in the cloud. We check the feasibility of using Blockchain in Cloud by comparing and analyzing various Security Requirements and Non-Functional Requirements in Blockchain and Cloud.

2.1   Blockchain and Cloud Technology

Blockchain technology is a decentralized storage that stores the records of assets and transactions across a peer to peer network. It is an open ledger of transaction showing the ownings and transactions of the entire member in the network. The transaction records are stored in blocks and these blocks of data are cryptographically secured and linked together [12]. Therefore, they cannot be changed or hampered. Every computer in the network maintains the copy of these records, which are frequently updated and remain consistent with other computers. Bitcoin digital currency was first proposed in [10] which are based on the blockchain technology. Apart from storing the assets of bitcoin, Blockchain can store other digital assets in cloud like Service Level Agreements (SLA), Policies, certificate, contract, real world objects, profile identity information of the Cloud Service Provider (CSP), the organization which are using the cloud's services etc. [11]. The open ledger can also store the security responsibilities offered to the cloud users in the cloud network and are replicated so that it's very secure and hard to tamper with. In this way, Blockchain lowers the uncertainty and therefore can transform the Cloud System in an evolutionary way. When the Cloud user gets access to some service from the CSP then it should be aware of the CSPs identity, their reviews, rating, checkmarks etc. Blockchain allows creating an open, global platform which can store any attestation about any CSP for any service. This allows the cloud users to create a user controlled and monitored adaptive portable identity about their private data. Through Blockchain, the Cloud owners can selectively reveal about their attributes and services that can help facilitate their trade or interaction, behavior and strengthening their relationship. The cloud owners can reveal their SLA's by revealing their cryptographic proof that these services exist and are signed off on. Having this kind of portable identity around the physical world and digital world can facilitate trust and profit. Secondly, when the cloud user does not have any degree of transparency to its data in cloud that how the data is moving inside cloud and who all are accessing the data. The cloud user requirement is to retrieve the same data, which he/she provisioned to the cloud. There should be some record or account of the users' data that the user does not want to be tampered with. The Cloud owner to receive feedbacks from their users about their services and the requirements that are still unfulfilled can also use Blockchain. Using Blockchain, cloud can create a shared reality across non-trusting entities. It is not necessary that all the users in the Cloud Platform need to know each other or trust each other because each of them have ability to monitor and validate the chain for them. Therefore, we don't require creating a central authority like the CSP as all the Cloud vendors and all companies can interact using the same database without trusting one another. The Cloud users can have lot more transparency because as their data travels inside cloud, they can see its digital certificate move on the blockchain, adding value as it goes.

Sometime the Cloud users face the problem of reneging, i.e. they do not receive the services which they were promised to by the CSP. In this condition, the tenants want their data back with integrity. Blockchain allows writing code, binding contracts between Cloud and guarantee that contracts will bear out without the CSP enforcer. The Blockchain lowers the cloud user's uncertainty because of the data and third-party transparency. The mutual distrust among the cloud users keeps the Blockchain secure and verified. The Blockchain enables the technological capability of creating a record of exchange of data and services between Cloud user and Cloud provider, all kinds of digital and physical assets in Cloud, Users personal attributes in a totally novel way.

2.2 Service Level Agreements for Cloud Security

As more consumers outsource their storage and computation to the cloud providers, such outsourcing is regularized by the Service Level agreements (SLA's) between the Cloud Consumer and the Cloud Provider. Service Level Agreement is a contractual relationship between the Cloud Consumer and the Cloud Service Provider. They contain certain legal requirements, agreed services to protect the personal data of the Cloud Consumer and provide Quality of Service (QoS) guarantees. Buyya et al. [4] explained that Service-Level Agreements (SLAs) acts as an important role in strengthening the commercial mainstream. SLA's provide trust between the Cloud users and Cloud Service Providers which helps cloud users to outsource their critical data on Cloud.

SLA Life Cycle is a costly and time taking process for provisioning of services, because of several phases involved between SLA development and the SLA Termination. Figure 1 shows the SLA life cycle phases.

In the SLA development phase, first an inquiry is done in-order to determine the business context of the user and to recognize their necessities. The provider identifies the service levels of the cloud user and exploits basic rules for coaction between the customer and the service provider. SLAs are then generically published by the provider in the SLA Publication phase. SLA Negotiation phase occurs when the user wants to consume some cloud service; she will negotiate on a specific SLA. In the Service Provisioning and Deployment Phase, the provider commits to provide the specific cloud service and the service is provisioned and deployed. In the next two phases, i.e. Service Execution and Monitor/Assessment phase the cloud user executes the provisioned service and monitors the service to check whether the negotiated SLA has been implemented or not. However, if the Provider does not commit to the negotiated SLAs then the cycle can return to SLA Negotiation phase from Monitor/assessment phase. The SLA lifecycle is a costly and time taking process, because of several phases involved between SLA development and the SLA Termination. Secondly, frequent user interaction with the system during SLA Negotiation and Service Execution, might holds up progress for the success of Cloud Computing. Thirdly, established SLAs may fail to agree due to changing functional and non-functional requirements, components, hardware/software failure, and workload [6, 8]. Therefore, there is an evolving need for a transparent, trustworthy, self-adaptive and secure service execution in a heterogeneous, distributed and service oriented environment like Cloud.

Fig. 1. SLA life cycle in cloud

- **SLA Components:** There are many literatures on the SLA components in both cloud computing and Web services. Well known SLA specification is WSLA (Web Service Level Agreement) Language Specification by IBM [19]. The Service level goals are defined in the SLA specifications which are officially agreed by the customer and the providers. It comprises of a set of service level indexes or Security and Non-Functional Requirements such as integrity, non-repudiation, privacy, reliability, availability, performance etc. Each service level has goal to complete with their legality [8].

3 Comparative Analysis Between Blockchain and Cloud

In this paper, we provide a comparative analysis of cloud computing and blockchain technology. We analyzed both technologies, in multiple manners in present scenario, such as, Application, Security Requirements, Non-Functional Requirements, Advantages and Disadvantages. We classified the security properties and non-functional requirements based on the design patterns of Blockchain and Cloud systems such as based on organizational structure (Centralized/Decentralized), Auditor (Single/Ad hoc), Data (No-chaining/Chaining), Computation (No-Chaining/Chaining) and Deployment Scope (Public/Community/Private) to classify and compare Blockchain and Cloud systems and get assistance with the design and assessment impact of their principal design decisions. When building Blockchain based Cloud system, we need to systematically consider the design features and configurations of blockchain and cloud and assess the impact of their features and configurations on security properties and non-functional requirements.

The four levels of grading (less favorable (+), neutral (++), more favorable (+++), most favorable (++++)) that we present in the paper signifies the impact of design features and configurations of Blockchain and Cloud Systems on the security properties and non-functional requirements. Our analysis is based on various research studies in [12, 14–18].

Table 1 shows the blockchain and cloud computing applications. The blockchain technology is very new technology compared to cloud computing, so cloud computing application areas are very broad but blockchain applications are limited. Presently, researchers are working and enhancing blockchain for various application fields.

Table 1. Applications in Cloud and Blockchain

Application	Cloud computing	Blockchain
IoT	Platform as a Service	Blockchain
Machine Learning	Robot as a Service	Blockchain
Autonomous Driving	Vehicular Cloud	Blockchain
Big Data	Cloud Storage	Blockchain
Cyber Security	Security as a Service	Blockchain

Cloud Computing: Provides the services for the multiple applications such as Platform as a service(Paas) Software as service (SaaS), Security as a Service (SecaaS) etc.

Blockchain Technology: Provides combined secure, distributed decentralized mechanism for applications according to application requirements

In Table 2, we analyze the major Security requirements such as Immutable, Non-repudiation, Data integrity, Data transparency, Equal rights and Trust of Cloud and Blockchain technologies and their impact on their design patterns such as Centralized,

Table 2. Comparative analysis based on Security Requirements in Cloud and Blockchain

Security requirements	Cloud	Blockchain	Cloud	Blockchain	Cloud	Blockchain	Cloud	Blockchain	Cloud			Blockchain		
Design pattern	Centralized	Decentralized	Auditor		Data		Computation		Deployment scope					
			Single	Ad hoc	No chaining	Chaining	No chaining	Chaining	Public	Community	Private	Public	Community	Private
Immutable	+	+++	++	+	+	++++	+	++++	+	+	+	+++	++	+
Non-repudiation	+	+++	++	+	+	++++	+	++++	+	+	+	+++	++	+
Data integrity	+	+++	++	+	+	++++	+	++++	+	+	+	+++	++	+
Data transparency	+	+++	++	+	+	++++	+	++++	+	+	+	+++	++	+
Equal rights	+	+++	++	+	+	++++	+	++++	+	+	+	+++	++	+
Trust	+	+++	++	+	+	++++	+	++++	+	+	+	+++	++	++

Where above mentioned symbol means as follows:

+ means less favorable; ++ means neutral; +++ means more favorable; ++++ means most favorable

Decentralized, Auditor (Single/Ad hoc), Data and Computation (Chaining/No chaining), and Deployment Scope (Public, Community, and Private). In the Table 2 we can see that Centralized Cloud is less favorable (+) and Decentralized Blockchain is more favorable (+++) for the security requirements. Cloud is less favorable and Blockchain is most favorable for Data and Computation security because data blocks in Blockchain are cryptographically secured and chained. For secure deployment, the private cloud is neutral (++) whereas the pubic blockchain is more favorable (+++) [15–17].

3.1 Non-functional Characteristics of Blockchain

Non-Functional requirements refer to the qualities that the system must possess and the constraints under which the system must function. Therefore, they impact the functionality of the system and can have greater impact on the system design. Below are discussed some non-functional attributes of blockchain.

- **Openness:** The nodes in the blockchain show interoperability that means that the nodes in the Blockchain have the ability to exchange and use information during transaction.
- **Concurrency:** Nodes process concurrently to enhance performance of the Blockchain.
- **Scalability:** Nodes can be added or removed to make the Blockchain flexible. Scalability considers three things:
  - *Size:* Mores nodes can be added easily in the Blockchain network.
  - *Distribution/Transaction Processing rate:* Geographical dispersion of the nodes does not degrade the performance of the Blockchain.
  - *Manageability/latency:* The Blockchain should be manageable as no. of nodes in the Blockchain increases and the different nodes are located in different parts of the world.
- **Fault tolerance:** The transactions in the Blockchain are immutable and any fault at any node will be transparent to all other nodes in the Blockchain.
- **Transparency:** Every transaction in the Blockchain is visible to each node in the Blockchain network.
- **Security:** The Blockchain uses strong Cryptographic protocols such as SHA-255 for securing the data in the Blockchain.
- **Quality of Service:** The quality of service (QoS) determines the reliability and a response time and throughput that is the system's ability to deliver its services dependably and with a response time and throughput that is satisfactory to the nodes in the Blockchain. Quality of Service is a critical parameter for the critical data transaction among the nodes.

- **Failure Management:** The Blockchain shall be designed such that it is resilient to the failures. There shall be mechanisms which can discover then cause of the failure and suggest recovery schemes so that the Blockchain can automatically recover from the failures.

3.2   Non-functional Requirements for Cloud

Below are discussed some major non-functional attributes of Cloud which impacts different design patterns of cloud.

- **Scalability:** There are millions of nodes or users in the Cloud Network utilizing the Cloud services.
- **Elasticity:** There is no fixed hardware architecture and the nodes can be scale in and scale out.
- **Privacy:** The personal information of the individual shall be protected, and every individual has the right to control his/her data.
- **Infinite Computing Resources:** The cloud users do not need to plan ahead for provisioning services from cloud.
- **Pricing:** Application and the services in the Cloud vary in cost and the payment is based on the resource utilization.
- **Utilization:** The resources can be dynamically reconfigured to adjust to a variable load (scale), allowing also for an optimum resource utilization.
- **Cost Efficiency:** Cloud provides the services on demand across the internet. This reduces the cost of software, maintenance and operations as there is no need of licensing the software or updating the software or making it compatible with the underlined hardware.
- **Performance:** Performance is normally measured by capabilities of applications running on the cloud system.
- **Flexibility:** It is the ability to share services or files over the internet. Cloud allows its customers to be more flexible.

Table 3 shows the comparative analysis of major Non-functional requirements such as Scalability, Privacy, Infinite computing resources, Pay for Use, Utilization, Cost Efficiency, Performance and Flexibility of Cloud and Blockchain and their impact on their design patterns such as Centralized, Decentralized, Auditor (Single/Ad hoc), Data and Computation (Chaining/No chaining), and Deployment Scope (Public, Community, and Private). In terms of Infinite Computing Resources, pay for use, Utilization, Cost Efficiency, Performance and Flexibility, the centralized Cloud is more favorable whereas the decentralized Blockchain is less favorable. Apart from that the centralized systems have a single point of failure [15–18].

Table 3. Comparative analysis based on Non-functional requirements in Cloud and Blockchain

Non-functional requirements	Design Pattern		Auditor		Data		Computation		Deployment scope					
	Cloud	Blockchain	Cloud	Blockchain	Cloud	Blockchain	Cloud	Blockchain	Cloud			Blockchain		
	Centralized	Decentralized	Single	Ad hoc	No chaining	Chaining	No chaining	Chaining	Public	Community	Private	Public	Community	Private
Scalability	+++	+++	++	+	+	++++	+	++++	+++	++	No	+++	++	+
Privacy	+	+++	++	+	+	++++	+	++++	+	+	++	+++	++	+
Infinite computing resources	+++	+	++	+	+	++++	+	++++	+++	++	+	+++	++	+
Pay for use	+++	+	++	+	++	+	+	++++	+++	++	+	+++	++	+
Utilization	+++	+	++	+	+	++++	+	++++	+++	++	~	+++	++	+
Cost efficiency	+++	+	++	+++	Insignificant	++	++++	+	+++	++	+	+	++	+++
Performance	+++	+	++	++	++++	+++	++++	+	+++	++	+	+	+	+++
Flexibility	+++	+	++	+	++++	+	++++	+	+++	++	+	+	++	+++

Where above mentioned symbol means as follows:

~ Means depends on company size; + means less favorable; ++ means neutral; +++ means more favorable; ++++ means most favorable

4   Blockchain Based Cloud

In this section, we apply the Blockchain use cases to Cloud.

4.1   Open Ledger

The Blockchain based Cloud storage is open and public to every Cloud user. Every Cloud user on the network can see the services cloud is providing, what will the Service Level Agreements (SLAs) and security requirements the cloud will provide. With this transparent and open specification of Cloud, the Cloud users can easily decide upon their preferences and the services they are looking for, without investing any money beforehand. Cloud users can compare the services of one Cloud with other Clouds. Cloud users who are already using the services of a cloud can validate the offerings provided by the cloud by giving their feedback/ratings, making it easier for other users to join the cloud network.

4.2   Distributed Ledger

All the copies of the ledger are synchronized, and all the cloud users can see the same copy/version of the ledger. The ledger will contain the current services (SaaS, PaaS, IaaS) used by cloud, SLAs, Policies and service usage amount information of each cloud user. Cloud users synchronize their ledger across itself using the concept of miners in Bitcoin [9]. Miners are special nodes which hold the ledger. In Fig. 2 Cloud user 1 and Cloud user 4 are miners. Miners will compete among themselves and the first miner to take the service (service requested by user or service provisioned by the cloud) and validate and place it into the ledger will get a financial reward like some digital money such as bitcoin. The job of miner is to validate the cloud user, service requested by cloud user, to check whether the cloud can provide with specific service, requirements or not. To find a special key that will enable the miner to take the previous service transaction, and to this previous service transaction, lock the new service/requirement transaction. The search for the key is random so in-order to find the key, the miner needs to invest

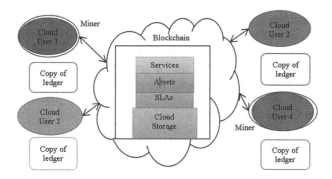

Fig. 2. Blockchain based Cloud

computational power and time. The miner is continuously guessing new keys till it finds the key that match the random puzzle. The first miner which will do that will get the financial reward. The key will enable every cloud user on the network to take the key and add on the ledger.

4.3 Decentralized Smart Contract

A Smart Contract in Blockchain is a piece of software that stores rules for negotiating the terms of a contract, automatically verifies the contract and then execute the agreed terms [13]. Blockchain coupled with smart contracts technologies enables more trust and transparency on CSP, TPA, AA parties. Smart Contracts are stored on the Blockchain which all cloud users have a copy of it. When the payment is confirmed the service is outsourced. All contract transactions are stored in chronological order on the Blockchain for future access along with the complete audit trail of events. If any party tries to change a contract on the Blockchain all other cloud users can detect and prevent it.

5 Blockchain Based Framework for Secure Cloud

The Blockchain based framework enables the cloud users to manage and control their private data on cloud. The framework is based on layered architecture. The four layers are show below in Fig. 3.

5.1 Cloud User Layer

The upper most layer known as Cloud user layer consists of individuals, organizations etc. who want to access services (SaaS, PaaS and, IaaS) from the cloud or wish to outsource their private data in the cloud.

5.2 Cloud Automation Layer

The second layer is the Cloud Automation layer which adaptively manages the cloud users request and response using the MAPE-K feedback loop. The MAPE-K loop has four phases and one Knowledge base. The Monitor phase monitors the request (Service, Quality of Service, user's requirements) of the cloud users. Each cloud user has a different request requirement. The requests are collected in the monitor Phase and forwarded to the Analyze phase. In the Analyze phase, the request is analyzed that what type of service (SaaS, PaaS, IaaS) the user is requesting and what are its Quality of Service requirements and other security and Privacy requirement. The next phase is the Plan phase in which, the response is planned according to the request of the user. In order to address the specific user requirements, the Plan phase uses the knowledge base, which contains the list of policies, Service Level Agreement and pricing for all services provided by Cloud. In the Execute Phase, the response adhered with the specific user requirement is provided to the cloud user.

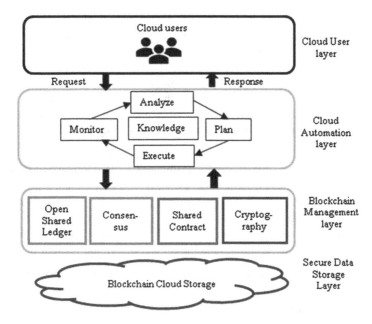

Fig. 3. Secure Blockchain based Cloud framework

5.3   Blockchain Management Layer

The third layer is the Blockchain Management Layer, which manages the Cloud and acts as a controller of the Cloud Network. Blockchain is the backbone of this framework as it provides much functionality such as access control, security, privacy etc. Each user of the Cloud can see what all services are provided by the Cloud, what are the policies of cloud, what are its service level agreements, compliance. The Knowledge base of the MAPE-K works with the use cases of Blockchain Management Layer. These use cases are Open Shared Ledger, Consensus, Shared Contract and Cryptography. The Blockchain management layer is the backbone of this framework as it manages all the layers of the framework using the Blockchain features. The Blockchain management layer uses the Blockchain functionalities which are defined below.

Open Shared Ledger: Cloud storage is open and public to every Cloud user. Every Cloud user on the network can see the services cloud is providing, what are security requirements the cloud can provide and can also compare it with other Cloud and then decide without investing any money beforehand. Other Cloud user using the services can validate the offerings provided by the cloud and give their feedback. Every cloud user on the network can see any invalidated SLAs.

Consensus: For every service request of the Cloud user and synchronization of the ledger, the concept of miner is used [9]. Miners are special nodes which can hold the ledger. Miners will compete among themselves and the first one to take the service provisioned by the cloud and validates and put it into the ledger will get a financial reward like bitcoin. Miners validate by calculating whether the cloud has the specific service or not. They find a special key that will enable them to take the previous service transaction and lock the new service/requirement transaction. In-order to find the key, the miner needs to invest computational power and time because the search for the key is random. The miner is repeatedly guessing new keys until it finds the key that match the random puzzle. The first miner to do that will get the financial reward. The key will enable every cloud user on the network to take the key and add on the ledger. There are various consensus protocols such as Proof of Work (PoW), Proof of Stake (PoS), Proof of Retrievability (PoR) which can be used for security [15].

Shared Contract: A Smart Contract is a piece of software that stores rules for negotiating the terms of a contract, automatically verifies the contract and then execute the agreed terms [13]. Smart Contracts are stored on the Blockchain which all parties have a copy of it. When the payment is confirmed the service is outsourced. All contract transactions are stored in chronological order on the Blockchain for future access along with the complete audit trail of events. If any party tries to change a contract on the Blockchain all other cloud users can detect and prevent it.

Cryptography: Blocks in the blockchain are cryptographically secured and linked.

5.4 Secure Data Storage Layer

The fourth layer is the Cloud storage layer. The Cloud storage layer is a Blockchain enabled storage layer, so this layer provides security by maintaining the confidentiality, integrity and Availability. The data stored in the Blockchain cloud is immutable and enriched with cryptographic techniques such as hashing, encryption/decryption, digital signatures for protection of the data.

6 Conclusion and Future Work

In this paper we have comparatively analyzed the blockchain and cloud to analyze the feasibility of blockchain in cloud. We discussed the preliminary study of the evolving Blockchain technology and its applications in Cloud to solve the current security and trust issues in cloud such as vulnerable third-party interference and costly SLA provision. We have introduced Blockchain based Cloud using the features of Blockchain to maintain trust, transparency and security in the Cloud. We have also introduced a novel four-layered conceptual model framework of Cloud based on the blockchain technology. The framework has exploited the Self-Adaptation MAPE-K approach for adaptively provisioning the request of the user based on its specific functional and quality requirements and has also used the Blockchain features to provide trust, transparency, security and privacy in the Cloud to maintain an open and trusted environment for reliable service provisioning and data tracking for cloud users. Blockchain speeds up the provisioning of services in cloud. The services, SLAs and other asset in cloud can be viewed by all cloud users and are immutable. This creates trust and reduces hazard and fraud.

We are at a very preliminary stage of using the blockchain technology and it will take some time for our Blockchain based Cloud framework to come to a maturity stage for adoption. For our future work, we need more research efforts at this stage to explore the primary exposition, new business. The main motive of our paper is to encourage innovative research and investigation for Blockchain based Cloud.

Acknowledgement. This research was supported by Basic Science Research Program through the National Research Foundation of Korea (NRF) funded by the Ministry of Education (NRF-2017R1D1A1B03034279).

References

1. Li, J., Jia, C., Li, J., Chen, X.: Outsourcing encryption of attribute-based encryption with MapReduce. In: Chim, T.W., Yuen, T.H. (eds.) ICICS 2012. LNCS, vol. 7618, pp. 191–201. Springer, Heidelberg (2012). https://doi.org/10.1007/978-3-642-34129-8_17
2. Hur, J., Noh, D.K.: Attribute-based access control with efficient revocation in data outsourcing systems. IEEE Trans. Parallel Distrib. Syst. (TPDS) **22**(7), 1214–1221 (2011)
3. Verizon 2015: 2015 Data Breach Investigations Report (2015). http://www.verizonenterprise.com/DBIR/2015/. Accessed 20 Sept 2017
4. Buyya, R., Yeo, C.S., Venugopal, S.: Market-oriented cloud computing: vision, hype, and reality for delivering it services as computing utilities. In: 10th IEEE International Conference on High Performance Computing and Communications, pp. 5–13. IEEE (2008)
5. Tang, J., Cui, Y., Li, Q., Ren, K., Liu, J., Buyya, R.: Ensuring security and privacy preservation for cloud data services. ACM Comput. Surv. (CSUR) **49**(1), 1–39 (2016)
6. Rong, C., Nguyen, S.T., Jaatun, M.G.: Beyond lightning: a survey on security challenges in cloud computing. Comput. Electr. Eng. **39**(1), 47–54 (2013)
7. Almorsy, M., Grundy, J., Ibrahim, A.S.: MDSE@R: model-driven security engineering at runtime. In: Xiang, Y., Lopez, J., Kuo, C.-C.J., Zhou, W. (eds.) CSS 2012. LNCS, vol. 7672, pp. 279–295. Springer, Heidelberg (2012). https://doi.org/10.1007/978-3-642-35362-8_22
8. Kertész, A., Kecskemeti, G., Brandic, I.: An interoperable and self-adaptive approach for SLA-based service virtualization in heterogeneous cloud environments. Future Gener. Comput. Syst. **32**, 54–68 (2014)
9. Aljoumah, E., Al-Mousawi, F., Ahmad, I., Al-Shammri, M., Al-Jady, Z.: SLA in cloud computing architectures: A comprehensive study. Int. J. Grid Distrib. Comput. **8**(5), 7–32 (2015)
10. Nakamoto, S.: Bitcoin: a peer-to-peer electronic cash system (2008)
11. Tschorsch, F., Scheuermann, B.: Bitcoin and beyond: a technical survey on decentralized digital currencies. IEEE Commun. Surv. Tutorials **1**(3), 2084–2123 (2016)
12. Swan, M.: Blockchain: Blueprint for a New Economy. O'Reilly Media, Inc. (2015)
13. Omohundro, S.: Cryptocurrencies, smart contracts, and artificial intelligence. AI Matters **1**(2), 19–21 (2014)
14. Ali, M., Nelson, J., Shea, R., Freedman, M.J.: Blockstack: a global naming and storage system secured by Blockchains. In: USENIX Annual Technical Conference, pp. 181–194 (2016)
15. Xu, X., Weber, I., Staples, M., Zhu, L., Bosch, J., Bass, L., Pautasso, C., Rimba, P.: A taxonomy of Blockchain-based systems for architecture design. In: 2017 IEEE International Conference on Software Architecture (ICSA), pp. 243–252. IEEE (2017)
16. Pilkington, M.: Blockchain technology: principles and Applications. In: Olleros, F.X., Zhegu, M., Elgar, E. (eds.) Research Handbook on Digital Transformations (2016). SSRN: https://ssrn.com/abstract=2662660. Accessed 2015

17. Xu, X., Pautasso, C., Zhu, L., Gramoli, V., Ponomarev, A., Chen, S.: The blockchain as a software connector. In: 13th Working IEEE/IFIP Conference on Software Architecture (WICSA), pp. 182–191. IEEE (2016)
18. Rimba, P., Tran, A.B., Weber, I., Staples, M., Ponomarev, A., Xu, X.: Comparing Blockchain and cloud services for business process execution. In: 2017 IEEE International Conference on Software Architecture (ICSA), pp. 257–280. IEEE (2017)
19. Ludwig, H., Keller, A., Dan, A., King, R.P., Franck, R: Web service level agreement (WSLA) language specification. IBM Corporation, pp. 815–824 (2003)

A Template for Writing Security Requirements

Massila Kamalrudin[1], Nuridawati Mustafa[2(✉)], and Safiah Sidek[1]

[1] Innovative Software System and Service Group (IS3), Universiti Teknikal Malaysia Melaka, Hang Tuah Jaya, 76100 Durian Tunggal, Melaka, Malaysia
{massila, safiahsidek}@utem.edu.my
[2] Universiti Teknikal Malaysia Melaka, Hang Tuah Jaya, 76100 Durian Tunggal, Melaka, Malaysia
nuridawati@utem.edu.my

Abstract. Quality security requirements contribute to the success of secure software development. However, the process of eliciting and writing security requirements is tedious and complex, It requires Requirements Engineers (RE) to have security experience in the process of eliciting consistent security requirements from the clients-stakeholders. Considering the requirements are derived from natural language, RE faced problems in eliciting and writing security requirements as they have the tendency to misunderstand the real needs and the security terms used. Motivated from these problems, this paper proposed a security requirements library and template to assist RE in writing security requirements. The library was built based on compilation of security attributes derived from syntax analysis and keywords matching. The realization of the library and writing template was demonstrated using two sets of scenario taken from real projects. The usage examples show that the template is able to help the RE to write security requirements by providing the relevant and suitable sentence structure as guidance.

Keywords: Security requirements · Security requirements template
Secure software

1 Introduction

Building secure software is becoming essential considering security is a crucial aspect of software in today's world. In the last decade, software system security has become an increasingly growing concern due to the large number of incidents and attacks targeting software systems. Attackers exploit software vulnerabilities and cause threats to the systems such as stealing sensitive information and manipulating data, resulting in denial of service [1]. According to [2], the US National Institute of Standards and Technology (NIST) estimates that the US economy loses $60 billion each year in costs associated with developing and distributing software patches and reinstalling systems that have been infected, as well as costs from the lost of productivity due to computer malware and other problems enabled by software errors.

Contextualized within this scenario, a better way to develop secure software is to incorporate security from the very beginning of software development. When building a secure software, it is helpful to take into account the security concerns right from the

M. Kamalrudin et al. (Eds.): APRES 2017, CCIS 809, pp. 73–86, 2018.
https://doi.org/10.1007/978-981-10-7796-8_6

beginning of the development process [3]. Based on Riaz et al., 46% of the sentences in requirement specification in healthcare domain were security-relevant [4]. Out of these, 28% explicitly mention security while 72% of the sentences are functional requirements with security implications. Therefore, early realization of the security is important so that security problems can be tackled early enough before proceeding further in the process; hence, any rework can be avoided [5, 6]. Most of the requirements engineers faced problems to elicit security requirements from the clients-stakeholders as there are instances of mismatch between the real needs and the security terms used [7, 8]. Therefore, a writing template that assists requirement engineers in writing security requirement engineering is needed so that a more systematic way for eliciting and writing security requirements can be performed. As such, this research aims to investigate the following research questions: (a) How can security requirements library and security requirement template facilitate in eliciting and writing security requirement?

This paper is organized as follows. After the Introduction, we discuss the background of and motivation for the research in Sect. 2. This is followed by Sect. 3, which proposes a new approach for security requirement template. In this section, we also define the security requirement library and explain the security templates. We describe two usage examples of requirements written in a form of requirements to demonstrate and describe the key features of our proof concept library and template in Sect. 4. Next, Sect. 5 presents the related works of this research. Finally, this paper ends with a conclusion and future works presented in Sect. 6.

2 Background and Motivation

We seek to improve the security requirements elicitation process by providing security requirements library and security requirements template to assist novice requirement engineers in writing the security requirements.

This research is motived by the findings drawn from our study that explores the problems faced by engineers when conducting the requirements engineering process. In our previous study [24], we conducted a quantitative survey with software companies in Malaysia, such as IBM Malaysia, Cyber Security Malaysia and other software companies.

The results from the survey identified three main problems faced by requirements engineers. The first problem is that most of the clients do not clearly understand the security needed by their systems. Secondly, requirements engineers face difficulties to understand the security terms in security standards documents. Finally, they have difficulties to write the security requirements. The study also identified several reasons for the existence of these problems. Firstly, it is not a common practice for IT practitioners to collect security requirements directly from the users and stakeholders. Secondly, the complexity and ambiguity of natural language commonly used for eliciting requirements may result in the elicitation of inconsistent security requirements.

With respect to writing security requirements, the survey also found that the majority (76%) of the respondents did not refer to any security requirement template. Only a small number of them refer to the companies' template and other existing standards, such as Federal Information Processing Standards Publication (FIPS),

Secure Sockets Layer (SSL), National Institute of Standards and Technology (NIST) and US Security Layer/Standards. The different security terms in the various standards resulted in the difficulties among requirement engineers to understand the security terms in the security standards documents. Additionally, most requirements engineers are not trained at all in security. In fact, those who have undergone the training were only given an overview of security architectural mechanisms, such as passwords and encryption rather than in actual security requirements [9].

Drawn from the above discussion, this research aims to provide a security requirements writing template that assists novice requirement engineers in writing security requirement. This writing template provides guideline for requirement engineers to elicit and write security requirements in a more systematic way. This research also aims to suggest a new practice of eliciting security requirements at the early stage rather than the later stage of product development. This approach is supported by Jindal et al. (2016) that argued the importance of addressing the security problems at the early phases of System Development Life Cycle (SDLC) process, especially during the requirement and analysis phases [10].

3 Security Requirements Template Approach

Security requirements is defined as constraints on the functions of the system, where these constraints operationalize one or more security goals and have traditionally been considered to be non-functional [11]. These requirements are not integrated into the mainstream of the requirements engineering activities since they are often developed independently from the rest of the requirements engineering activities. As a consequence, security requirements that are specific to application software or system and the protection of essential services and assets are often neglected. Many requirements engineering researches and practices have addressed the capabilities that a software or system should provide. Although, much attention has been given to the system's functional requirements from the perspectives of the user, less attention has been given to security requirements [3]. Therefore, this template focuses on the functional security requirements since it describes the desired security behavior of a system as in [12].

Motivated from the findings of the study, we developed a template that is able to assist requirements engineers to write security requirements aligned with the needs of a security standards. This template is drawn from the Common Criteria standards [12, 13]. It is believed that this approach could improve the quality of the elicited security requirements for secure software development. The process to elicit security requirements using the template is as shown in Fig. 1:

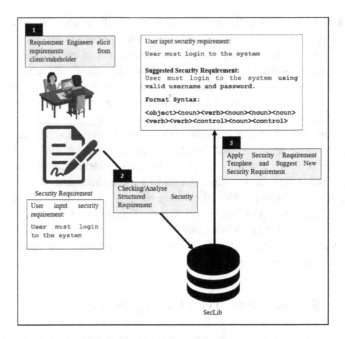

Fig. 1. The proposed approach

With reference to Fig. 1, the process to elicit security requirements can be described based on the following three steps:

(1) Requirements engineers (RE) elicit requirements from the client/stakeholders. The collected security requirements are in the form of textual natural language requirements.
(2) Then, the textual security requirements are analyzed based on two aspects. First, each sentence is analysed using syntax analysis to identify the components needed to be in the structure of functional security requirement. The sentence structure is then analysed to determine the security keyword and security mechanism.
(3) Next, keyword matching is applied to search for the associated security keywords and mechanism through the SecLib.
(4) The security requirements template is used to guide the writing of security requirements. The template provides the generic structure of the security requirements used by the RE.

3.1   Security Requirements Library

To define the relevant security attributes for each of the requirements, we developed a security requirements library called SecLib. In our work, the security properties are defined based on ISO/IEC 27000 [14], as shown in Table 1. Here, the security properties are the elements that should be addressed in the context of an overall security policy as a protection of system data against disclosure, modification or destruction.

Table 1. Security properties definitions

Security properties	Definition
Authentication	Provision of assurance that a claimed characteristic of an entity is correct
Integrity	Property of safeguarding the accuracy and completeness of information and processing methods
Confidentiality	Property that information is not made available or disclosed to unauthorized individuals, entities, or processes
Availability	Property of being accessible and usable upon demand by an authorized entity
Non-repudiation	Ability to prove the occurrence of a claimed event or action and its originating entities

To do this, we first explored the most highly considered security properties for developing a secure software. In this paper, we focused on three most highly considered security properties, which are authentication, integrity and confidentiality. We categorized each of the security properties with its associated security keywords as described in [12]. We used security keywords defined by the Common Criteria to develop a library of security keywords for security requirement from business requirements.

As shown in Table 2, each security properties is associated with one to many (1..M) security keywords. We then identified the security attributes in Common Criteria that are associated to each security properties. For example, the security property "Authentication" is associated with security keywords "Verify" and "Privilege" as per

Table 2. Security properties, Keywords, Attributes and Synonym

Security properties	Security keywords	Security attributes	Security keywords synonym
Authentication	(a) Verify (b) Privilege	(a) Username (b) Password (c) Encrypted time-stamps, (d) Random numbers from a secret lookup table	(a) Register (b) Valid (c) Login (d) Appropriate (e) Required (f) Log In
Integrity	(a) Modification (b) Deletion (c) Insertion (d) Replay	(a) Source trusted (b) Manner protected (c) Modification/Deletion/ Insertion/ Replay error	(a) Update (b) Document (c) Perform (d) Purchase (e) Confirm
Confidentiality	(a) Transmit (b) Receive	(a) Identity (b) Unauthorized User (c) Unauthorized subject (d) Unauthorized disclosure (e) Manner protected	(a) Print (b) Display

defined in Common Criteria. However, more security keywords synonyms were found in normal business requirements "Authentication", such as "Register", "Valid", "Login", "Appropriate", "Required" and "Log In". These additional keywords synonym were extracted using keyword matching of security attributes found in Common Criteria for each of the security properties.

3.2   Development of Security Requirements Template

Further, we have developed security requirements template to assist RE to write security requirement. We used syntax analysis and keyword matching to parse the textual natural language security requirements into functional security requirements key textual structures to the check the structure of the security requirements.

This template utilizes the SecLib, especially the Security Keywords and Security Keyword synonyms. Next, we analyzed a few sets of functional business requirements that consist of security concerns. Here, we analyzed the sentence structures for each of textual requirement from multiple domains of applications. The key textual structures or the syntax that define the security requirement are shown in Fig. 2 below:

The **<Subject>** should **<Verb/Security Keyword>** to the **<Object>** **<Security Keyword>** **<Security Mechanism>** in order to **<Adjective Phrase>**.

Fig. 2. Security requirements key textual structures

The definition of the terms used in this template is shown in Table 3.

Table 3. Security requirements sentence structural definition

Term	Descriptions
Subject	The person or thing that the sentence is about. It's often the person or thing that performs the action of the verb in question and it usually (but not always) comes before the verb
Verb/Security keywords	Describes what a person or thing does or what happens. It relates to the activity that involves security concern
Security mechanism	Describe the type of method used for security activity. For example: Username/Password, Biometric (Voice Recognition, Fingerprints, Face scanning) and Eye prints (Retina and Iris Scans)
Object	The person or thing affected by the Verb/Security Keywords
Adjective phrase	A group of words that describes a noun or pronoun in a sentence

Example 1

<Subject>	<Verb>	<Object>	Security keyword	Security mechanism	<Adjective phrase>
[The] customer	**should register**	[to] the system	**using unique**	**username and password**	in order to proceed to book ticket service

Based on Example 1, we found that the sentence structure of security requirements is more complex than the normal functional requirements as the security keyword and security mechanism components are embedded in the sentence structure. The difference between the normal business requirements and security requirement is shown in the tree structures below (Fig. 3):

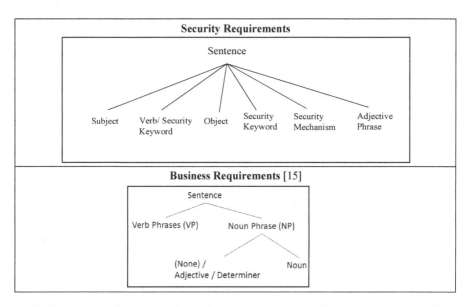

Fig. 3. Key textual structure of security requirement (a) and Business requirements (b)

4   Usage Examples

This section demonstrates the realization and usage of our security requirements template approach that consists of security requirements library and security template. For this purpose, we used two sets of requirements based on real project: The first set of requirements is for "Booking Flight Ticket" [16] and the second set of requirements is for "Electronic Health Record (EHR)" [17]. The two systems, the airline reservation system and electronic health record system were selected as they are considered as applications that has critical effect on the business performance of the respective domains. Any failure or interruptions in the systems may result in a great loss to the business entity. Therefore, we expected that security requirements have significant effect on the development of application. Here, we demonstrate the utilities of the library based on this research question: "How can our security requirements library and security requirement template facilitate the elicitation and writing of security requirement?"

4.1 Requirements 1: Booking Flight Ticket

In this section, we demonstrate the usage of our library and template using a set of requirements scenario of an online flight booking application [16]. The requirements are designed for adoption of SOA methodology (SOMA) from IBM and realizing its applicability in the domain of airline reservation services. The requirements have been classified to four services consists of Customer Service, Flight Service, Reservation Services and Payment Service. For the demonstration purpose, we focused on the Customer Service and Flight Service for Register Profile business scenario and Book Ticket scenario only. The descriptions of this scenario is shown in Fig. 4.

Register Profile
1.0 The customer should register himself in order to proceed to book ticket service.
2.0 The customer needs to input all the required particular details during the registration process.
3.0 The web service will perform validation checks on customer input and length constraints.
4.0 Upon successful login, the customer will be registered officially to the web service and he can login using his username and password.
Book Ticket
1.0 From the Check Flight, the customer is required to log in and the web service will prompt the customer to confirm the flights.
2.0 The web service will then ask the customer whether to update his profile details or not.
3.0 Subsequently, the customer will be asked to purchase and confirm the selected flights.

Fig. 4. Flight ticket booking [16]

Firstly, RE elicits security requirements from the scenario in Fig. 4. Next, the RE key-in the requirements in the text editor provided in the template as shown in Fig. 5(a). The template then checks and analyzes the key textual structures of the elicited security requirement according to sentence structural terms definition in Table 3. Next, the keywords stated in the Verb/Security Keyword column are used to determine and choose the matching security template. Finally, as shown in Fig. 5(a), the template shows the corrected security requirement and the amendment, which are highlighted in red color. In addition, the selected template is displayed together with the matching security attributes.

4.2 Requirements 2: Electronic Health Record (EHR)

This section demonstrates the utilization of the library and template for writing security requirements based on the second set of requirements, the Electronic Health Record (EHR) determined by the Statewide Collaboration Process (SCP) [17]. The requirements are designed for the technical implementation of the projects for the Statewide Health Information Network, New York (SHIN-NY) and interoperable electronic health

User key-in requirement:

< Subject >	<Verb/ Secu-rity Keyword>	<Object>	<Security Key-word>	<Security Mechanism>	<Adjective Phrase>
The customer	should register	himself			in order to proceed to book ticket service information.

Check Format

Suggested Security Requirement:

< Subject >	<Verb/ Secu-rity Keyword>	<Object>	<Security Key-word>	<Security Mechanism>	<Adjective Phrase>
The system	should register	to the system	using unique	username and password	in order to proceed to book ticket service information.

Applied Security Requirement Template:

The <subject> should <verb/security keyword> **using unique** <security mechanism>

Security Attributes: Authentication

Fig. 5(a). Suggestion from security library and security template for booking flight ticket (Color figure online)

User key-in requirement:

< Subject >	<Verb/ Secu-rity Keyword>	<Object>	<Security Key-word>	<Security Mechanism>	<Adjective Phrase>
The system	can verify and document	patient			eligibility and patient demographic information.

Check Format

Suggested Security Requirement:

< Subject >	<Verb/ Secu-rity Keyword>	<Object>	<Security Key-word>	<Security Mechanism>	<Adjective Phrase>
The system	should verify	patient eligibility	using unique	id	

Applied Security Requirement Template:

The <subject> should <verb/security keyword> **using unique** <security mechanism>

Security Attributes: Authentication

Fig. 5(b). Suggestion from security library and security template for EHR (Color figure online)

Eligibility
1.0 The system can verify and document patient eligibility (e.g. insurance information) and patient demographic information.
2.0 The system shall provide the ability to display medical eligibility obtained from patient's insurance carrier, populated either through data entry in the system itself or through an external application interoperating with the system.
Patient Demographic and Financial Information
3.0 The system shall allow appropriate clinical staff to document and/or update patient identifying and financial information.
Printing Patient Data
4.0 Appropriate clinical staff can print out medication and diagnosis list and other applicable information for patient.

Fig. 6. Electronic Health Record (EHR) [17]

records. The requirements have been classified into ten areas that correspond to EHR functional categories. For the demonstration purpose, we focused on the Administration Requirements only. The description of this user scenario is shown in Fig. 6.

First, RE elicits the security requirements from the scenario in Fig. 6. Next, the RE key-in the security requirements in the text editor provided in the template as shown in Fig. 5(b). The template then checks and analyzes the key textual structures of the elicited security requirement according to sentence structural terms definition in Table 3. Next, the keywords stated in the "Verb/Security Keyword" column are used to determine and choose the matching security template. Finally, as illustrated in Fig. 5(b), the template shows the corrected security requirement, which is highlighted in red. In addition, the selected template is displayed together with the identification of relevant security attributes.

Based on the two user scenarios presented above, we found that most of the business requirements comprise multiple security requirements. Further, it can be concluded that the template is relevant and suitable to be used for writing security requirements, using different types of security attributes and keywords.

5   Related Works

Riaz et al. proposed a framework, named Discovering Goals for Security (DIGS) that models the key entities in information security, including assets and security goals. The researchers developed a set of security goal patterns that captures multiple dimensions of security for assets [18]. They also developed and utilized a systematic process to identify security requirements patterns from the existing knowledge sources [19]. Riaz et al. also developed a tool-assisted process using machine learning techniques to aid requirements engineers in producing a more comprehensive and classified set of security requirements by: (1) automatically identifying security-relevant sentences in natural language requirements artifacts; and (2) providing context-specific security requirements templates to help translate the security-relevant sentences into functional security requirements [4]. Riaz et al. further improved the security requirements elicitation process by suggesting appropriate security requirement templates based on the existing functional requirements [20]. The statements with security implications are statements suggesting a need for security. However, the proposed template is applicable for health domain and cover limited security properties only.

Jindal et al. on the other hand, treated the security requirements by mining the descriptions of requirements that pertain to security related issues specified in Software Requirement Specification (SRS) document using text mining. They classified them using J48 decision tree method provided by WEKA software into their respective categories of security requirements [10]. Yet, no security template has been highlighted to assist in writing the security requirements.

Motil et al. proposed a security pattern selection method based on classification according to properties and application domain called Pattern-based System and Software Engineering (PBSE). This method is guided by security risk analysis. The selection follows two steps: First, the selection of abstract patterns responding to identified security requirements issued by a risk analysis; and second, the use of constraints introduced by relevant concrete patterns to refine the selection. They used SysML as a modeling language for illustration [21].

Haley et al. proposed a framework for security requirements elicitation and analysis based on constructing a context for the system, representing security requirements as constraints, and developing satisfaction arguments for the security requirements. The system context is described using a problem-oriented notation, which is then validated against the security requirements through the construction of a satisfaction argument [11]. In contrast to our work, there is no template or guideline to write security requirements. Therefore, the process of elicitation following this framework is still not promising and difficulty to be used by novice engineers.

Likewise, El-Hadary and El-Kassas proposed a methodology for security requirement elicitation based on problem frames. The proposed the methodology aims at early integration of security with software development. It considers security while eliciting the requirements of software systems using problem frames [1]. However, no template is provided to ease the security requirements elicitation process.

Further, Beckers et al. presented a catalog of security requirements patterns for the domain of cloud computing. This catalog is part of the ClouDAT framework, which is a holistic method. It also includes tool support for evaluating cloud computing with regard to security. This catalog is currently composed of 78 security requirements in 10 different protection categories along with a structured method for mining the patterns and validated the catalog via discussions with the industrial partners of the ClouDAT project [22]. Overall, they only focus more on the elicitation of domain knowledge rather than providing guidance in writing security requirements.

Yahya et al. proposed a new approach of capturing security requirements using an extended Essential Use Cases (EUCs) model [23]. Using the essential interactions patterns and essential use case patterns, they developed a tool called SecMereq. Their tool allows requirements engineers to automate the elicitation process for capturing security requirements. However, they did not perform any security templates that can support the security requirement elicitation process.

In a similar context, Yusop et al. proposed an automated approach and tool, called MobiMEReq that helps to capture and validate the security attributes requirements of mobile apps. They employed the concept of Test Driven Development (TDD) with a model-based testing strategy using Essential Use Cases (EUCs) and Essential User

Interface (EUI) models [24]. However, they did not perform any security templates that can support the security requirement elicitation process.

Salini and Kanmani improved the elicitation of security requirement by proposing MOSRE framework for web applications that can be used to elicit and model the Security Requirements for E-Health system. By considering the Security requirements as functional requirements in the Requirement phases, the Security requirements and domain knowledge for E-Health system can be captured in a well-defined model [25]. However, they did not provide the security template to assist in writing the security requirements.

Houmb et al. proposed SecReq by combining three techniques: the Common Criteria (CC), the heuristic requirements editor (HeRA), and UMLsec. SecReq makes a systematic use of the security engineering knowledge contained in the CC and UMLsec, as well as security-related heuristics in the HeRA tool [7]. This research supports the elicitation process and derives the security-related heuristics based on the UMLsec stereotypes. However, their tool does not have any guidance or template on how to write security requirements.

6   Conclusion and Future Works

This study is motivated by the findings of the literature review and survey. From the findings of the existing literature and survey, we concluded that there are limited solutions that cater for writing security requirements. Although writing templates has been proposed, the template has been drawn from a particular standard; hence covering limited security properties in healthcare domain. As for future work, we are motivated to enhance this template to incorporate more standards such as Common Criteria (CC), National Institute of Standards and Technology (NIST) and International Organization for Standardization (ISO) to provide more generic template to support all these three standards. A possible extension of this work is to provide support consistency checking between the generated security requirements and the identified security requirements by the templates. An automation tool will be developed to support larger and multiple set of security requirements. Further, the template will be included with feature selections technique and cover more rigorous security properties. We strongly believe that this approach will simplify the way of writing security requirement to support the novice requirement engineers.

Acknowledgment. I would like to thank UTeM and MoE for the funding research: FRGS/1/2015/ICT01/FTMK/02/F00291.

References

1. El-Hadary, H., El-Kassas, S.: Capturing security requirements for software systems. J. Adv. Res. **5**(4), 463–472 (2014)
2. Zhivich, M., Cunningham, R.K.: The real cost of software errors. IEEE Secur. Priv. **2**(2), 87–90 (2009)

3. Salini, P., Kanmani, S.: Survey and analysis on security requirements engineering. Comput. Electr. Eng. **38**, 1785–1797 (2012)

4. Riaz, M., King, J., Slankas, J., Williams, L.: Hidden in plain sight: automatically identifying security requirements from natural language artifacts. In: IEEE 22nd International Requirements Engineering Conference, RE 2014, pp. 183–192 (2014)

5. Yu, E.S.K.: Towards modelling and reasoning support for early-phase requirements engineering. In: IEEE 3rd International Symposium on Requirements Engineering, ISRE 1997, pp. 226–235 (1997)

6. Mellado, D., Blanco, C., Sánchez, L.E., Fernández-Medina, E.: A systematic review of security requirements engineering. Comput. Stand. Interfaces **32**, 153–165 (2010)

7. Houmb, S.H., Islam, S., Knauss, E., Jürjens, J., Schneider, K.: Eliciting security requirements and tracing them to design: an integration of common criteria, heuristics, and UMLsec. Requir. Eng. **15**(1), 63–93 (2010).

8. Banerjee, A., Sharma, M., Banerjee, C., Pandey, S.K.: Research on security requirements engineering: problems and prospects. MATRIX Acad. Int. Online J. Eng. Technol. **3**(1), 32–35 (2015)

9. Firesmith, D.G.: Engineering security requirements. J. Object Technol. **2**(1), 53–68 (2003)

10. Jindal, R., Malhotra, R., Jain, A.: Automated classification of security requirements. In: International Conference on Advances in Computing, Communications and Informatics (ICACCI 2016), pp. 2027–2033 (2016)

11. Haley, C.B., Laney, R., Moffett, J.D., Nuseibeh, B.: Security requirements engineering: a framework for representation and analysis. IEEE Trans. Softw. Eng. **34**(1), 133–153 (2008)

12. CCRA: Common Criteria for Information Technology Security Evaluation (Part 2: Security Functional Components) (2017)

13. CCRA: Common Criteria for Information Technology Security Evaluation (Part 1: Introduction and General Model) (2017)

14. ISO/IEC: International Standard ISO/IEC 27000 (Information Technology — Security Techniques — Information Security Management Systems — Overview and Vocabulary) (2016)

15. Kamalrudin, M., Grundy, J., Hosking, J.: Tool support for essential use cases to better capture software requirements. In: ACM the International Conference on Automated Software Engineering, ASE 2010, pp. 255–264 (2010)

16. Chua, F.-F., Ngazizan, S.A., Hassan, M.: Design and implementation of airline reservation web services using service-oriented architecture. In: World Congress on Engineering 2010 (2010)

17. S.C.P. (SCP): EHR Functional Requirements (2009). https://nyehealth.org/wp-content/uploads/2012/07/Version_2_2_EHR_Functional_Requirements-16_Nov_09.pdf. Accessed 30 Aug 2017

18. Riaz, M., Stallings, J., Singh, M.P., Slankas, J., Williams, L.: DIGS – a framework for discovering goals for security requirements engineering. In: ACM International Symposium on Empirical Software Engineering and Measurement (ESEM 2016) (2016)

19. Riaz, M., Elder, S., Williams, L.: Systematically developing prevention, detection, and response patterns for security requirements. In: The 3rd International Workshop on Evolving Security and Privacy Requirements Engineering (ESPRE) (2016)

20. Riaz, M., Slankas, J., King, J., Williams, L.: Using templates to elicit implied security requirements from functional requirements - a controlled experiment. In: ACM the 8th International Symposium on Empirical Software Engineering and Measurement, ESEM 2014, p. 22 (2014)

21. Motil, A., Hamid, B., Lanusse, A., Bruel, J.-M., Motii, A., Hamid, B., Lanusse, A., Jean-Michel, B.: Guiding the selection of security patterns based on security requirements and pattern classification. In: ACM the 20th European Conference on Pattern Languages of Programs, EuroPLoP 2015, pp. 10:1–10:17 (2015)
22. Beckers, K., Côté, I., Goeke, L.: A catalog of security requirements patterns for the domain of cloud computing systems. In: ACM the 29th Symposium on Applied Computing, pp. 337–342 (2014)
23. Yahya, S., Kamalrudin, M., Sidek, S., Grundy, J.: Capturing security requirements using Essential Use Cases (EUCs). In: Zowghi, D., Jin, Z. (eds.) Requirements Engineering. CCIS, vol. 432, pp. 16–30. Springer, Heidelberg (2014). https://doi.org/10.1007/978-3-662-43610-3_2
24. Yusop, N., Kamalrudin, M., Sidek, S., Grundy, J.: Automated support to capture and validate security requirements for Mobile Apps. Commun. Comput. Inf. Sci. **671**, 97–112 (2016)
25. Salini, P., Kanmani, S.: Elicitation of security requirements for e-health system by applying Model Oriented Security Requirements Engineering (MOSRE) framework. In: ACM the Second International Conference on Computational Science, Engineering and Information Technology, CCSEIT 2012, pp. 126–131 (2012)

A Security Requirements Library for the Development of Internet of Things (IoT) Applications

Massila Kamalrudin[1], Asma Asdayana Ibrahim[2(✉)], and Safiah Sidek[1]

[1] Innovative Software System and Service Group,
Universiti Teknikal Malaysia Melaka, 76100 Durian Tunggal, Melaka, Malaysia
{massila, safiahsidek}@utem.edu.my
[2] Faculty of Information and Communication Technology,
Universiti Teknikal Malaysia Melaka, 76100 Durian Tunggal, Melaka, Malaysia
asmaasdayana@gmail.com

Abstract. In today's era, there is a rapid increase in the demand for IoT applications. Thus, securing the information content delivered among various entities involved in the IoT applications development has become an important issue. It is also identified that there is a high cost of implementing a secured IoT application as it requires efforts, skills and knowledge to understand the security concern, especially when developers and requirement engineers do not have any formal training in software engineering and eliciting security requirements. In addition, requirements engineers who are unfamiliar with the IoT applications confront problems to elicit accurate security requirements to avoid misinterpretations. Motivated by these issues, this paper presents the development of a new IoT security requirements library of security requirement for the development of IoT applications. Using an industry scenario, the utilities of the library demonstrated the elicitation of security requirements for each of the IoT attributes of specific business applications domains.

Keywords: Security requirement · Eliciting · Application development
Internet of Things (IoT) · IoT applications

1 Introduction

Internet of Things (IoT), is currently growing at a rapid rate in all business applications. IoT is defined as a coordination of multiple machines, devices and appliances connected to the Internet through multiple networks [1]. These devices include everyday objects such as tablets and consumer electronics. Other machines such as vehicles, monitors and sensors equipped with communication capabilities that allow them to send and receive data are also considered as IoT devices. Based on recent reports, the number of connected 'things' is set to explode and expected to reach 100 billion by 2025 [2]. With a rapid increase in the demand for IoT applications, securing the information content delivered among various entities involved in IoT applications development has become an important issue. Further, the problem of IoT security has

© Springer Nature Singapore Pte Ltd. 2018
M. Kamalrudin et al. (Eds.): APRES 2017, CCIS 809, pp. 87–96, 2018.
https://doi.org/10.1007/978-981-10-7796-8_7

become more and more challenging, especially on ensuring the use of secured and safe applications. It is also identified that the implementation of secured IoT applications is costly [3] since it requires efforts, skills and knowledge to understand the security attributes of IoT [4]. It is found that 70% of the most commonly used IoT devices contain security vulnerabilities due to the lack of consideration on the security issues during the development of these devices [2, 5]. It is also found that most of the requirements engineers fail to capture and elicit correct security related requirements during the eliciting phase as they face difficulties to understand the terms and knowledge of security [6, 7]. Further, it has been a common practice to seek the service of security engineer after the implementation stage of the application development. This practice leads to the validation of security errors at the later stage, causing the development of insecure application [8, 9]. Considering the abovementioned challenges, there is a need to elicit security related requirements at the early stage of IoT application development. In this respect, a simple method to identify the security properties for each of the IoT requirements during the requirements engineering process is necessary.

To address the issues above, an approach to facilitate the identification of security properties for the development of IoT applications has been proposed. Specifically, this paper describes a library of security requirements that supports the identification of the security properties for each of the associated IoT requirements. We posit that this library facilitates the elicitation of the security concern at the early stage of the IoT applications development. This paper is organized in five sections. After the introduction section, we present the background of and motivation for this study in Sect. 2. This is followed by the demonstration of our security library for IoT application in Sect. 3. Next, we present the realization of the library using a usage example in Sect. 4, and the related works in Sect. 5. Finally, the conclusion and future works are presented in Sect. 6.

2 Background and Motivation

2.1 IoT Applications

IoT has a huge potential for developing new intelligent applications in nearly every field, and it has been used in various domains, such as personal, social, societal, medical, environmental, logistics and many others. Irrespective of its application in various fields, it has one common aim that is to enhance the quality of every-day life. Hence, it has a profound impact on the economy and society. The application of IoT can be grouped into three major domains: (1) industrial domain, (2) smart city domain, and (3) health well-being domain [10]. As shown in Table 1, each of the three domains is sub-divided into two levels. For the first level, the three domains are divided between three to four categories. For example, the industrial domain is divided into three, which are: (i) logistic and product lifetime management, (ii) agriculture and breeding, and (iii) industrial processing. The smart city domain is divided into four, which are: (i) smart mobility and smart tourism, (ii) smart grid, (iii) smart homes/building, and (iv) public safety and environment monitor. Finally, the health well-being domain is further divided into two domains, which are: (i) medical and healthcare, and (ii) independent living. Further, each of the sub-categories of the three domains are further divided into three categories. Table 1 shows the three IoT domains and their sub-categories domains together with their related business applications [10]. For example, the tracking of products is common between the industrial and the health well-being domains as it can be used for monitoring cargos or foods as well as monitoring the delivery of pharmaceutical products.

Table 1. IoT related domains and business applications [10]

IoT domain	Related domain	Business applications
Industrial domain	Logistic and product lifetime management	Identification of materials/goods/product deterioration
		Warehouse management, retail, inventory
		Shopping operation, fast payment
	Agriculture and breeding	Animal tracking, animal certification, animation trade control
		Irrigation, monitoring agriculture production & feed
		Farm registration management
	Industrial processes	Real-time vehicle diagnostic, assemblage process, assistant driving
		Luggage management, boarding operation, mobile tickets
		Monitoring industrial plants
Smart city domain	Smart mobility and smart tourism	Traffic management, bike/car/van sharing, multi-modal transport
		Road condition monitoring, parking system, waste collection
		Payment systems, entertainment/tour guide services
	Smart grid	Power generation/distribution/storage, energy management
		Sustainable mobility, booking charging slots, customer recognition
		Load management, storage service, entertainment services
	Smart home/building	Plant maintenance HVAC/lighting/irritating, energy management
		Video surveillance, access management, children protection
		Entertainment, comfortable living
	Public safety and environmental monitoring	Environmental & territorial monitoring
		Video/radar/satellite surveillance
		Emergency site/rescue personal tracking, emergency plan

(*continued*)

Table 1. (*continued*)

IoT domain	Related domain	Business applications
Health well-being domain	Medical & healthcare	(Remote) monitoring medical Parameters, diagnostics
		Medical equipment tracking, secure/access indoor environment management
		Smart hospital services, entertainment services
	Independent living	Elderly assistance, disabled assistance
		Personal home, mobile assistance, social inclusion
		Individual well-being, personal behaviour impact on society

2.2 IoT Attributes and Security Properties

IoT consists of different suite of supporting technologies. It serves two main purposes: Firstly, it illustrates how various technologies relate to each other. Secondly, it communicates the scalability, modularity and configuration of IoT deployments in different scenarios. Typically, IoT is expected to offer advanced connectivity of devices, systems, and services that goes beyond machine-to-machine (M2M) communications and covers a variety of protocols, domains, and applications [11, 12]. The interconnection of these embedded devices (including smart objects) is expected to usher in automation in nearly all fields, while enabling advanced applications like smart grid, and

Table 2. Examples of IoT attributes and security requirement/properties

IoT attributes/Key technologies	Descriptions	IoT applications	Security requirement/properties
Sensors	Sensors are currently used in various fields like healthcare, military, and industry. Each sensor network consists of a large number of sensing nodes, in addition to a special node called sink, where the sink node is used to collect sensing results reported by other nodes in the network [13]	Healthcare [14–16], smart hospital [17] military, and industry, parking smart system [18], smart home [19], tracking system [20, 21]	Data privacy [15], data integrity [14–16], data freshness [15, 16], authentication [14–16, 21], anonymity [15], secure localization [15], data confidentiality [14, 16, 21], authorization [14, 16], forward security [14], architecture scalability [14], lightweight solutions [14], access control [14], availability [16]

expanding to areas such as smart cities. These devices collect useful data with the help of various existing technologies and then, autonomously flow the data to other devices. It is crucial for requirements engineers to understand all of the related technologies during the process of developing a secure application. In this regard, they need to have some experiences in the customer's domain to understand these requirements [9]. The commonly available methods for eliciting requirements, such as interviews and brainstorming are found to be time-consuming, and they fail to accurately identify security requirements. Therefore, eliciting security requirements using the present approaches and techniques are prone to be inaccurate, inconsistent and incomplete, leading to instances of insecure software and application development [5].

3   Development of IoT Security Library

Our approach is to elicit security requirements of IoT application in the early phase of application development [22]. In this paper, our focus is to develop a security requirement library of IoT applications using keyword matching that categorizes IoT applications based on its security properties. This library is aimed to assist the requirements engineers to elicit and identify correct security properties for each of the related IoT application requirements, also referred as attributes. With this library, requirements engineers can easily match the relevant security property that can be applied to each of IoT attributes. To do this, security requirements related to IoT applications development were collected and categorized according to two categories: IoT application and security properties. Table 2 shows an example of IoT attributes, 'sensor' and its related categorization. We also identified that each of the IoT attributes are associated with one or many security properties, as shown in Fig. 1.

Fig. 1. Relation of IoT attributes and security properties

We define the association and constraints among the IoT attributes and the security properties using a mathematical formulation as below:

$$F : Req_i \rightarrow A, \text{ where } i = \{1, 2, 3....n\} \text{ which is a set of IoT attributes}$$
$$\text{and } A = \{j, k, l\} \text{ which is a list of IoT security properties}$$

The rule is obtained once the relationship between the IoT attributes and security properties are established. Table 3 shows the examples of security properties and IoT attributes available in the library.

Table 3. Example of IoT security library: Security properties and IoT attributes

Examples of IoT attributes	Example of security properties
Mobility networks	Authentication
RFID systems	Confidentiality
WiFi	Integrity
Bluetooth	Authorization
Sensors	Access control
Wireless sensor network	Availability
Actuators	Data Integrity
Cloud	Anonymization
GPS	Identification
Embedded system	

Here, the library will suggest a security requirements based on selected IoT application. For example, if the user (requirement engineer) intends to develop a Smart home application (IoT application), the library will give the following suggestion:

$$\text{Smart home application} = \{\text{Bluetooth, mobility network}\}$$

Let us assume that the user choose Bluetooth as the attribute for the application. Based on the user's selection, the library will suggest the most suitable and correct security properties for Bluetooth, using keyword matching as below:

$$\text{Bluetooth} = \{\text{Authentication, Confidentiality, Authorization}\}$$

4   Usage Example

We used a scenario based on a real project of "Smart Parking System" [18] to demonstrate the realization and the usage of our security requirements library for IoT application development. Here, we demonstrate the utilities of the library based on this research question: "How can our security requirements library help to elicit and identify the security properties for each of the IoT attributes?". It is also important to note that the IoT attributes used in the description of the scenario are written in bold to highlight the use of the attributes in our security requirements library.

This scenario is a research project developed by Khanna and Anand [18] of an IoT based cloud integrated smart parking system. The proposed Smart Parking system consists of an on-site deployment of an IoT module used to monitor and signalize the state of availability of each single parking space. A mobile application that allows an end user to check the availability of parking space and book a parking slot accordingly is also provided. This parking system uses **sensors** like Infrared, Passive Infrared (PIR) and Ultrasonic Sensors. These **sensors** have similar function: To sense the parking area and to determine whether a parking slot is vacant or not. For this purpose, ultrasonic **sensors** are used to detect the presence of a car. The ultrasonic sensors are wirelessly connected to raspberry pi using the ESP8266 chip. An ESP8266 **WiFi** chip comprises of a self-contained SOC with integrated TCP/IP protocol stack that allows any microcontroller to access a **WiFi** network. The sensors are connected to a 5 V supply either from raspberry pi or an external source, considering the external source being more preferable.

Based on this scenario, the requirement engineer or application developer can use the suggestion from our security library to develop the smart parking system. As shown in Fig. 2, the requirements engineer needs to firstly choose the IoT domain "Smart City", then choose the suitable related applications, such as "Smart mobility and smart tourism". Then, the requirements engineer is able to choose the most relevant application based on the eight possible options related to business applications, which is "Parking system". Based on the selected application, IoT attributes related to "Parking system" will be displayed. Next, the library will show two matching IoT attributes of parking system, which are the "sensors" and the "WIFI". In this case, three security properties suitable for "sensors" are "authentication", "authorization" and "integrity". Meanwhile, two security properties suitable for "WIFI" are "Authentication" and Data Confidentially".

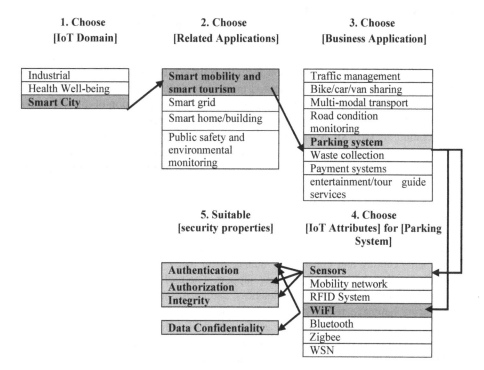

Fig. 2. Suggestion from the library for Smart Parking System

In summary, this scenario has demonstrated that our IoT security library is able to assist the requirements engineers to elicit security requirements by matching relevant security properties for each of the identified IoT attributes with the business application domains and type of applications. This process is believed could simplify and ease the elicitation of security requirements of the IoT requirements.

5 Related Works

Work by Kabir and Rahman [23] concentrated only on those approaches that proactively address the issue of security. They addressed a variety of approaches that could be adapted by engineer security requirements. They also specified a model for security requirements elicitation and presentation. The work has provided the knowledge of security requirements elicitation and presented approaches for requirements phase in software development life cycle. However, this model is limited to the security of functional requirements only: They did not consider other approaches. They also did not propose security requirements for IoT applications.

Beckers et al. [24] proposed a structured, pattern-based method for eliciting security requirements and selecting security measures called Cloud System Analysis Pattern. The method guides potential cloud customers to model the application of their business case in a cloud computing context using a pattern-based approach. Then, the information of the instantiated pattern can be used to fill-out the textual security requirements patterns and individually defined security requirement patterns. This work also designed a tool that supports the instantiation of the cloud system analysis pattern and automatically transfers the information from the instance to the security requirements patterns. They demonstrated their method using an online-banking system. However, this work only covers cloud computing domain, hence the application of this approach and tool in IoT application is beyond the scope of their work.

By combining CLASP, Misuse cases and Secure TROPOS, Islam and Qureshi [25] proposed a framework that contains the strengths of three security requirements elicitation techniques. They also included the security requirements categorization to make the proposed framework even more effective. The framework is flexible and contains fifteen steps to elicit security requirements. In addition, it allows iterations to improve the security in a system. However, this framework does not support elicitation techniques in security requirement of IoT applications.

Kamalrudin et al. [26–28] developed a technique and toolset, MaramaAI to support requirements capture and consistency management using EUCs. This tool is supplemented by end-to-end rapid prototyping support. The tool uses EUC patterns to validate requirements consistency, completeness, and correctness. Nonetheless, it focuses on capturing language requirements only, hence the application of this tool in IoT application security requirements is past the extent of their work.

Yusop et al. [29] proposed an automated approach and tool, called MobiMEReq that helps to capture and validate the security attributes requirements of mobile apps. They employed the concept of Test Driven Development (TDD) with a model-based testing strategy using Essential Use Cases (EUCs) and Essential User Interface (EUI) models. They also conducted an evaluation to compare the performance and correctness of the tool in various application domains. The results of the study showed that their tool is able to help requirements engineers to effectively capture and validate security-related requirements of mobile applications. However, they did not address the task to elicit requirements of IoT applications.

6 Conclusion and Future Work

Due to the fluid function of IoT, security requirements is one of the most important intangible requirements that needs to be taken into consideration at the early stage of developing IoT applications. To develop secured applications, it is essential to correctly focus on the essential security needs and rules. Therefore, this study presents a library of security requirement for IoT application that is able to assist the requirements engineers to elicit security requirements by matching relevant security control for each of the identified IoT attributes with the business application domains and type of applications. It is argued that the library is able to assist in developing a more secure IoT application. The library facilitates requirements engineer to elicit security requirements for IoT applications at the initial step of application development. For future work, a mapping of security properties with a specific security policy will be conducted. Further, the function of the library will be realized with an automated tool to help requirements engineers and application developers to automatically elicit and identify the security requirement at the early stage of IoT application development.

Acknowledgements. The authors would like to acknowledge Universiti Teknikal Malaysia Melaka (UTeM) and Ministry of Higher Education (MoHE) for its support and the funding of this FRGS research grant: FRGS/1/2016/ICT01/FTMK-CACT/F00325.

References

1. GSM Association, IoT Security Guidelines Overview Document (2016)
2. Rose, K., Eldridge, S., Chapin, L.: The Internet of Things: An Overview Understanding the Issues of a More Connected World (2015)
3. Maskani, I., Boutahar, J., El Houssaini, S.E.G.: Analysis of security requirements engineering: towards a comprehensive approach. Int. J. Adv. Comput. Sci. Appl. **7**(11), 38–45 (2016)
4. Borgohain, T., Kumar, U., Sanyal, S.: Survey of security and privacy issues of Internet of Things. Cryptogr. Secur., 7 (2015)
5. Tankard, C.: The security issues of the Internet of Things. Comput. Fraud Secur. **2015**(9), 11–14 (2015)
6. Ramesh, M.R.R., Reddy, C.S.: A survey on security requirement elicitation methods: classification, merits and demerits. Int. J. Appl. Eng. Res. **11**(1), 64–70 (2016)
7. Ikram, N., Siddiqui, S., Khan, N.F.: Security requirement elicitation techniques : the comparison of misuse cases and issue based information systems, pp. 36–43 (2014)
8. Oltsik, J.: The Internet of Things: a CISO and network security perspective. ESG White Paper, October 2014
9. Russell, B., Garlati, C., Lingenfelter, D.: Security guidance for early adopters of the Internet of Things (IoT). Mob. Work. Gr. Peer Rev. Doc., April 2015
10. Borgia, E.: The Internet of Things Vision: key features, applications and open issues. Comput. Commun. **54**, 1–31 (2014)

11. Zolanvari, M.: IoT security: a survey, pp. 1–15 (2010)
12. Patel, K.L., Patel, S.M.: Internet of Things-IOT : definition, characteristics, architecture, enabling technologies, application & future challenges. Int. J. Eng. Sci. Comput. **6**(5), 6122–6131 (2016)
13. Alqassem, I., Svetinovic, D.: A taxonomy of security and privacy requirements for the internet of things (IoT). In: 2014 IEEE International Conference on Industrial Engineering and Engineering Management (IEEM), pp. 1244–1248 (2014)
14. Rahimi, S., Nguyen, T., Rahmani, A.M.: End-to-end security scheme for mobility enabled healthcare Internet of Things. Futur. Gener. Comput. Syst. **64**, 108–124 (2016)
15. Gope, P., Hwang, T.: BSN-Care: a secure IoT-Based modern healthcare using body sensor network. IEEE Sens. J. **16**(5), 1368–1376 (2016)
16. Islam, S.M.R., Kwak, D., Kabir, H.: The Internet of Things for health care: a comprehensive survey. IEEE Access **3**, 678–708 (2015)
17. Dhariwal, K., Mehta, A.: Architecture and plan of smart hospital based on Internet of Things (IOT). Int. Res. J. Eng. Technol. **4**(4), 1976–1980 (2017)
18. Khanna, A., Anand, R.: IoT based smart parking system. In: International Conference on Internet of Things and Applications (IOTA), pp. 266–270 (2016)
19. Aravindan, V., James, D.: Smart homes using Internet of Things. Int. Res. J. Eng. Technol. **4**(4), 1725–1729 (2017)
20. Lau, H., Zhu, M., Ye, S.: An intelligent tracking system based on Internet of Things for the cold chain. Internet Res. **26**(2), 435–445 (2016)
21. Ukil, A., Bandyopadhyay, S., Bhattacharyya, A., Pal, A., Bose, T.: Lighweight security scheme for iot application using CoAP. Int. J. Pervasive Comput. Commun. **10**(4), 372–392 (2014)
22. Ibrahim, A.A., Kamalrudin, M., Abdollah, M.F.: Postgraduate research seminar 2017 (PGRS 2017). In: Proceeding of Postgraduate Research Seminar in Conjuction with ISORIS 2017, pp. 235–242, July 2017
23. Kabir, A., Rahman, M.: A survey on security requirements elicitation and presentation in requirements engineering phase. Am. J. Eng. Res. **2**(12), 360–366 (2014)
24. Beckers, K., Heisel, M., Côté, I., Goeke, L., Güler, S.: A structured method for security requirements elicitation concerning the cloud computing domain. Int. J. Secur. Softw. Eng. **5**(2), 24 (2014)
25. Islam, G., Qureshi, M.A.: A Framework for Security Requirements Elicitation (2012)
26. Kamalrudin, M.: Automated Support for Consistency Management and Validation of Requirements (2011)
27. Kamalrudin, M., Hosking, J., Grundy, J.: MaramaAIC: tool support for consistency management and validation of requirements. Autom. Software Eng. **24**(1), 1–45 (2016)
28. Kamalrudin, M., Grundy, J.: Generating essential user interface prototypes to validate requirements. In: Proceedings of the 2011 26th IEEE/ACM International Conference on Automated Software Engineering, ASE 2011, pp. 564–567 (2011)
29. Yusop, N., Kamalrudin, M., Sidek, S.: Automated support to capture and validate security requirements for mobile apps. Requir. Eng. Towar. Sustain. World **671**, 97–112 (2016)

Crowd-Sourcing

Eliciting Activity Requirements from Crowd Using Genetic Algorithm

Chunhui Wang[1,2,3], Wei Zhang[1,2], Haiyan Zhao[1,2], and Zhi Jin[1,2(✉)]

[1] Key Laboratory of High Confidence Software Technology (MoE),
Peking University, Beijing, China
{ciecwch,zhangw.sei,zhhy.sei,zhijin}@pku.edu.cn
[2] Institute of Software, School of EECS, Peking University, Beijing, China
[3] Computer and Information Engineering College,
Inner Mongolia Normal University, Hohhot, China

Abstract. Web-based software systems face a wide range of users and situates in different context. Developing such systems needs to deal with the diversity and variability of requirements. Crowd-based requirements engineering performs requirements engineering activities, such as elicitation requirements from the crowd of stakeholders. That leads to the collected requirements being more diverse and wider coverage. However, the requirements elicited from crowd are not directly available and need to be merged into system requirements. It is a tedious and error-prone work without the help of automatic method. System requirements can be expressed in a variety of ways, of which activity diagram is widely used. This paper provides a method based on genetic algorithm. This approach targets to solve two key issues about the individual requirements representation and the requirements synthesis, one is using a triangular matrix encoding scheme to ensure completeness and uniqueness of genetic representation of solution, the other is proposing a generalized information entropy as fitness function to measure candidate solutions. A simple but meaningful example has been used to demonstrate the feasible of this approach. Moreover, during the synthesis of activity diagrams, the information source's IDs are kept. This can be used for building the traceability links between the system requirements and their source. That will be helpful to requirements management and evolution.

Keywords: Crowd-based requirement elicitation · Activity diagram
Genetic algorithm

1 Introduction

At present, many of application software are web-based, facing a wide range of users and running in an open and dynamic environment [1]. The users of such a system may come from everywhere in the world, i.e., they are highly distributed form a large, heterogeneous online group, and then may have different kinds of needs and desires, and the system need to satisfy these different kinds of requirements [2–5]. For example, online payment systems are intended to be used by various kinds of users. These users may have different preferences on payment ways, like using credit cards, Alipay, WeChat,

© Springer Nature Singapore Pte Ltd. 2018
M. Kamalrudin et al. (Eds.): APRES 2017, CCIS 809, pp. 99–113, 2018.
https://doi.org/10.1007/978-981-10-7796-8_8

money transfer and so on. For developing any system, the developers need first to gather the requirements of all these potential users of wide diversity and build a system model that can satisfy as many as possible the users' needs.

Traditional requirements engineering approaches generally elicit requirements through face-to-face meetings, interviews, brainstorming sessions, focus groups, and so on [6]. In such way, the number and the distribution of the participants are limited. Crowd-based requirements engineering utilizes the power of the crowd in contributing information, then discover creative requirements [7–9]. It gives the software developers the opportunity accessing to a wide diversity of potential users.

For allowing the crowd to be involved in requirements elicitation and making the eliciting results being usable directly by the developers, some issues need to be solved. The first could be how the participants describe their needs in an understandable way to help the requirements elicitation? Some crowd based approaches accept the users' feature comments and feedbacks in natural language and the developers manually analysis the comments and feedbacks to decide the system requirements. They use linguistic analysis techniques [11] for analysis crowd feedback. However, it is difficult identifying all the relevant information and automatically analyzing feedback from great amount of noisy feedbacks. The manual analysis is time-consuming and error-prone and the developers' burden is heavy.

Asking the crowd to use some structured or semi-structured way, e.g., some kind diagram or pseudo natural language, to describe the pieces of requirements is a promising way to solve the representation problem. In addition, using structured representation can enable the automated merging of the pieces of requirements and resulting in the system requirements.

This paper uses activity diagram as the interactive process requirements description language. Activity diagram is a widely-used graphical representation of workflows of stepwise activities and actions [12]. It can simply and quite plainly show how things work and easily comprehensible. Additionally, it can describe the requirements of different levels, e.g., the entire system, a use case, or a user story. Moreover, using activity diagram makes it possible to automatically combine the massive pieces of requirements. Many existing works have shown this possibility in the tasks of automated test case synthesis, test case generation, and fault checking [13–16].

The second question is how to combine the massive individual pieces of requirements to create the system requirements in an automated or semi-automated way? This paper proposes to use genetic algorithm to produce the system activity diagram from the set of activity diagrams. Here, there two key issues that need to be solved, i.e., the chromosome encoding and the fitness function. The chromosome encoding is for defining the genetic representation of the solution. In order to ensure the completeness and uniqueness of encoding and to save space effectively, a triangular matrix encoding scheme is proposed to represent the diagram merging solution. Fitness function is for evaluating the solution. A generalized entropy is proposed to measure the solution's fitness, so that it can measure the divergence degree of the merged node, i.e., the divergence of name and incoming edge and outgoing edge.

This paper uses a simple but meaningful case study to demonstrate the feasible of this approach. The result shows that our method can obtain a synthesis diagram from a set of activity diagrams. Moreover, during the synthesis of activity diagrams, the informant's IDs are kept. This information can be used for building the traceability links between the system requirements and their source. That will be helpful to requirements management and evolution.

The rest of the paper is organized as follows: Sect. 2 describes a motivation example to explain our work. Section 3 introduces crowd-based requirements elicitation approach. Section 4 presents genetic algorithm for activity diagram automatic merging, including the main idea, algorithm overview, encoding scheme, fitness function, and genetic operators. Section 5 a case study is designed to investigate the feasible of merging approach. Finally, we summarize our study and future work.

2 A Motivating Example

An example scenario is chosen as a running case, where developers intend to build a web-based online book store. For enhancing the competitiveness, they hope their system can be a crowd oriented application by catering for the needs of more wide range of people. They decide using a crowd-based method to elicit requirements. They post the requirements question to the crowd, e.g. "what is the best way for you to choose books to your shopping cart?". They ask the participants to use activity diagram with a narrative comment to describe their needs. Then they gather the feedbacks from crowd. They get lots of answers. The following are three answers among others:

- As a user, I want to search books, then the books I need will be added to the shopping cart.
- As a user, I want to browse the recommended books on the site, then the books I need will be added to the shopping cart.
- As a user, I want to browse the recommended books on the site, then the books will be added to the shopping cart if they are stockout.

These requirements descriptions can be depicted as activity diagrams respectively, as shown in Fig. 1.

For developing the system requirements of "adding a book to the shopping cart", the developers need to merge all the diagrams they received together to obtain the system activity diagram. So that the to-be system can satisfy the needs of potential users by following the system activity diagram.

The manual analysis is time-consuming and error-prone. The developers want to have an automatic method to help them to synthesize these individual activity diagrams. The result needs to be still an activity diagram with one initial node and one final end. Meanwhile, the duplicate activities (nodes) and controls (edges) are eliminated (seeking the same), and all activities proposed by the crowd are retained (saving the difference). Concretely, they want to have an activity diagram merging algorithm to help them.

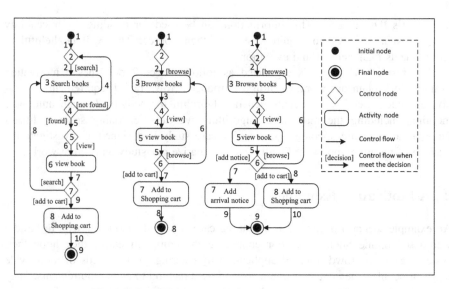

Fig. 1. Three activity diagrams gathering from a crowd

3   Crowd-Based Requirements Elicitation

Crowd-based requirements engineering (CrowdRE) is performing RE activities such as elicitation from the crowd of stakeholders [7–9]. It turns RE into a participatory effort, leads to more accurate requirements, and ultimately boosts software quality. It is used for obtaining and analyzing a continuous flow of user feedback and monitoring data on the usage context, with the goal of deriving validated user requirements. CrowdRE depends on a continuous flow of user feedback.

- Motivating Crowd Members: Crowdsourcing has recently been recommended as a relatively cheaper and time-saving way to gather more requirements [7–9]. To abstract more participation, some reward mechanisms have been provided [17].
- Eliciting Feedback: Crowd members can report on a variety of aspects, including requirements questions. CrowdRE providing multiple feedback channels let developers consider crowd members' individual backgrounds and needs regarding feedback communication.
- Analyzing Feedback: To analyze the feedback gathered from different channels, CrowdRE predominantly uses linguistic analysis techniques [7]. This analysis filters out irrelevant data(statements) and automatically classifies the remaining data.
- Monitoring Context and Usage Data: Depend on sensors in highly distributed environments, Crowd-based monitoring results can be aggregated with multi-modal feedback from users to quantify and better understand similarities and differences.

To analyze the large amount of data obtained from the crowd, automated approaches are key. Current efforts use techniques, such as text mining [11], and speech-act-based analysis [18], to deal with participants' natural language feedbacks or comments. Developers still need to pay great efforts on understanding these feedbacks for producing the system requirements. It is needed to combine the individual feedbacks automatically into an integrated view. Such an automated synthesis method is still missing.

Of course, for automatically combining the individual requirements (from the crowd), representing the individual requirements in a structured way would make the thing easier. That is why we choose activity diagram to describe the individual requirements. With a set of activity diagrams coming from the crowd, we propose a genetic algorithm based approach to merge the activity diagrams and generate a synthetic solution which can serve a crowd consensus about requirements question. Next section will discuss this approach.

4 Genetic Algorithm Based Approach for Activity Diagram Merging

The synthesis of individual activity diagram is a combinatorial optimization problem. It is trying to combine nodes in individual activity diagrams iteratively, until find a best combination solution, in which all of duplicate nodes are combined together. Genetic algorithms (GA) is a metaheuristic inspired by the process of natural selection. They are commonly used to generate high-quality solutions to optimize and search problems by relying on bio-inspired operators such as selection, crossover and mutation [19]. Before describing details of the algorithm, we first discuss the main idea of activity diagram synthesis approach.

4.1 Main Idea

Given a set of activities diagrams $S = \{G_i | i = 1, 2, \ldots, N\}$, $G_i = \{V_i, E_i\}$ is an activity diagram in S, and $V_i = \{n_{i,j} | i = 1, 2, \ldots, N, j = 1, 2, \ldots, k_i\}$ is a set of nodes in G_i and $E_i = \{e_{i,j} | i = 1, 2, \ldots, N, j = 1, 2, \ldots, l_i\}$ is a set of edges in G_i. The number of nodes in G_i is k_i, and the edge number is l_i, e.g., Fig. 2 shows three activity diagrams G_1, G_2 and G_3.

Nodes in these diagrams are merged firstly, then edges are merged according to the merged nodes. To represent how to merge nodes in multiple diagrams, we first construct a matrix M with N lines and $c(c = k_1 + k_2 + \ldots + k_N)$ columns, then place successively each node n_{ij} in a cell which position is (i, r), where r is a random number between 1 to c. After all of nodes in these diagrams are placed in M, a merged way of these nodes is represented by the matrix, where each column is a merged node. For example, in Fig. 2, all of nodes of G_1, G_2 and G_3 are placed in a matrix with 3 lines and 7 columns, and there are four merged nodes which are $\{1.2, 2.2\}, \{1.3, 3.1\}, \{3.2\}$ and $\{1.1, 2.1\}$. According to this merging solution, edges are added to the merged nodes based on its source and target, then the edges with the same source and target are merged together, such as $\{e_{11}, e_{21}\}$, then a merged diagram will be obtained. We can see that the key issue of synthesis of individual activity diagram is finding an optimal combination of nodes merging.

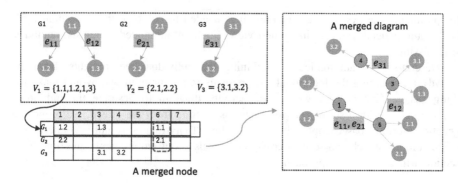

Fig. 2. The main idea of merging method

What is the time complexity of finding the optimal solution for the nodes merging? Suppose there is an optimal solution, which is represented by a matrix, and the problem of finding the optimal solution is transformed into the problem of constructing this matrix, that is, arranging the combinatorial problem. We calculate the combination numbers of getting the optimal solution by placing each node of diagrams in the fit position. The complexity of merging one diagram is $O(c!)$. There are N diagrams, so the complexity of finding the optimal solution is $O(C!^N)$. It is NP hard problem to find an optimal solution. Genetic algorithms are commonly used to generate high-quality solutions to optimization and search problems, so we use genetic algorithm to solve merging problem of multiple diagrams.

There are three concerns when utilize genetic algorithm for automatic requirement merging: the first is how to encode a chromosome for genetic representation, the second is how to measure the fitness of candidate chromosomes, the third is how to evolve chromosomes using the genetic operators. Encoding is the genetic representation of activity diagram merging. Although the matrix in Fig. 2 completely represents the merging way of multiple activity diagrams, we do not use directly the matrix as encoding, but use a triangular matrix to encode a chromosome. The triangular matrix is derived from the matrix and it have some good performance in integrity, uniqueness and more space saving, and it will be described in Sect. 4.3.

A fitness function is designed to evaluate each chromosome. The divergence in a merged node may occur due to attributes of nodes, e.g., name, type, incoming edges and outgoing edges. For a best chromosome, the divergence of each merged node needs to be minimal. That means after moving away a node from a merged node to another merged node, the divergence becomes larger. A generalized information entropy is proposed as a fitness function to measure the divergence. The smaller the divergence is, and the smaller the generalized entropy is. The generalized entropy is described in Sect. 4.4.

Genetic algorithm proceeds to initialize a population of chromosomes and then to improve it through repetitive application of the crossover, mutation, and selection operators. The process is introduced in Sect. 4.2, and the crossover and the mutation are described in Sect. 4.5.

4.2   Overview of the Approach

Genetic algorithm generates a set of initial solutions, evolves over generations, and terminates when meeting the stopping condition. A good enough solution is returned as a consequence. Algorithm 1 shows this top-level process.

Algorithm 1. Genetic Algorithm for activity diagram synthesis.

Input: a set of activity diagrams
Output: a merged activity diagram
1: create initial population of fixed size;
2: repeat
3:     for i=1 to n do
4:         choose $parent_1$ and $parent_2$;
5:         $offspring_i \leftarrow crossover(parent_1, parent_2)$;
6:         $mutation(offspring_i)$;
7:     end for
8:     choose elites from n offspring;
9:     reproduce next population by replacing chromosomes with elites;
10: until stopping condition
11:return the best chromosome

The genetic algorithm has five key aspects:

- Initial population: When genetic algorithm starts, chromosomes of fixed size are created at random.
- Chromosome Fitness: Generalized information entropy is proposed to measure the fitness.
- Stopping condition: The algorithm limit the number of repetitive of genetic operators as stopping condition.
- Genetic Operators: The operators include selection, crossover and mutation. After doing these operators, the new population is obtained.
- Elitism: Better chromosomes (the fitness is smaller) from the new population become elites to replace the worse chromosomes (the fitness is larger) in previous population.

4.3   Encoding Scheme

Type of node is considered in our encoding, because only the same type of node can be merged and evolved. Nodes with the same type are clustered, then encode for each set. Given a set of $V = \{V_i | i = 1, 2, \ldots, N\}$, the number of node type is T. In the example of Fig. 1, there are four kinds of node type: initial node, final node, control node and activity node. Supposed V_i^j is a set of nodes with j type in V_i, and j is between 1 to T. $V^j = \{V_i^j | i = 1, 2, \ldots, N, j = 1, 2, \ldots T\}$ represents a set of nodes with j type in the group of diagrams. Each subset V_i^j is encoded and combined together to get a chromosome.

Each subset of nodes with the same type is encoded with a way to facilitate the genetic operators. A matrix based on the method in Sect. 4.1 is constructed, e.g., in Fig. 3, the matrix is got by generating randomly in the subset $\{V_1^2, V_2^2, V_3^2\}$. Observing this matrix reveals that it is disorder of the merged nodes, so this representation is not a one-to-one correspondence with the merging solution. To obtain a one-to-one correspondence representation, the matrix is sorted on the merged nodes. In each line, the nodes are placed according to its id's sequence, that is the nodes in the first diagram are placed at a position from 1 to k_1, and the nodes in the second diagram are placed at a position from $k_1 + 1$ to $k_1 + k_2$, and other nodes are placed in the same way. If some node is merged to other column, the position is vacancy. For example, a sorted matrix is constructed, as shown in the middle diagram in Fig. 3. The shaded part has no element, because all of the nodes in V_i have been sorted and placed at the front cell. So the encoding is a triangle matrix, and it is more space saving. Some special values are filled in some empty cells. -1 means that no node of V_i is merged to the column. 0 is flagged means that the column is empty.

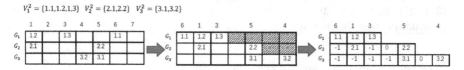

Fig. 3. An example of constructing a triangular matrix encoding

4.4   Fitness Function

According to a merged solution(chromosome), a merged graph is obtained by merging the edges as described in Sect. 4.1. The fitness function is calculated to quantify the degree of divergence of the merged diagram. The information entropy is used to calculate the probability distribution of a state, and then measure the amount of information that is conflict before reception [10]. The state in merging problem is merged nodes, and the information refer to the attributes of merged nodes, such as name, incoming edges and outgoing edges. So we chose the information entropy as the fitness function to measure the merged diagram. However, the information entropy does not take into account the similarity between states, e.g., the similarity of "browse books" and "search books" is different with the "browse books" and "search orders". The similarity between states is influential to merging problem, so it is increased to the information entropy. The entropy increased the similarity is more general to measure the differences in state, so it called as the generalized entropy (following abbreviated as entropy) which is described in Eq. (1) (n is the number of states of some attribute).

$$H(v_i) = -\sum_{k=1}^{n}\left(p(x_k) * \log\left(\sum_{t=1}^{n}p(x_t)s(x_k, x_t)\right)\right) \tag{1}$$

Next, we provide an example of using the Eq. (1) to compute the entropy of a merged node. Figure 4 shows two different merged nodes (the yellow node shows a merged node). In the left-hand side of Fig. 4, the encoding of the merged node is $\{2, -1, 1\}$ represented a merging of u'_1s 2 node (the node's name is "search books") and u'_3s 1 node (the node's name is "browse books"). Similarly, in the right-hand side, the encoding of the merged node is $\{2, 1, 1\}$ which combines u'_1s 2 node (whose name is "search books"), u'_2s 1 node and u'_3s 1 node (whose names are "browse books").

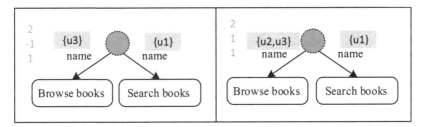

Fig. 4. Two examples of calculating generalized entropy of name edge

To get the entropy of a merged node, the distribution $p(x)$ of state X is calculated firstly. In the two images shown in Fig. 4, there are two states about name attribute: $X_1 =$ "*browse books*", $X_2 =$ "*search books*". The distributions of X in the left-hand side are $p(X_1) = 1/2$ and the $p(X_2) = 1/2$. The distributions in the right-hand side are $p(X_1) = 2/3$ and the $p(X_2) = 1/3$.

We use Eq. (2) to measure these similarity, such as the similarity of "browse books" and "search books" is 1/3.

$$s(x_k, x_t) = \frac{|token_{x_k} \cap token_{x_t}|}{|token_{x_k} \cup token_{x_t}|} \tag{2}$$

Using the Eq. (1), the entropy of the left-hand side of Fig. 5 is:

$$H(v_i) = -\sum_{k=1}^{n}\left(p(x_k) * \log\left(\sum_{t=1}^{n} p(x_t)s(x_k, x_t)\right)\right)$$

$$= -\frac{1}{2} * \log\left(\frac{1}{2} + \frac{1}{2}*\frac{1}{3}\right) - \frac{1}{2} * \log\left(\frac{1}{2} + \frac{1}{2}*\frac{1}{3}\right) = 0.176$$

The entropy of the right-hand side of Fig. 5 is:

$$H(v_i) = -\sum_{k=1}^{n}\left(p(x_k) * \log\left(\sum_{t=1}^{n} p(x_t)s(x_k, x_t)\right)\right)$$

$$= -\frac{2}{3} * \log\left(\frac{2}{3} + \frac{1}{3}*\frac{1}{3}\right) - \frac{1}{3} * \log\left(\frac{1}{3} + \frac{2}{3}*\frac{1}{3}\right) = 0.158$$

From this example, we can see that the right-hand image has better fitness than the left-hand side if we only consider the attribute of name. There are some other attributes which may be divergence due to merging nodes, and expressed in the distribution of edge. For example, in Fig. 5, there are two control edges (1 and 2) which target node is "search books" in u_1 and one control edge (2) which target node is "browse books" in u_3. So there are two kinds of state about the edges with the control flow type in the crowd, one is $\{1,2\}(u_1)$ and $\{2\}(u_3)$, and their similarity is 1/2.

We also use the Eq. (1) to calculate the entropy of the edge with control flow type. Here, the states are $X_1 = \{1,2\}$ and $X_2 = \{2\}$. The probabilities of distribution of these states are $p(X_1) = 1/2$ and $p(X_2) = 1/2$.

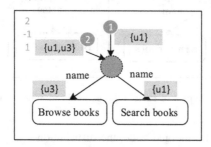

Fig. 5. An example of calculating generalized entropy of the same type edge

Entropy of a merged node is the sum of entropy of edge with the same type (including the "name" edge, and calculating with Eq. (3), in which the m is the number of edge distributions type). Entropy of a chromosome is the sum of all of the merged nodes, calculated with Eq. (4) ($|\dot{E}|$ means the number of merged nodes).

$$H(v_i) = - \sum_{j=1}^{m} \left(\sum_{k=1}^{n} \left(p(x_k) * \log \left(\sum_{t=1}^{n} p(x_t) s(x_k, x_t) \right) \right) \right) \qquad (3)$$

$$F(\delta) = \left(\sum_{i=1}^{N} (H(v_i)) \right) * |\dot{E}| \qquad (4)$$

4.5 Genetic Operators

Genetic operators including selection, crossover and mutation. Selection operator uses a roulette selection method. Crossover operator will recombine merged nodes of two chromosomes to generate new offspring. Mutation operator introduces changes in chromosome and reduces the chances of finding local solutions. After genetic operators, a new population will be generated.

Crossover operator. Figure 6 illustrates the crossover operator. After selecting two chromosomes, a *crossover position* is randomly selected, such as the random number 2. Then two chromosomes swap all of their elements after the second bit position in each encoding. In Fig. 6, the left-hand side is the two parent chromosomes and the right-hand side is two offspring.

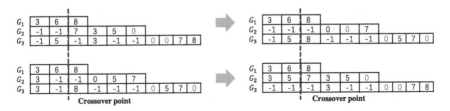

Fig. 6. An example for crossover operator

The swapping operation could be make the encoding no longer satisfy the encoding properties. For example, for the left-hand side in Fig. 7, there is no 5 in the third line, and there two 3 in the second line. Algorithm 2 is designed to make the encoding fit its constraint.

Fig. 7. An example for crossover correction

Algorithm 2: correct the encoding after crossover operator
Input: a chromosome encoding
Output: a chromosome encoding satisfied the encoding constraint
1: for each row in the triangular matrix
2:     elements = {each node of individual diagram}
3:     for each number(element) < 1
4:         remain only one element, and other bits are set to
5:     for each number(element) = 0
6:         add the element at a random position

Mutation operator. We take two kinds of mutation strategy, split and exchange, e.g. Fig. 8. Split is the decomposition of a merged node, and the exchange is a reorganization of a chromosome.

5   Case Study

In this section, we give an example for evaluating our approach. As we described in previous section, our approach has two significant features for enhancing activity requirements elicitation. One is that a synthesis activity diagram can be obtained automatically from a set of individual activity diagrams. The other is that the requirements provider IDs can be recorded in synthesis activity diagram. Such traceability information can facilitate the change impact analysis. The following three questions can be used to demonstrate these features.

- Q1. Dose genetic algorithm get a good enough fitness solution?
- Q2. Dose the merged diagram represent a synthesis activity diagram?
- Q3. Dose the merged diagram support traceability?

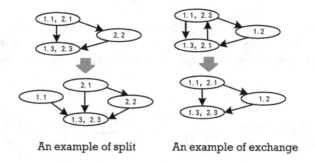

An example of split   An example of exchange

Fig. 8. Two examples of mutation strategy

Algorithm 1 produces a solution with the three example activity diagrams in Sect. 2 as input. Figure 9 shows the solution. The left-hand side of the figure is the encoding representation of the solution and the provider IDs of synthesis diagram. The right-hand side of the figure shows the synthesis activity diagram.

A checklist is designed to answer these three questions. The checklist is provided to the model users, allowing them to evaluate the synthesis diagram and give the answers. The answers in the checklist are "yes", we can see that the synthesis diagram answers the three questions raised above (Table 1).

The synthesis diagram combines the nodes and the edges of each individual activity diagram. Duplicate nodes and duplicate edges are synthesized together. All nodes and all edges of each individual diagram are preserved. The synthesis diagram is structured as an activity diagram. At the same time, the information source's IDs are recorded in the synthesis diagram.

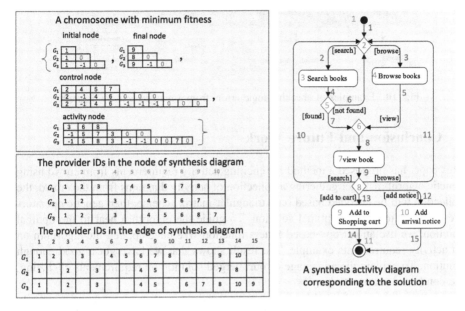

Fig. 9. A synthesis activity diagram of Fig. 1.

Table 1. Feasibility investigation of a synthesis activity diagram

	Question	Answer
Q1	Is it automated to obtain a synthesis diagram?	yes
Q2	Are the duplicate nodes or the duplicate edges synthesized and saved only one duplicate?	yes
Q2	Is any node and any one edge of each individual diagram presented in the synthesis diagram?	yes
Q3	Is there only an initial node and a final node in the synthesis diagram?	yes
Q3	Is there at least a path from initial node to final node in the synthesis diagram?	yes
Q3	Can an individual diagram be extracted from the synthesis diagram?	yes

In addition, during the synthesis of diagrams, some errors in input diagrams can be found. For example, Fig. 10 shows some errors:

- Case 1: The same decision (edge) from a source of the activity has a different activity target.
- Case 2: There are two mutual exclusion decisions (edges) from an activity source to an activity target.
- Case 3: The description of a decision is irrelevant with the activity name.
- Case 4: There are two reverse flows between two activities.

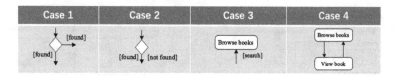

Fig. 10. Examples of checking logic errors from a merged activity diagram

6 Conclusion and Future Work

This paper has proposed a method for eliciting activity requirements from crowd using genetic algorithm. After gathering a collection of activity diagrams from the crowd, the collection will be encoded based on a triangular matrix scheme, then genetic operators are executed to find an optimal solution. To guide the algorithm near to the optimal solution, we use an entropy-based fitness function. We have applied the algorithm on an activity requirements example. The result shows that we have got a good enough solution. To explain the advantage of our merged solution on requirements elicitation, we conducted a case study.

Our algorithm is affected by the no-normalized description about name in activity diagram, such as "view book", "watch book", "look book". Although different name maybe expresses the same semantic, our algorithm can't identify them, so algorithm can't merge them together. However, if the relevance of these descriptions is given in advance, our algorithm can handle such problems.

In our future work, we plan to carry out more empirical research on this approach, and conduct more in-depth study on the requirements description of individual activity diagram and the analysis of synthesis diagram.

Acknowledgments. This work is supported by the National Basic Research Program of China (the 973 Program) under grant 2015CB352201, the National Natural Science Foundation of China under grant 61620106007 and 61432020.

References

1. Sampaio, A., Vasconcelos, A., Sampaio, P.R.F.: Assessing agile methods: an empirical study. J. Braz. Comput. Soc. **10**(2), 21–48 (2004)
2. Ali, R., Solis, C., Omoronyia, I., Salehie, M., Nuseibeh, B.: Social adaptation: when software gives users a voice. In: Proceedings of the 7th International Conference on Evaluation of Novel Approaches to Software Engineering (ENASE), June 2012
3. Gultekin, P., Bekker, T., Lu, Y., Brombacher, A., Eggen, B.: Combining user needs and stakeholder requirements: the value design method. In: Markopoulos, P., Martens, J.-B., Malins, J., Coninx, K., Liapis, A. (eds.) Collaboration in Creative Design, pp. 97–119. Springer, Cham (2016). https://doi.org/10.1007/978-3-319-29155-0_6
4. Tuunanen, T., Rossi, M.: Engineering a method for wide audience requirements elicitation and integrating it to software development. In: Hawaii International Conference on System Sciences, 10 p. IEEE (2004)

5. Stakeholders, S., Barber, K.S., Graser, T.: Effective representation and search in intelligent requirements management and query tools supporting system stakeholders (2000)
6. Sommerville, I.: Software engineering (6th edition). IT Prof. **8**(2), 57 (2001)
7. Groen, E.C., Seyff, N., Ali, R., et al.: The crowd in requirements engineering: the landscape and challenges. IEEE Softw. **34**(2), 44–52 (2017)
8. Srivastava, P.K., Sharma, R.: Crowdsourcing to elicit requirements for MyERP application. In: IEEE International Workshop on Crowd-Based Requirements Engineering, pp. 31–35. IEEE (2016)
9. Hosseini, M., Shahri, A., Phalp, K., et al.: Configuring crowdsourcing for requirements elicitation. In: IEEE International Conference on Research Challenges in Information Science, pp. 133–138. IEEE (2015)
10. Farhang-Mehr, A., Azarm, S.: Entropy-based multi-objective genetic algorithm for design optimization. Struct. Multi. Optim. **24**(5), 351–361 (2002)
11. Maalej, W., Rashid, A.: When users become collaborators: towards continuous and context-aware user input. In: Companion to the ACM Sigplan Conference on Object-Oriented Programming, Systems, Languages, and Applications, OOPSLA 2009, 25–29 October 2009, Orlando, Florida, USA, pp. 981–990. DBLP (2009)
12. Activity diagram, 11 March 2017. In Wikipedia, The Free Encyclopedia. Accessed 16:48, 15 Sept 2017
13. Nayak, A., Samanta, D.: Synthesis of test scenarios using UML activity diagrams. Softw. Syst. Model. **10**(1), 63–89 (2011)
14. Chen, M., Qiu, X., Xu, W., et al.: UML activity diagram-based automatic test case generation for java programs. Comput. J. **52**(5), 545–556 (2009)
15. Eshuis, R., Wieringa, R.: Tool support for verifying UML activity diagrams. IEEE Trans. Software Eng. **30**(7), 437–447 (2004)
16. Eshuis, R.: Symbolic model checking of UML activity diagrams. ACM Trans. Software Eng. Methodol. **15**(1), 1–38 (2006)
17. Hosseini, M., Phalp, K., Taylor, J., et al.: The four pillars of crowdsourcing: a reference model. In: IEEE Eighth International Conference on Research Challenges in Information Science, pp. 1–12. IEEE (2014)
18. Morales-Ramirez, I., Perini, A., Ceccato, M.: Towards supporting the analysis of online discussions in OSS communities: a speech-act based approach. In: Nurcan, S., Pimenidis, E. (eds.) CAiSE Forum 2014. LNBIP, vol. 204, pp. 215–232. Springer, Cham (2015). https://doi.org/10.1007/978-3-319-19270-3_14
19. Simon, D.: Evolutionary Optimization Algorithms. Biologically Inspired and Population-Based Approaches to Computer Intelligence. Genetic Programming (2013)

Crowd Vigilante

Detecting Sabotage in Crowdsourcing

Muneera Bano[1,2(✉)] and Didar Zowghi[2]

[1] Faculty of Science, Engineering and Technology,
Swinburne University of Technology, Melbourne, Australia
mbano@swin.edu.au
[2] Faculty of Engineering and Information Technology,
University of Technology Sydney, Ultimo, Australia
{Muneera.Bano,Didar.Zowghi}@uts.edu.au

Abstract. Crowdsourcing is a complex and sociotechnical problem solving approach for collaboration of geographically distributed volunteer crowd to contribute to the achievement of a common task. One of the major issues faced by crowdsourced projects is the trustworthiness of the crowd. This paper presents a vision to develop a framework with supporting methods and tools for early detection of the malicious acts of sabotage in crowdsourced projects by utilizing and scaling digital forensic techniques. The idea is to utilize the crowd to build the digital evidence of sabotage with systematic collection and analysis of data from the same crowdsourced project where the threat is situated. The proposed framework aims to improve the security of the crowdsourced projects and their outcomes by building confidence about the trustworthiness of the workers.

Keywords: Crowdsourcing · Requirements · Sabotage · Digital forensic

1 Introduction

The advent of web 2.0 has enabled the creation of socio-technical environment to foster participatory culture by masses on the Internet. The increase in usage of online communities is facilitated by the features such as anonymity, ease of access and interaction among users, as well as temporal flexibility. This has led to formation of online social communities with exponential growth in user generated contents on the Internet.

Online social communities are considered as rich sources of information and innovation for businesses [1]. The user-generated contents (i.e. reviews, comments and feedback) have been observed to be a major source of evolution in product line release in case of mobile apps [2]. In recent years a great deal of research has been dedicated to propose methods, tools and techniques in making the best use of the raw unstructured data and morph it into meaningful resources with business value [3].

In early 2000, there was a surge of interest by organizations to utilize the collective intelligence from online social communities in order to achieve their business goals [4, 5]. Platforms were provided for large communities across the globe to interact for problem solving. The collaboration of geographically distributed volunteer crowd contributing in

© Springer Nature Singapore Pte Ltd. 2018
M. Kamalrudin et al. (Eds.): APRES 2017, CCIS 809, pp. 114–120, 2018.
https://doi.org/10.1007/978-981-10-7796-8_9

achievement of a common task in an online environment or platform provided by an organization for mutual benefits is known as *'Crowdsourcing'* [6]. Various successful examples of crowdsourced projects emerged over time, such as financial reward based crowdsourcing (i.e. Amazon Mechanical Trunks), or collaborative volunteer crowdsourcing (i.e. Wikipedia).

Success in crowdsourcing outcomes depends on various factors such as technical design, collective cognition of participating individuals, social interaction, collaboration and coordination among the workers. In crowdsourcing, the projects are open for anyone who is willing and able to participate. One of the major issues faced by crowdsourced projects is the trustworthiness of the crowd [7]. The outcomes of crowdsourcing approach can be nullified by the behavioural aspects of the crowd such as low quality of work by volunteers, bad collaboration, or the malicious act of sabotage [8]. There is a risk of many unqualified workers hindering the task by unusable or substandard contributions. Due to the ease of access, crowdsourced projects are vulnerable for sabotage for the politically or financially motivated saboteur to contribute false information through the relevant platforms [9, 10].

The field of 'Digital Forensics' uses scientifically derived methods for analyzing digital sources in order to prepare digital evidence in helping to anticipate unauthorized actions that can disrupt the normal sequence of an operation [11]. This involves a systematic identification, collection, validation, analysis, interpretation, documentation and presentation of digital evidence derived from digital sources. The existing digital forensics technologies do not scale up to the requirements of crowdsourced projects [11, 12].

This paper presents our vision for the development of a framework with supporting methods and tools to tackle the malicious acts of sabotage in crowdsourced data. The idea is to use crowdsourcing approach to build the digital evidence against the saboteur. This implies systematic elicitation and analysis of data from the same crowd where the threat is situated. The expected outcomes of this project vision are:

- Analyzing current digital forensics methods, tools and techniques in order to elicit the requirements that would enhance, improve and scale them for the detection of potential threats in crowdsourced projects,
- A framework with supporting methods and tools for application of digital forensics in the field of crowdsourcing,
- Evaluating the effectiveness of the proposed framework by assessing the trustworthiness of a crowdsourced project with potential threats of sabotage.

The paper is organized as following: Sect. 2 provides brief overview of the background of the research domain and the motivation for current research project. Section 3 describes the vision for proposed framework. Section 4 enlists the open research questions for discussion and Sect. 5 provides conclusion and overview of future directions of the proposed project.

2   Background and Motivation

The term crowdsourcing was first coined by Jeff Howe [13] based on the book of James Surowiecki "wisdom of the crowd" [14]. Over the period of time various researchers tried to present a concise definition of what crowdsourcing is [6]. Crowdsourcing can be defined as [4]:

> *"an online, distributed problem-solving and production model that leverages the collective intelligence of online communities to serve specific organizational goals. Online communities, also called crowds, are given the opportunity to respond to crowdsourcing activities promoted by the organization, and they are motivated to respond for a variety of reasons."*

In software engineering, the concepts of crowdsourcing were adopted to recruit online workers across the globe to perform various software engineering tasks in order to reduce time, effort and cost of the development [5]. Some of the successful examples are: TopCoder, AppStori, UTest and TestFlight [5]. Various initiatives have been taken in requirements engineering research community to utilize crowdsourcing [15], e.g. StakeNet [16] and StakeSource [17].

Crowdsourcing comes with its own set of challenges such as crowd management and concerns over the quality of results. Arguably one of the important challenges for a crowdsourcing project is its vulnerability due to its open access making it an easy target for deliberate attacks from competing agents with political [18, 19] or financial motivations [9]. Researchers are focusing on detection and measurement of the maliciousness in the crowd, by analyzing the work contributed by the individual workers [7, 8]. But tracing the outcomes back to the originator of the work by observing the behavior of a distributed crowd working collaboratively on a project over the Internet is a very complex task [20]. The very limited time and resources available further exacerbate this difficulty.

One of the major impacts of sabotage in crowdsourcing project is the destruction of the user-base by degrading the motivation and confidence of the volunteer crowd. Research has highlighted the importance of this multifaceted security threat in their crowdsourcing projects where one individual sabotaged the work of the others in order to deliberately make the project fail [9]. It was reported that the saboteur hired hackers for the attack over the period of time and was being paid by a competitor. Though the crowd adjusted itself initially to the sabotage and identified the saboteur but the attacks continued and the work of the crowd was being nullified by the end of the day [9].

It is noteworthy that in formal digital forensic investigation techniques the digital evidence is built around the *'person of interest(s)'* who would be known [19]. In crowdsourced projects the saboteur is not known from the outset of investigation. Not much research focus has been paid when the attacker is unknown and mixed in the crowd. This requires investigative methods and techniques to discover evidence indicating sabotage and link it back to the perpetrator through the digital traces left in the collaborative work.

With huge amount of data, and human resources working on a common task in distributed environments, this form of 'sabotage' is extremely difficult to identify. The increase in cybercrimes and the exponential growth in user generated contents in recent years make it extremely challenging to process the data and build digital evidence in timely manner in order to make appropriate actions [21]. There is a need for research to enable the early apprehension of such threats that corrupt the output from the collective intelligence of the crowd. This has motivated us to work on developing practical solutions to this problem that is both economically viable while yielding timely results for outsourced projects.

3 Proposed Conceptual Model

The project addresses a cutting edge research issue in crowdsourcing and proposes a novel approach by scaling digital forensics to mitigate the risks associated with sabotage. This project aims to develop a framework with supporting methods and tools to address the malicious acts of sabotage in crowdsourced projects. The interaction among the workers of the crowd generates two types of data: text data in natural language (e.g. reviews, reports, chats etc.) and log data (e.g. mouse clicks, duration timers etc.). The text data is analyzed with text mining techniques (for analyzing the contents) and log data requires usage mining techniques (for analyzing the behavioral patterns) [26]. There is a need for mobilization of crowd with some form of incentive in order for data generation beyond what is already available [27].

The idea is to utilize the data and the crowd of the same project where a threat of sabotage is apprehended. Thus putting the crowd on vigilance and making them to contribute to crowdsource digital evidence. The digital evidence is thus built from the same crowd based on the analysis of the data and contribution of the volunteer crowd. Figure 1 shows the abstract concept of the proposed framework.

Unanticipated delays observed in crowdsourced projects that have been managed well with adequate allocated resources could indicate a potential threat of sabotage. This can be one of the triggers to initiate the sabotage detection process for timely analysis and action. The conceptual model in Fig. 1 presents the view where the sabotage is apprehended in crowdsourced project. We propose to follow this process in order to build the digital evidence *from the crowd and by the crowd*.

The raw data (reviews, projects documents, text from forums and chat rooms etc.) is retrieved from the crowdsourcing platforms in unstructured format. The data is to be parsed and classified based on the sentiments of threats. These threats are identified by analyzing the interactions or linguistic expressions in communication of the workers. This ultimately leads to identification of the workers that are either considered by others as untrustworthy or are considered to be generating contents, which are (explicitly or implicitly) impacting the overall performance of the project.

Further evidence is to be acquired around those potential 'suspects' in the crowd and the crowd is put on vigilance. In this context, gathering information from the selected workers in the crowd can be likened to eliciting requirements from the relevant stakeholders. Text mining and usage mining techniques are to be employed to discover the behavioral patterns of the suspected section of the crowd. At this stage of the process, additional investigative artifacts can be developed for further knowledge acquisition from the crowd which will contribute towards digital evidence. The analysis continues over a period of acceptable time to build the confidence that there is an act of sabotage in crowdsourced project. Various stages of the analysis and evidence building

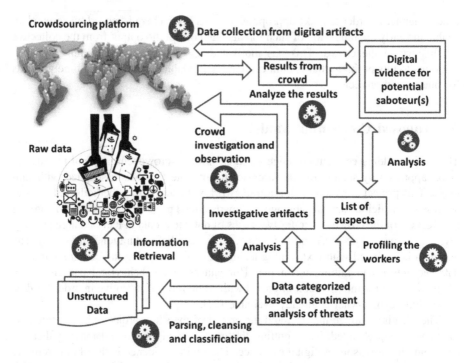

Fig. 1. Process of detecting sabotage with the help of crowd in crowdsourced project

will require support of automated tools for information retrieval, parsing, sentiment analysis and profiling.

4 Open Questions

With the conception of the vision of the process model formulated, we are currently analyzing how requirements engineering (RE) methods and tools can assist in various stages of analysis for sabotage detection in the crowdsourced projects. Various initiatives have already been taken to address the RE in crowdsourced projects such as data-driven RE [22], Feedback-based RE [23], Crowd-centric RE [24], and Crowd-based RE or CrowdRE [25]. The open questions for the development of this framework are:

- What RE techniques for identifying relevant stakeholders can be utilized at different stages of the process for the identification of potential suspects?
- How do we build the profile of the potential suspects from their digital footprints in the crowd?
- Which of the RE techniques can be applicable in crowdsourced projects for eliciting the information from the crowd when building digital evidence?
- What are the requirements for the supporting automated tools within this framework?

- What are the ethical considerations while the crowd who is helping to find the culprits don't have any knowledge of their involvement?

How do the scrutinizing of the project data and observing the workers in the crowd impact the outcomes of the overall project in terms of quality?

5   Conclusion and Future Work

In this paper we have presented our vision for addressing the issue of sabotage in crowdsourced projects. The proposed framework is based on building digital evidence from the same crowd where sabotage is apprehended.

Currently we are in the initial stages of gathering requirements for the conception of this framework based on existing case studies. The project is exploratory in nature and will be analyzing relevant data from existing crowdsourced projects with reported sabotage to identify the core elements for consideration.

References

1. Maalej, W., Hadeer, N.: Bug report, feature request, or simply praise? On automatically classifying app reviews. In: 2015 IEEE 23rd International Requirements Engineering Conference (RE), pp. 116–125. IEEE (2015)
2. Carreño, L.V.G., Winbladh, K.: Analysis of user comments: an approach for software requirements evolution. In: Proceedings of the 2013 International Conference on Software Engineering. IEEE Press (2013)
3. Guzman, E., Maalej, W.: How do users like this feature? A fine grained sentiment analysis of app reviews. In: 2014 IEEE 22nd International Requirements Engineering Conference (RE) (2014)
4. Brabham, D.C.: Crowdsourcing. MIT Press, Cambridge (2013)
5. Mao, K., Capra, L., Harman, M., Jia, Y.: A survey of the use of crowdsourcing in software engineering. J. Syst. Softw. **126**, 57–84 (2017)
6. Estellés-Arolas, E., González-Ladrón-de-Guevara, F.: Towards an integrated crowdsourcing definition. J. Inf. Sci. **38**(2), 189–200 (2012)
7. Gadiraju, U., et al.: Understanding malicious behavior in crowdsourcing platforms: the case of online surveys. In: Proceedings of the 33rd Annual ACM Conference on Human Factors in Computing Systems. ACM (2015)
8. Dwarakanath, A., et al.: Trustworthiness in enterprise crowdsourcing: a taxonomy & evidence from data. In: Proceedings of the 38th International Conference on Software Engineering Companion. ACM (2016)
9. Stefanovitch, N., et al.: Error and attack tolerance of collective problem solving: The DARPA Shredder Challenge. EPJ Data Sci. **3**(1), 1–27 (2014)
10. Johnson, C.W.: Anti-social networking: crowdsourcing and the cyber defence of national critical infrastructures. Ergonomics **57**(3), 419–433 (2014)
11. Raghavan, S.: Digital forensic research: current state of the art. CSI Trans. ICT **1**(1), 91–114 (2013)
12. Garfinkel, S.L.: Digital forensics research: the next 10 years. Digital Investigation **7**, S64–S73 (2010)
13. Howe, J.: The rise of crowdsourcing. Wired **14**(6), 1–4 (2006)

14. Surowiecki, J.: The Wisdom of Crowds: Why the Many Are Smarter Than the Few and How Collective Wisdom Shapes Business, Economics, Society and Nations. Little, Brown, New York (2004)
15. Breaux, T.D., Schaub, F.: Scaling requirements extraction to the crowd: experiments with privacy policies. In: 2014 IEEE 22nd International Requirements Engineering Conference (RE) (2014)
16. Lim, S.L., Quercia, D., Finkelstein, A.: StakeNet: using social networks to analyse the stakeholders of large-scale software projects. In: Proceedings of the 32nd ACM/IEEE International Conference on Software Engineering-Volume 1. ACM (2010)
17. Lim, S.L., Quercia, D., Finkelstein, A.: StakeSource: harnessing the power of crowdsourcing and social networks in stakeholder analysis. In: Proceedings of the 32nd ACM/IEEE International Conference on Software Engineering-Volume 2. ACM (2010)
18. Lesk, M.: The new front line: Estonia under cyberassault. IEEE Secur. Priv. 5(4), 76–79 (2007)
19. Compton, D., Hamilton, J.: An examination of the techniques and implications of the crowd-sourced collection of forensic data. In: 2011 IEEE Third International Conference on Privacy, Security, Risk and Trust (PASSAT) and 2011 IEEE Third International Conference on Social Computing (SocialCom) (2011)
20. Ghosh, A., Kale, S., McAfee, P.: Who moderates the moderators?: Crowdsourcing abuse detection in user-generated content. In: Proceedings of the 12th ACM Conference on Electronic Commerce. ACM (2011)
21. Pasquale, L., et al.: Adaptive evidence collection in the cloud using attack scenarios. Comput. Secur. 59, 236–254 (2016)
22. Maalej, W., et al.: Toward data-driven requirements engineering. IEEE Softw. 33(1), 48–54 (2016)
23. Hosseini, M., et al.: Towards crowdsourcing for requirements engineering. In: 20th International Working Conference on Requirements Engineering: Foundations for Software Quality, Empirical Track (2014)
24. Snijders, R., et al.: Crowd-centric requirements engineering: a method based on crowdsourcing and gamification. Technical Report Series (UU-CS-2015-004) (2015)
25. Groen, E.C., Doerr, J., Adam, S.: Towards crowd-based requirements engineering a research preview. In: Fricker, S.A., Schneider, K. (eds.) REFSQ 2015. LNCS, vol. 9013, pp. 247–253. Springer, Cham (2015). https://doi.org/10.1007/978-3-319-16101-3_16
26. Pachidi, S., Spruit, M., Van De Weerd, I.: Understanding users' behavior with software operation data mining. Comput. Hum. Behav. 30, 583–594 (2014)
27. Groen, E.C., Koch, M.: How Requirements Engineering can benefit from crowds. The Magazine for RE Professionals from IREB. http://re-magazine.ireb.org/issues/2016-2-take-the-broader-view/how-requirements-engineering-can-benefit-from-crowds/. Accessed 27 June 2016

Requirements Challenges

A Systematic Mapping Study of Empirical Research in GORE

Anbreen Javed$^{(\boxtimes)}$, Naveed Ikram, and Faiza Ghazanfar

Riphah International University, Islamabad, Pakistan
anbreenjaved@ymail.com, naveed.ikram@riphah.edu.pk,
faizaghazanfar@gmail.com

Abstract. Goal Oriented Requirements Engineering (GORE) has the potential to fulfill customer's needs. It is an emergent field in requirements engineering (RE) because it helps to achieve the intended objectives of the system under consideration. A large number of Conferences and Journals have reported GORE work regarding different techniques, tools, frameworks, and methods with various processes. However, there is little effort to aggregate GORE existing empirical work, identify knowledge gaps, trends, and patterns by using an unbiased, comprehensive and systematic methodology. Therefore, there is a need to evaluate GORE empirical research to show its affluence. We conducted Systematic Mapping Study (SMS) to analyze empirical research in GORE. An analysis on extracted data showed the great increase of GORE empirical work in the year 2012 and the most focused area is Requirements Analysis (63%), and Elicitation (20%) while the Modeling (70%) is a trendy concept in Requirements Analysis. The most used research method in GORE empirical studies was the experiment. Our study did not find any empirical work in the GORE area of Validation and Verification. A large percentage of studies presented methods as the output of research and validated these methods empirically. To develop the reliability and integrity of research outcomes, the researchers need to perform evaluative empirical research. The practitioners are required to share their experiences of using various modeling tools and techniques the community.

Keywords: Requirement Engineering · Mapping study · GORE
Empirical literature

1 Introduction

Traditionally Requirements Engineering (RE) activities focus on "what" question of the system and ignore "why" question. The focus of (GORE) on "why" question helps to identify the intended objectives of the system. The term "Goal" plays a vital role in RE activities [1] because they are the intended objectives of the system under consideration/functional concerns or quality attributes/high-level concerns to low-level concerns. Typically, GORE starts at early-phase RE activities whereas traditional RE is the late-phase RE activities.

GORE has taken its roots from Artificial Intelligence [2]. A lot of GORE empirical literature exists due to its increasing importance in both academia and industry that is not aggregated and classified up till now. Therefore, it is essential to summarize it to

© Springer Nature Singapore Pte Ltd. 2018
M. Kamalrudin et al. (Eds.): APRES 2017, CCIS 809, pp. 123–139, 2018.
https://doi.org/10.1007/978-981-10-7796-8_10

identify knowledge gaps, to find out the current state of GORE field and scope for future research directions. Many researchers indicate the need and importance of systematically aggregate empirical evidence in RE [3, 4]. Most of the researchers reported the status of the GORE field and reported the state-of-the-art in GORE as well; and several studies do summarize and classified the existing research and identified future directions, but those were not about the empirical evidence.

Goals played the most significant role in the RE process which has widely recognized by RE research [5–11]. Such RE recognition has directed towards an entire stream of research on goal elicitation, goal modeling, goal-based reasoning and goal specification for a number of purposes, and also in multiple forms. Various literature surveys worked on multiple goals perspectives in requirements engineering, goal modeling, goals specification, significance and techniques of GORE [12, 13] and a systematic roadmap [14] also exist. A critical study synthesized the underlying principles and concepts of GORE, and then performed the comprehensive concept-centric evaluation of GORE techniques [15]. A survey provided the classification of different GORE methods using multiple criteria [16].

The studies mentioned above gathered the existing GORE literature and each study has different objectives and varying in scope. All of these studies presented the normal surveys and literature reviews without following the guideline of SLR process. However, Horkoff et al. produced a Systematic Literature Map (SLM) [17] in 2016 and an extended SMS [18] in 2017 which focused only on 246 highly-cited GORE related research papers according to SCOPUS but did not consolidate the evidence-based GORE literature. They searched SCOPUS, Google Scholar, and Web of Science on 16th December 2015 with 966 results initially in order to extract and compare citation data. They classified the included studies according to paper types, paper types per year, evaluation types per year, total papers topics, top five total papers topics per year, framework used in 246 publications, top 12 publications venue, 20 top-cited GORE publications ranked according to SCOPUS, Web of Science citations and explored increasing interest in GORE risen from 2008 to 2012. Evaluation of empirical evidence is important for both academia as well as industry [17, 18]. Systematically aggregating and summarizing the evidence-based empirical literature will help researchers in identifying future research directions and practitioners will also formulate intelligent and knowledgeable decisions.

More specifically, we have explored the state-of-the-art and strength and effectiveness of empirical evidence considered in empirical studies in GORE. The main motivation behind this mapping study is to aggregate and synthesize the complete evidence-based GORE discipline.

The research questions devised for this research are about state-of-the-art and strength of empirical evidence. These research questions were adapted from other systematic reviews [19, 20]. The research questions are:

RQ1: What is the state-of-the-art in empirical studies in GORE?
RQ2: What is the strength and effectiveness of empirical evidence considered in empirical GORE literature?

RQ1 aim is to assess the status of the GORE field with empirical evidence and provide future directions in this field. RQ2 aim is to find out the strength of empirical evidence in terms of the source of evidence and methods used.

RQ1 is divided into following sub-questions:

- Which era of GORE has maximum progress and advancement?
- What are the sources and major publication channels of GORE empirical studies?
- Which country and institution is actively involved in GORE empirical research?
- What are the most investigated RE areas and sub-areas that have been covered by GORE and where more consideration is required?
- Which empirical studies have top citation count?
- Who are the top authors in terms of publication frequency?
- What types of solutions have been investigated or proposed in GORE research?

RQ2 is also divided into sub-questions which are as follows:

- Which research method has been used more frequently in GORE empirical studies?
- Which data collection method has been used more frequently in GORE studies to collect data?
- Which type of research participants are actively involved in empirical studies?

This paper presents interesting results of the SMS to provide GORE state-of-the-art by highlighting different trends and opportunities. The paper structure is as follows: Sect. 2 describes the research process; Sect. 3 presents the results; further discussion is provided in Sect. 4; Study limitations are highlighted in Sect. 5; lastly Sect. 6 concludes the research.

2   Research Process

For this Systematic Mapping Study (SMS), we followed the Petersen et al. [21, 22] guidelines for performing SMS. We have described the activities of our research process over here.

2.1   Protocol Development

Firstly we have developed the protocol for this SMS that included the research question, decisions for search strategy, inclusion/exclusion criteria, data extraction strategy and data synthesis strategy.

2.2   Search String

There was only one search term for this mapping study, and it was Goal Oriented Requirements Engineering. The alternatives of our major search terms are as Goal-oriented requirements engineering, Goal-oriented RE, Goal-based requirements engineering, Goal-based RE, Goal-driven requirements engineering, Goal-driven RE, Goal-directed requirements engineering, Goal-directed RE, GORE. Finally, we have developed a generic search query for all databases as *(("goal-oriented" OR "goal-driven" OR "goal-based" OR "goal-directed" OR "GORE") AND ("requirement")).*

2.3 Search Resources

We used four major databases IEEE, ACM, EI Compendex, and SCOPUS in order to search the studies. We searched for journal articles, workshops, and conference papers.

2.4 Inclusion and Exclusion Criteria

The studies retrieved after applying search string on the databases were screened for inclusion and exclusion criteria. We removed editorials, prefaces, discussions, comments, summaries of tutorials, workshops briefs, panels and duplicate papers before applying inclusion/exclusion criteria for the selected studies. The inclusion criterion was complete research papers in the area of empirical studies GORE from the open-ended period publication.

2.5 Data Extraction Strategy

We extracted data based on research questions as defined in the introduction section by using data extraction form. We have stored the extracted data in the MS Excel and assigned each paper with unique study ID. We updated the list of extracted data items during the conduct of SMS. We have consulted REBOK [23] and SWEBOK [24] in order to find RE main and sub-areas in the data extraction strategy. While the research method had been devised in accordance to the research methods presented in the [25]. However, the data extraction form contained information as follows:

I. General Bibliographic Information of the Study

- Paper Title
- Author(s)
- Source (i.e. Conference or journal)
- Search String(s) or Keywords used to retrieve an article
- Year of Paper Publication
- Affiliation Organization
- Geographical area

II. Specific Information about the Study

- Research Method
- Research Study Area
- Study Participants
- Data Collection Method
- Research Highlights
  - Main Area of RE
  - Sub-Area of RE
  - Solution Type
  - Number of Citations

2.6 Execution of Mapping Study

On 15th April 2015, both researchers applied the search string on four databases. The initial application of query on the four databases obtained results, as ACM 487 results, IEEE 383 results, EI Compendex 236 results, and SCOPUS 1190 results. The references obtained from the search string result was imported into Reference Management Software, we used Excel Sheet in our case. The obtained results were imported and saved into excel sheet. We obtained a total of 2296 results. There were some duplicates within ACM and SCOPUS. After duplicates removal, we have merged studies from all four databases. After merging, 901 duplicates found and excluded from the library. Then we performed study screening in two phases. In the first phase of screening, we have checked title and abstract of the obtained studies for the relevancy of the study. If any study was irrelevant to GORE, then we excluded that study from the main library. We placed the studies in another library which were relevant to the GORE. This screening process continued until all studies were checked. We found 543 studies that were unable to evaluate upon the title and abstract screening for relevance to GORE; these studies were placed for introduction and conclusion screening phase. In the second phase, the screening performed through reading of introduction and conclusion to check about the inclusion/exclusion of the study. The studies which were unclear for inclusion/exclusion in this phase were decided in consensus meeting to be included or excluded. We faced a difficulty during inclusion/exclusion in categorizing the research method where studies claimed "case studies" as the method. We came across many studies in which researchers used examples to elaborate their research work, but they claimed it as a case study. As our focus was empirical work, that's why we needed to critically consider each aspect of such studies to decide that evidence provided is empirical or just example explanation. Figure 1 shows the whole process of screening. We have attached the list of included studies in the Appendix. We excluded most of the studies during this screening process and 310 studies made up to the final inclusion. These studies were then placed in the new library and assigned them Study Ids.

We performed the data extraction on 310 included primary studies based on RQ1 and RQ2. An excel sheet was used to extract and store data about the title, its generic information, intervention type, citation count, RE main and sub-area, data collection method, research method, research participants, and study area. The two researchers independently extracted the data. Then matched the results of both to validate the extracted data. Moreover, the dependency between various data extraction results also shows the validity of the extracted data. After data extraction of 310 studies, we got 268 studies in which authors claimed that they used case study as research methodology but in actual they didn't conduct any case study in their work and presented the case studies or used some other authors' case studies just to illustrate their approaches. Then we excluded those 268 studies because they were non-empirical. In the end, we have 42 studies of which six were duplicate studies. After removal of studies duplication, we got 36 empirical studies.

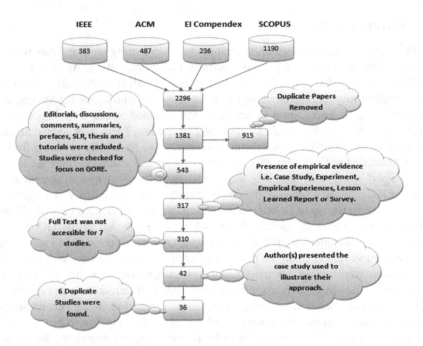

Fig. 1. Study screening process

3 Results

This section presented the analysis and results of the quantitative extracted data to answer the research questions stated in this mapping study.

3.1 State-of-the-Art in the Empirical Studies of GORE (RQ1)

We have designed a few sub-questions to answer RQ1 and also investigated different aspects of included empirical studies. The detailed results of the state-of-the-art in GORE are as follows:

Which era of GORE has maximum progress and advancement? This mapping study includes 36 primary studies from last one decade. Figure 2 presents the number of empirical publications reported in the time span from 2001 up to 2015. GORE empirical work has been started since 2001. However from 2007, researchers take an interest in GORE empirical research, and by the end of 2012, the six empirical studies were found that is the highest number of publications.

What are the sources and major publication channels of GORE empirical studies? We got 44% conference publications, 42% journal publications, and 14% workshop publications as shown in Fig. 3. We have seen a sharp increase and decrease in conference publications because some conferences held after two or three years. Apart from this, the major conference publication channel was the International Conference on Requirements Engineering Conference (ICRE) with 17% studies. And the major journal publication channel was the Journal of Systems and Software with

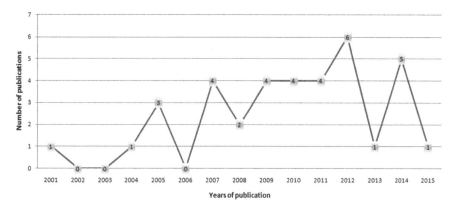

Fig. 2. GORE empirical publication trend

14% primary studies. Other most significant conference publication channel includes International Conference on Requirements Engineering: Foundation for Software Quality (REFSQ) with 5% empirical studies while the other considerable journal channel includes Journal of Requirement Engineering (RE) with 8% studies as shown in Fig. 4. However, 56% empirical studies in multiple conference and journal publication channels. These publication channels of GORE can be useful for GORE researchers to search for the desired GORE empirical work and also for getting an opportunity to publish new empirical work in GORE.

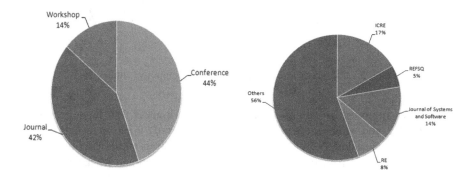

Fig. 3. Types of publication channels   **Fig. 4.** GORE major publication channels

Which country and institution is actively involved in GORE empirical research? Figure 5 depicted that sixteen different countries involved in GORE empirical research activities. The maximum number of GORE reported empirical work is in Canada (5studies), UK (5 studies), Italy (5 studies), Japan (5 studies) and China (5 studies). All of these countries share the same percentage of studies. However, the University of Ottawa and University of Toronto in Canada and Tokyo Institute of Technology in Japan worked independently while The Open University in the UK worked in collaboration with Fudan University in China on three empirical studies and Center for Information Technology (CIT-IRST) of FBK in Italy reported one empirical study in collaboration with the Technical University of Catalonia in Spain and one University of Haifa in Israel. The results show that USA, Europe and Asia (Japan and China) are the most active regions in carrying out GORE empirical research. It is interesting to note that the authors with the largest number of GORE publications are also from Europe and Asia.

Fig. 5. Country-wise distribution of GORE empirical studies

What are the most investigated RE areas and sub-areas that have been covered by GORE and where more consideration is required? Figure 6 reveals that the most foused RE areas in GORE are the Requirements Analysis and Elicitation. A little amount of attention is paid to the Requirements Specification and Management, but nothing was done in Validation and Verification. We got only two studies focusing on Requirements Traceability which is the sub-area of Requirements Management. Only five studies deal with Requirements Specification in which the most focused area is the Formal Specification. The results depicted that out of 29 studies of Requirements Analysis 22 studies were on Modeling that is the highest percentage of our included empirical studies.

Which empirical studies have top citation count? Citation count represents the quality and popularity of the empirical study. We have shown top six citation ranks of the empirical studies in Fig. 7. We have found that only one primary study has above 100 citation counts and one study has approximately 100 citation counts. We have

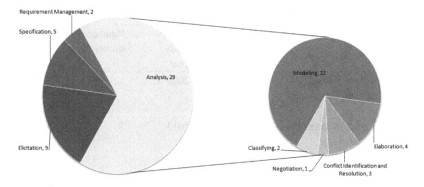

Fig. 6. Distribution of studies on RE areas

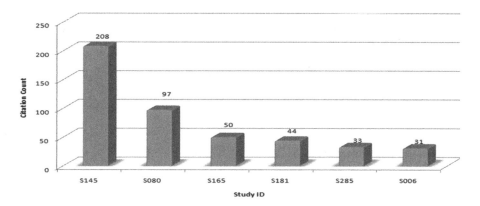

Fig. 7. Top citation count

found three empirical studies with no citation and four studies with only one citation. The study with highest citation counts is important because authors discussed their work from research to practice [S145] while some authors presented their experiences about the management of large collection of scenarios during the activities of requirements specification for e-commerce applications [S080]. The results show that most cited studies are from USA [S080] and Europe [S145] which are the most active regions in carrying out GORE empirical research whereas one study was journal publication [S080] and two studies were conference publications [S145]. However, the researchers shared their experiences in an industrial domain in the two most cited studies [S080, S145]. These studies covered the Requirements Analysis area of RE.

Who are the top authors (number of publications)? We have identified top authors according to the frequency of publications. Table 1 shows that top most authors are having three publications each but their publication period varies. Saeki M. has four years of publication period while other top authors have two to three years. Their current affiliation is from Asia and Europe which are among the top most regions in terms of a number of publications. Perini A. and Susi A. worked in collaboration with

Table 1. Top authors according to publication frequency

Authors name	Current affiliation	First study year	Last study year	Number of studies	Study ID (s)
Saeki M.	Tokyo Institute of Technology, Japan	2005	2009	3	S170, S073, S165
Perini A.	Center of Information Technology (CIT-Irst) of FBK, Italy	2011	2013	3	S285, S234, S070
Susi A.	Center of Information Technology (CIT-Irst) of FBK, Italy	2011	2013	3	S285, S183, S070
Peng X.	Fudan University, Shanghai, China	2011	2014	3	S057, S251, S295
Yu Y.	The Open University, UK	2011	2014	3	S057, S251, S295
Zhao W.	Fudan University, China	2011	2014	3	S057, S251, S295
Chen B.	Fudan University, China	2011	2014	3	S057, S251, S295

each other on two empirical studies in the Center of Information Technology (CIT-Irst) of FBK, Italy and their publication period was only three years from 2011 to 2013. However, Peng X., Zhao W., Chen B. and Yu Y. worked collaboratively on three empirical studies in the Fudan University, China and The Open University, UK. One of their publications is from conference channel and two studies are from journal publication.

What types of solutions have been investigated or proposed in GORE research? There are various solutions proposed in GORE empirical studies (see Fig. 8). We got eight studies in which no new solution was presented, and authors were either sharing their experiences of using different GORE techniques through a case study or evaluating/comparing the different GORE techniques and tools. The researchers most widely used methods and frameworks. Eleven primary studies presented new methods and nine empirical studies proposed new frameworks. Other solution types that GORE researchers mostly used and proposed were new tools and models. The least frequency of studies produced processes and techniques.

*N/A (Empirical studies did not present any solution and authors were either sharing their experiences or evaluating/comparing the different GORE techniques and tools).

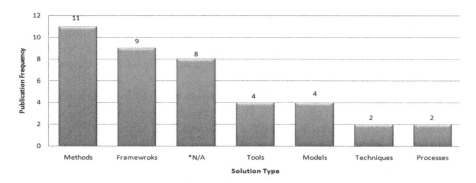

Fig. 8. Solution types in empirical studies

3.2 Strength of Empirical Evidence (RQ2)

The focus of this research question is to identify the strength of GORE empirical evidence according to the source of evidence along with the data collection methods and research methods used. This section presents different sub-question to investigate the strength of GORE empirical studies.

Which research method has been used more frequently in GORE empirical studies? It is evident from the Fig. 9 that most of the studies used experimentation as a research method. It might be due to the rationale that most of the researchers wanted their research in the industrial/real world environment. Case study and empirical experience were also among the leading research methods. We have recorded sixteen experiments from GORE empirical research. A low percentage of an experiment in an industrial context is because probability of experiment failure is larger than the case study failure and industry doesn't want to bear such failures. Though selected studies reported nine case studies and eight empirical experiences. GORE researchers conducted a large proportion of case studies in an industrial context and a very few in academia context. This reveals that we could conducted case study more conveniently

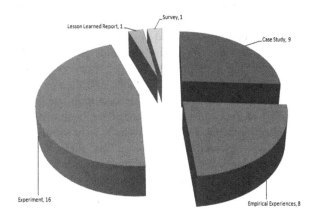

Fig. 9. Research methods

in real world/industry. We also found one lesson learned report and one survey in GORE publications. In Surveys, we excluded the literature surveys and included only those industrial and academic surveys which reported the practitioner's experiences. Only one empirical study reported experiment collaboratively with the lesson learned report.

Which type of research participants are actively involved in empirical studies? Extracted data depicts that most of the GORE empirical research is going on in an industrial/real world context. It is quite a good sign that we have found eighteen empirical studies from industrial context as shown in Fig. 10. Academia involved in fourteen of the selected studies and both academia and industrial/real world contexts collaboratively worked in only one empirical study. The study area of three studies was not available. These statistics show that implication of this SMS is mostly for the GORE practitioners in industrial/real world context rather than in academic context. Academic and industrial/real world context need to work in collaboration with each other for the betterment of GORE area.

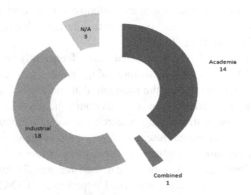

Fig. 10. Study area of the empirical studies

Which data collection method has been used more frequently in GORE studies to collect data? Figure 11 shows that most of the included studies used interview and questionnaire, but the data collection method of three GORE empirical studies was not available. These studies did not talk about regarding any data collection method, procedures to get data and the tools for data storage. However, some of the included studies not only stated the data collection methods and data storage tools but also mentioned the sequence where different data collection tools used. It happened in the studies in which combined data collection methods have been used. GORE empirical studies where data collection method was not available were mostly the "experiments" and "case studies." It has observed that whenever any study did not describe data collection method then it also lacks some other contextual as well as methodological details. These details of the case study measure the quality of the study and such lacks of information decreases the quality score.

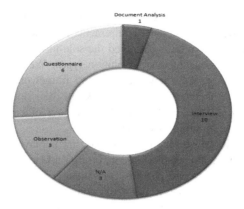

Fig. 11. Data collection methods

Some studies used two or more than two combined methods for data collection. The empirical studies in which data is collected by using combined data collection methods and multiple sources associated with the strength of evidence; and it is also believed to be a repeatable process. Most of the empirical studies preferred observations and interviews with the combination of other data collection methods. Observations and interviews used together in four studies. Only one study used interview, observation, and document analysis to collect the data. Focus group, observation, and questionnaire were also used in only one study. Brainstorming was only used with interviews in only one study. Interviews were used in combination with a questionnaire in four empirical studies. Interviews and document analysis were also used in two studies. In one study questionnaire was combined with observation. Observations and document analysis collectively used in two primary studies.

4   Discussion

This section discusses the major findings of the two research questions RQ1 and RQ2 to provide future directions to the GORE researchers. From the results of RQ1, we found that the research in GORE has taken its roots in the early 20s and flourished in 2012. Most active research institutions and communities working in the empirical GORE are mostly on the continent of USA, Europe, and Asia. Canada, Italy, UK, China, and Japan are the geographic locations of well-known research institutions of Goal-oriented Requirements Engineering. The University of Ottawa, University of Toronto, Center of Information Technology (CIT-IRST) of FBK, Fudan University, The Open University, and Tokyo Institute of Technology is the leading institutes involved in GORE empirical research. However, top authors in terms of publications frequency are also from Europe and Asia. IEEE Conference on Requirements Engineering and Journal of Systems and Software are the most relevant publication channels for the coverage of GORE research. We obtained most of our included studies from these publications. Overall GORE is in emerging phase and on its way towards maturing. The consistently researched and matured area of RE in GORE is the Requiremenent Analysis. However, in Requirements Analysis the researchers mostly focused only on Modeling. We have classified the solution of the empirical studies in some general and most extensively used solution types. We found that most of the researchers are widely proposing new methods and frameworks. The whole GORE community applies these methods and frameworks in their domain and shares their experiences. Moreover, GORE is dynamically implying emerging trends and new applications within the computing discipline.

From the results of RQ2, we found that the industry is playing the most significant role in GORE research. Academia needs to pay more attention towards GORE publications so that practitioners can benefit from their research. Most of the GORE published literature was in real world/industrial context although academia also contributed to GORE literature, but comparatively small part of the published literature was from academia. The obtained studies for this systematic mapping study were all empirical studies, and the majority of these studies were experiments. Researchers do not strictly follow the quality criteria for conducting empirical research. The second largest proportion of empirical studies used case studies. A large number of claimed case studies could not be concluded as empirical because most of the researchers have demonstrated case scenarios and implications of examples to illustrate their results, but they referred these studies as real-world case studies. About 9% GORE studies didn't report the tools that are used to collect data. While in rest of the 91% studies used single as well as multiple data collection methods and tools. Researchers used interview, observation, document analysis, and questionnaire most extensively data collection tools.

This systematic mapping study depicts the complete picture of empirical research done in GORE so far. So, it is significant for both GORE researchers and practitioners because they can easily get information about the entire area, its affluence, and limitations. Evidence-Based Software Engineering (EBSE) is rapidly gaining importance now a day. A lot of empirical research has already done in the field of GORE but this literature is not aggregated. We aggregated this empirical literature in one study so that researchers can find future research directions through this single aggregation rather than finding and consulting all the empirical work.

New problems on modeling are arising within the GORE, therefore, it is good ground for practitioners in order to see whether all modeling problems can be handled with GORE or some specific. Certain aspects of GORE reported well in empirical literature. Hence, it is beneficial for industry to use GORE. There is a need for industrial tools support for GORE so that practitioners will use GORE. Practitioners can use the solutions which researchers have made and provide them feedback for further improvements.

5   Study Limitations

Another limitation is that we got a quite small size of final primary studies as compared to other mapping studies due to the limited empirical work in GORE. The threats to validity are as follows:

We faced many challenges while query string designing. We identified and applied all possible keywords/terms used for Goal Oriented Requirements Engineering like "Goal-based", "Goal-driven" and "Goal-directed" in order to cover complete literature. We used these terms to ensure the maximum coverage of GORE literature and this also resulted in a large number of studies from different engineering disciplines. We have done tedious work during inclusion/exclusion phase to screen out studies obtained from other engineering disciplines but did not exclude those terms/keywords from the search string. We have made this judgment particularly to reduce the chances of skipping any paper relevant to GORE. Moreover, most database sources have limitations on a number of search keywords/terms used and also on the number of characters. For that we have broken down our search string into sub-strings to accommodate these types of limitations. We performed pilot testing for query string and data extraction form to increase their reliability and modified them according to results of pilot testing.

6   Conclusion

We have performed this SMS to find out state-of-the-art in GORE where the focus was only on empirical evidence. We used four databases (IEEE, EI Compendex, SCOPUS, and ACM) to search and found 36 empirical studies from 2001 to April 2015. We found Requirements Analysis and Elicitation the most researched RE areas. From the quantitative analysis, it revealed that modeling was the trendiest area in GORE discipline and researchers solved many problems related to modeling languages, but still a large number of their problems remained unsolved.

However, GORE researchers paid little attention to Requirements Specification and Management, but did not find any work reported on Validation and Verification. Apart from this, a large proportion of solutions proposed by different researchers were methods and frameworks for goal modeling and validated them through case studies and experiments. And the industry is playing the most significant role in GORE research rather than academia. The most frequent research method found in GORE discipline was an experiment. In this work we have reported the positive aspects of our collected data in terms of strength and effectiveness, in future, we will come with weaknesses and limitations of the included studies as well. In future, we should investigate why there is a divergence in goal-oriented modeling languages instead of convergence. Further studies should be conducted to see why case studies were rarely performed in GORE. A survey should also be conducted to explore that how industry considers GORE.

Appendix

The list of included primary studies available at link:
    https://drive.google.com/open?id=0BwAn-a1YARAma0lzbEYyaXVsRVU

References

1. Letier, E., Lamsweerde, A.V.: Agent-based tactics for goal-oriented requirements elaboration. In: 24th International Conference on Software Engineering, pp. 83–93. IEEE CS, USA (2002)
2. Regev, G., Wegmann, A.: Where do goals come from: the underlying principles of goal-oriented requirements engineering. In: 13th International Requirements Engineering Conference, pp. 353–362. IEEE CS, France (2005)
3. Ghanavati, S., Amyot, D., Peyton, L.: A systematic review of goal-oriented requirements management frameworks for business process compliance. In: 4th International Workshop on Requirements Engineering and Law (RELAW), pp. 25–34. IEEE CS, Italy (2011)
4. Bano, M., Zowghi, D., Ikram, N.: Systematic reviews in requirements engineering: a tertiary study. In: 4th International Workshop on Empirical Requirements Engineering (EmpiRE), pp. 9–16. IEEE CS, Sweden (2014)
5. Yue, K.: What does it mean to say that a specification is complete? In: 4th International Workshop on Software Specification and Design. IEEE CS, USA (1987)
6. Robinson, W.N.: Integrating multiple specifications using domain goals. In: 5th International Workshop on Software Specification and Design, pp. 219–226. ACM, USA (1989)
7. Berzins, V.A., Luqi, L.: Software Engineering with Abstractions. Addison-Wesley, MA (1991)
8. Dardenne, A., Fickas, S., Lamsweerde, A.V.: Goal-directed concept acquisition in requirements elicitation. In: 6th International Workshop on Software Specification and Design, pp. 14–21. IEEE CS, Italy (1991)
9. Mylopoulos, J., Chung, L., Nixon, B.: Representing and using nonfunctional requirements: a process-oriented approach. IEEE Trans. Softw. Eng. **18**(6), 483–497 (1992)
10. Jarke, M., Pohl, K.: Vision-driven system engineering. In: Proceedings of the IFIP Wg8.1 Working Conference on Information System Development Process, pp. 3–20. Elsevier, Italy (1993)
11. Zave, P.: Classification of research efforts in requirements engineering. ACM Comput. Surv. **29**(4), 315–321 (1997)
12. Aljahdali, S., Bano, J., Hundewale, N.: Goal oriented requirements engineering - a review. In: 24th International Conference on Computer Applications in Industry and Engineering, CAINE, pp. 328–333. IEEE CS, USA (2011)
13. Sen, A.M., Hemachandran, K.: Goal oriented requirement engineering: a literature survey. Assam Univ. J. Sci. Technol. Phys. Sci. Technol. **6**(2), 16–25 (2010)
14. Horkoff, J., Li, T., Li, F.-L., Salnitri, M., Cardoso, E., Giorgini, P., Mylopoulos, J., Pimentel, J.: Taking goal models downstream: a systematic roadmap. In: 8th International Conference on Research Challenges in Information Science. IEEE CS, Morocco (2014)
15. Anwer, S., Ikram, N.: Goal oriented requirement engineering: a critical study of techniques. In: 13th Asia Pacific Software Engineering Conference (APSEC), pp. 121–130. IEEE CS, India (2006)
16. Vinay, S., Aithal, S., Adiga, S.: Identification of research challenges and classification schema for goal-oriented requirements engineering methodologies. In: National Conference on Artificial Intelligence and Software Engineering, Bangalore (2011)
17. Horkoff, J., Aydemiry, F.B., Cardosoy, E., Liy, T., Matéyz, A., Pajay, E., Salnitriy, M., Mylopoulos, J., Giorginiy, P.: Goal-oriented requirements engineering: a systematic literature map. In: 24th International Requirements Engineering Conference. IEEE CS, China (2016)

18. Horkoff, J., Aydemiry, F.B., Cardosoy, E., Liy, T., Matéyz, A., Pajay, E., Salnitriy, M., Mylopoulos, J., Giorginiy, P., Piras, L.: Goal-oriented requirements engineering: an extended systematic mapping study. Requirements Eng. J. 1–28 (2017)
19. Ambreen, T., Ikram, N., Usman, M., Niazi, M.: Empirical research in requirements engineering: trends and opportunities. Requirements Eng. J. **21**(3), 1–33 (2016)
20. Smite, D., Wohlin, C., Gorschek, T., Feldt, R.: Empirical evidence in global software engineering: a systematic review. J. Empirical Softw. Eng. **15**(1), 91–118 (2010)
21. Petersen, K., Feldt, R., Mujtaba, S., Mattsson, M.: Systematic mapping studies in software engineering. In: 12th International Conference on Evaluation and Assessment in Software Engineering (EASE), pp. 68–77. ACM, Italy (2008)
22. Petersen, K., Vakkalanka, S., Kuzniarz, L.: Guidelines for conducting systematic mapping studies in software engineering: an update. J. Inf. Softw. Technol. **64**, 1–18 (2015)
23. Aoyama, M., Nakatani, T., Saito, S., Suzuki, M., Fujita, K., Nakazaki, H., Suzuki, R.: A model and architecture of REBOK (Requirements Engineering Body of Knowledge) and its evaluation. In: 17th Asia Pacific Software Engineering Conference (APSEC), pp. 50–59. IEEE CS, Australia (2010)
24. Bourque, P., Dupuis, R., Abran, A., Moore, J.W.: Guide to the software engineering body of knowledge (SWEBOK). IEEE CS (2004)
25. Wieringa, R., Maiden, N., Mead, N., Rolland, C.: Requirements engineering paper classification and evaluation criteria: a proposal and a discussion. Requirements Eng. J. **11**(1), 102–107 (2005)

Challenges in Context-Aware Requirements Modeling: A Systematic Literature Review

Yuanbang Li, Rong Peng[✉], and Bangchao Wang

State Key Lab of Software Engineering, Wuhan University,
Wuhan 430072, People's Republic of China
{lybang, rongpeng, wangbc}@whu.edu.cn

Abstract. Context-aware applications are becoming increasingly popular as they can adapt their behaviors to situations. However, the modeling of context-aware requirements is challenging owing to the inherent complexity and dynamicity of the context. Therefore, learning from existing studies can help academia and industry overcome the challenges. The primary objectives of this study are as follows: (1) survey the state-of-the-art of context-aware requirements modeling; (2) determine the challenges in context-aware requirements modeling and the extent to which the challenges have been addressed; (3) explore the future research directions of context-aware requirements modeling. We adopt the method of systematic literature review to retrieve relevant studies and extract available data aimed at the objectives. Seventy-two studies are finally selected. After data synthesis, we identify 4 categories of 13 challenges in context-aware requirements modeling. Based on the findings, we analyze the extent to which the challenges have been addressed and suggest future research directions.

Keywords: Systematic literature review · Context aware
Requirement modeling · Challenges

1   Introduction

Requirements engineering (RE) is the first stage in the software development process, which aims to clarify stakeholders' requirements and analyze and synthesize the requirements to create a requirements document. Requirements modeling is an important activity in RE.

With fierce competition in the mobile market, being aware of the changes in the context and modifying behaviors accordingly is becoming increasingly important for context-aware applications to attract end users. Owing to the intrinsic diversity and uncertainty of the context, the modeling of context-aware requirements is considerably challenging. Several researchers have focused on the investigation of this problem to address the challenges. Sutcliffe A. et al. extended the goal-oriented method to model context-aware requirements [1]. Frece A. used business process modeling notation (BPMN) to model context-aware requirements [2], and Choi J. used extended UML to model them [3].

© Springer Nature Singapore Pte Ltd. 2018
M. Kamalrudin et al. (Eds.): APRES 2017, CCIS 809, pp. 140–155, 2018.
https://doi.org/10.1007/978-981-10-7796-8_11

This study conducts a systematic literature review (SLR) to identify the challenges in context-aware requirements modeling, clarify the status of these challenges, and determine future research directions.

The rest of the paper is structured as follows: Sect. 2 introduces the research method, Sect. 3 elaborates the survey results, Sect. 4 discusses the threat to validity, Sect. 5 presents the related work, and Sect. 6 describes the conclusion and future work.

2 Research Method

This section provides a detailed description of the review process adopted to make the investigation more accurate, complete, and comprehensive [4]. The process complied with the method of an SLR [5, 6].

2.1 Research Questions

The following three questions are considered to achieve the objectives mentioned above:

(a) What are the times/venues/organizations/authors of the studies?
(b) What are the challenges in context-aware requirements modeling?
(c) To what extent have the challenges been addressed?

2.2 Review Process

As shown in Fig. 1, the review process includes the following phases:

Phase 1: Keyword-based literature retrieval
Retrieval keywords are selected according to the research questions from the following databases: ACM Digital Library, IEEE Xplore, Springer, EI Compendex, ISI Web of Science, and Elsevier ScienceDirect (http://www.lib.whu.edu.cn/web/dzzy/detail.asp?q=IDN=WHU01329&s=detail&full=Y). The search string is applied only to the title and abstract as a full text search would yield a large number of irrelevant results [7]. The literature is from Jan. 2007 to Dec. 2016.

Phase 2: 1st round of literature filtering
The titles, abstracts, and keywords of all potential primary studies are checked by the first and third authors against inclusion and exclusion criteria. If it is difficult to determine whether a paper should be included or not, it is reserved for the next phase.

Phase 3: 2nd round of literature filtering
In this round, the first and third authors read the full text to determine whether the paper should be included or not according to the inclusion and exclusion criteria. When an agreement cannot be reached, they are asked to state the reasons of inclusion/exclusion to an arbitration panel. The arbitration panel includes all members of the RE group, which consists of 1 doctoral supervisor, 3 doctoral candidates, and 3 master's students.

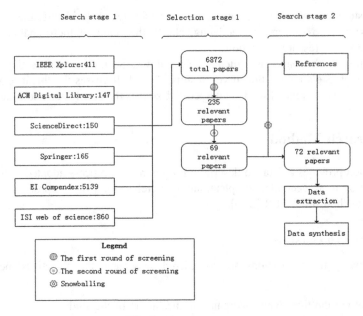

Fig. 1. Survey process

Phase 4: Snowballing

After the filtering, "snowballing" is conducted to find omitted papers. We adopt the snowballing process proposed by Claes Wohlin [8] to iteratively search the reference list and papers cited in a study until no new papers are found. Then, the new papers are checked against the inclusion and exclusion criteria. After the "snowballing," 3 papers were added to the final set.

Phase 5: Data extraction

After the filtering process, data are extracted from the selected studies to answer RQ1 to RQ3. The data extraction forms are not provided here because of the space limit. Detailed information can be found at http://www.pengronggroup.org/table.doc.

Phase 6: Data synthesis

The data extracted from the previous phase are synthesized to answer the research questions.

2.3 Search Strategy

A detailed and comprehensive identification of research papers is one of the factors that differentiate a systematic review from a conventional review. Based on the research questions, keywords are extracted and used to search study sources. The search string consists of two parts. The first part is "requirements modeling" as population, and the second part is "context aware" as intervention. Through the investigation of articles on context awareness [9–11] and requirements modeling [12–14], the keywords and their alternatives are extracted. The search terms used for population and intervention are as follows:

(requirement model OR requirement modeling) AND (context aware OR scenario aware OR ubiquitous computing OR pervasive computing)

2.4   Inclusion and Exclusion

Once potentially relevant studies have been obtained, their actual relevance must be assessed. Bases on the SLR guidelines, the following inclusion and exclusion criteria are defined to select studies from the search results [6]:

(1) **Inclusion criteria**

I1.   The papers that were written in English and published from Jan. 2007 to Dec. 2016.
I2.   Only research papers from peer reviewed journals or conferences.
I3.   For duplicate papers, one is retained and the rest are excluded.
I4.   The papers with the potential of answering at least one of the 3 research questions

(2) **Exclusion criteria**

E1.   Papers that are not written in English or not published between Jan. 2007 and Dec. 2016.
E2.   Tutorials, papers, and editorials that are less than 4 pages.
E3.   Papers whose full texts are inaccessible.
E4.   Papers that cannot answer any research questions.
E5.   Papers that cannot meet the inclusion criteria

2.5   Quality Assessment

Assessing the quality of the primary studies is important for performing an SLR. Several quality assessment questions were formulated to evaluate the selected studies. These questions are presented in Table 1. Each question has three optional answers, i.e., "Yes", "Partly", or "No", which are scored as follows: "Yes" = 1, "Partly" = 0.5, and "No" = 0. The quality score for a particular study is a sum of the scores of the answers to the questions.

Table 1. Quality assessment questions

Number	Questions
No. 1	Is the challenge clearly articulated?
No. 2	Is the proposed method of addressing the challenge clearly described?
No. 3	Is the method validated empirically or theoretically?
No. 4	Is the validated process clearly described?
No. 5	Are the limitations of the study discussed explicitly?

3 Results and Analysis

Seventy-two studies are identified using the abovementioned search strategies and the inclusion/exclusion criteria. Owing to the space limit, the list of papers is provided at http://www.pengronggroup.org/literatures.doc. The following results are obtained by analyzing the extracted data:

3.1 What Are the Venues/Authors of the Studies?

The answers are important for understanding the state-of-the-art.

3.1.1 What Are the Venues of the Studies?

The 72 papers are distributed over 59 publication sources (29 journals and 30 conferences). As shown in Figs. 2 and 3, the CAiSE, APSEC, CIT, and RE@RunTime conferences and the BPMDS, REJ, REFSQ, CONTEXT, and INFORM SOFTWARE TECH journals have published more than 1 paper. This indicates that context-aware requirements modeling is a widespread area of interest in the research community. It is being investigated not only by the software engineering domain but also by other domains such as human–computer interactions and pervasive computing.

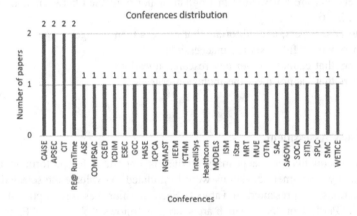

Fig. 2. Conferences in which the studies are published

3.1.2 What Are the Authors of the Studies?

The 72 primary studies were produced by 62 authors. Figure 4 presents the authors that published more than one paper. Raian Ali is the most productive author; his research interest focuses on how to use the goal-based method to meet the challenges in context-aware requirements modeling. The most frequently used method is proposed by Tomás Ruiz-López, i.e., the model-driven requirements modeling method.

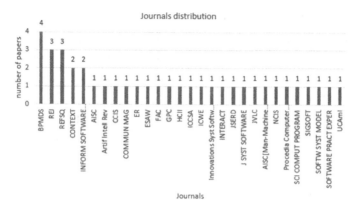

Fig. 3. Journals in which the studies are published

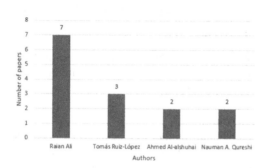

Fig. 4. Authors of the studies

3.2 What Are the Challenges in Context-Aware Requirements Modeling?

Context-aware requirements modeling is critical to the success of context-aware systems. However, owing to the intrinsic diversity, complexity and uncertainty of the context, the modeling of context-aware requirements is considerably challenging. We analyzed and summarized these challenges and classified them into 4 classes of 13 items, which are specified below.

3.2.1 Challenges of Diversity

(i) *Challenges of environment diversity*

In context-aware systems, the environment has an extremely strong impact on requirements [15]. However, the environments in which systems run are diverse. For example, for a smart health care system, a patient may be at home or at a mall, perhaps even in a street or in a deserted area [16]. The patient's requirements will vary with the environments.

(ii) *Challenges of source diversity*

In context-aware systems, there are a large number of requirements from multiple sources [17]. A few of them are necessary while others are not. Modeling the source diversity of the requirements is a major challenge.

(iii) *Challenges of domain diversity*

With the continuous development of context-aware applications, software has penetrated into multiple domains such as ambient intelligence [18] and motion-based games [19]. Modeling the specific concepts and characteristics of each domain is challenging.

(iv) *Challenges of format diversity*

Context-aware systems frequently consist of multiple distributed components. In a few cases, requirements are documented informally and even in the form of multimedia and multiple modalities [20]. Modeling format diversity is challenging.

(v) *Challenges of user diversity*

Context-aware systems involve complex relationships among users and the system. Each user has a personal background, social role, requirements, and preferences [21]. Modeling user diversity is challenging.

3.2.2   Challenges of Dynamicity

A context-aware system should monitor and adapt to an open and dynamic environment, in which the environment changes inherently, users join and leave the system at will, initial assumptions might be eventually invalid in unexpected circumstances, and system resources vary.

(i) *Challenges of environment dynamicity*

A context-aware system describes scenarios in which people are pervasively surrounded by senses and mobile devices. The requirements of a person may change because the context of such devices changes continuously [22]. For example, in context-aware mobile phones, in a typical case, the system should notify a user of a phone call by ringing, and when he walks into a meeting room, the system should notify him through vibration or reject the phone call and send an SMS to the caller [3].

(ii) *Challenges of user dynamicity*

Context-aware systems are always heterogeneous and dynamic. Users join and leave the system at will [16], and their interests and activities vary according to changes in time or location [23]. This leads to challenges in context-aware requirements modeling.

(iii) *Challenges of resource dynamicity*

Context-aware systems may be distributed, and computing resources change constantly [24]; a few requirements cannot be satisfied until others have been met because of resource constraints. Thus, modeling resource dynamicity is challenging.

(iv) *Challenges of assumptions dynamicity*

Requirements engineers frequently make initial assumptions in context-aware systems. However, these assumptions might become invalid when the context of the system changes [25]. Monitoring these assumptions and detecting invalid assumptions is challenging.

3.2.3 Challenges of Consistency

(i) *Challenges of external consistency*

External consistency implies that the requirements in the SRS exclude conflicts with any project documentation [26]. The relationships between the requirements and other components in context-aware systems are complex. A single requirement may be associated to a number of components and each component may include the elements of several requirements [27]. Maintaining the consistency of requirements and components consistent is challenging.

(ii) *Challenges of internal consistency*

Internal consistency implies that there is no subset of requirements in the SRS that includes conflicts [26]. The requirements model of a context-aware system combines the variability of the context and requirements [28]; this is error prone. Maintaining the consistency of requirements is challenging.

3.2.4 Challenges of Uncertainty

(i) *Challenges of environmental uncertainty*

Context-aware systems must adapt to the environment and realize users' requirements. However, the environment of a system is uncertain owing to various factors such as lack of information. In addition, the context items influenced by the status of the environment may be uncertain [29]. Modeling the uncertainty of the environment is challenging.

(ii) *Challenges of requirements uncertainty*

Requirements uncertainty implies that requirements are not known until it is practically used, which results from software requirements creating an ill-defined problem [30]. One requirement may be redundant under a specific environment, whereas it may be important in other environments but difficult to realize. Modeling requirements uncertainty is challenging.

3.3 To What Extent Have the Challenges Been Addressed?

We analyzed the extent to which the challenges identified above have been addressed. Detailed information is provided in Table 2.

Table 1 shows that the challenges of dynamicity have been considered in most studies (45 papers), followed by the challenges of diversity (23 papers); the challenges

Table 2. Challenges and the corresponding studies

Challenges	Sub-challenges	Number	Studies
Diversity	Environment diversity[a]	4	p27, p34, p59, p66
	Source diversity	2	p17, p28
	Domain diversity	6	p4, p9, p21, p30, p49, p61
	Format diversity	5	p1, p5, p67, p68, p71
	User diversity	6	p19, p20, p26, p48, p51, p56
Dynamicity	Environment dynamicity	30	p2, p3, p7, p10, p12, p13, p14, p15, p16, p25, p29, p31, p32, p33, p36, p37, p38, p39, p41, p42, p43, p46, p47, p50, p54, p55, p58, p63, p64, p65
	User dynamicity	11	p18, p24, p39, p43, p46, p55, p58, p60, p64, p69, p72
	Resource dynamicity	3	p43, p50, p64
	Assumption dynamicity	1	p22
Consistency	External consistency	5	p11, p44, p45, p50, p70
	Internal consistency	2	p35, p53
Uncertainty	Environment uncertainty	6	p6, p8, p23, p52, p57, p62
	Requirements uncertainty	1	p40

of consistency and uncertainty have been considered only in a few studies. Several methods have been used to address these challenges.

The primary approach of addressing the challenges of environmental diversity is to use scenarios, such as extended UML use cases, to describe environmental diversity [31] and specify requirements in different context scenarios [15, 32]. The challenges of source are addressed by modeling human–computer interaction formally and verifying it automatically [33]. The challenges of domain diversity are addressed using a framework or process for a specific domain, such as ambient intelligence [18], motion-based games [19], context adaptive systems [34], ambient intelligent systems [35], ubiquitous systems [36], and interactive TV applications [37]. The challenges of format diversity are addressed using layered thought [38, 39], adding an intermediate layer to handle diverse requirements, or using a model to handle multiformat requirements, such as the VoiceToModel framework that handles requirements in the voice form [40]. The challenges of user diversity is are addressed by introducing human-centered design into requirements engineering to model the characteristics and preferences of users [1, 41] or use a preference model to model the diversity in the preferences of users [42].

The challenges of environment dynamicity are addressed by perceiving the changes in the context and incorporating them into different requirements models such as the goal-based requirements model [43–52], UML requirements model [53–56], and requirements model in the BPMN form [2, 57], or by supporting adaptation. The representative method of addressing the challenges of user dynamicity is to capture the changes in the location, preference, or other context dimensions of a user and model and analyze these changes to realize dynamic requirements [58–62]. The primary method of addressing the challenges of resource dynamicity is to define the provider and requester of resources and dynamically maintain resource usage [24]. The challenge of assumption dynamicity is addressed by monitoring the assumptions in the requirements model at runtime and evolving the model to reflect the validity level of the assumptions [25].

Model-driven development is used to address the challenge of external consistency [63] as it can describe and link user-level requirements and other components. The challenge of internal consistency is addressed by defining a set of rules to express the relationships and constraints of requirements and determining internal consistency according to the rules [28].

The challenge of environment uncertainty is addressed by assigning a value to represent the reliability of context information [64]. The challenge of requirement uncertainty is addressed by introducing a context snapshot model to represent the uncertainty in requirements with domain knowledge [30].

The results show that the research on context-aware requirements modeling is at an early stage. Diversity is the basic feature of context-aware requirements modeling. Environment dynamicity and user dynamicity are necessary functions of system operation; they are indispensable for context-aware systems, and there are several studies on them. Assumptions define the initial constraints of the system. Addressing these assumptions, consistency, and uncertainty requires detailed analysis. Even though the solutions to these challenges are not essential for system operation, they are important for improving the stability and quality of the system, and there are only a few studies on them.

4   Threats to Validity

Even though we conducted the review in a rigorous manner, the threats to validity are inevitable, which are as follows:

Missing primary studies: Even though commonly used digital libraries are selected, the possibility of missing important papers still exists. In addition, the snowballing methods are adopted to reduce risk. Only papers written in English are collected and analyzed. As English is the most commonly used language in academia, the threat is acceptable.

Potential bias: Bias from researchers may affect analysis results. To mitigate the bias, the first and third authors conduct filtration and data extraction independently. In addition, they submit disagreement to the arbitration panel when agreement cannot be achieved.

5 Related Work

During the last decade, several surveys have been published in this field. As shown in Table 3, [65] primarily discusses the role of uncertainty in self-adaptation systems, related research challenges, and existing solutions, [66] elaborates the challenges in RE for cyber-physical systems, [67] focuses on the modeling methods, RE activities, requirements quality attributes, application domains, and research topics of self-adaptive systems, and [68] focuses on how existing requirements modeling methods address the challenges caused by self-adaptation and the advantages and disadvantages of their solutions. However, it is not an SLR and the research scope is small. The research questions and interests of these studies are considerably different from ours.

Table 3. Related works.

	Methods	Topics
71	Survey	Requirements for self-adaptation
72	Survey	RE for cyber-physical systems
73	SLR	Modeling methods, RE activities, requirements quality attributes, application domains, and research topics of self-adaptive systems
74	Survey	Requirements modeling methods for self-adaptive software systems and the advantages and disadvantages of their solutions

Context-aware systems should be aware of the changes in the context and change behaviors accordingly. Owing to the intrinsic diversity, dynamicity, inconsistency and uncertainty of the systems, modeling context-aware requirements is considerably challenging. Identifying and classifying these challenges can enable researchers to determine the current problems that must be addressed. In this study, we adopt the method of an SLR to survey the challenges in context-aware requirements modeling, analyze the extent to which the challenges have been addressed, and suggest future research directions.

6 Conclusion and Future Work

The state-of-the-art of context-aware requirements modeling research is as follows: (1) This field has attracted widespread interest in the software engineering domain and other domains such as human–computer interactions. (2) Raian Ali from Bournemouth University is the most productive author, and his research interest focuses on the modeling of context-aware requirements using the goal-based method. (3) The challenges in context-aware requirements modeling include diversity, dynamicity, consistency, and uncertainty. There are numerous studies on solving the challenges of diversity, environment, and user dynamicity and a few studies on addressing the challenges of assumption dynamicity, consistency, and uncertainty. This indicates that the research on context-aware requirements modeling is at an early stage.

Based on the abovementioned findings, the following research directions require further attention:

(1) How to verify the correctness and credibility of the context information around the requirements should be take into account more.
(2) The assumptions and initial constraints of requirements should be examined in detail as they may be invalid because of the changes in the context.
(3) The consistency between requirements and other artifacts should be considered to improve the robustness of the system.

Acknowledgments. This work was supported by National key research and development plan of China (No. 2016YFB0501801). The work also was supported by National Natural Science Foundation of China under Grant No. 61170026.

References

1. Sutcliffe, A., Sawyer, P.: Modeling personalized adaptive systems. In: Salinesi, C., Norrie, M.C., Pastor, Ó. (eds.) CAiSE 2013. LNCS, vol. 7908, pp. 178–192. Springer, Heidelberg (2013). https://doi.org/10.1007/978-3-642-38709-8_12
2. Frece, A., Juric, M.B.: Modeling functional requirements for configurable content-and context-aware dynamic service selection in business process models. J. Vis. Lang. Comput. **23**(4), 223–247 (2012)
3. Choi, J.: Context-driven requirements analysis. In: Gervasi, O., Gavrilova, M.L. (eds.) ICCSA 2007, Part III. LNCS, vol. 4707, pp. 739–748. Springer, Heidelberg (2007). https://doi.org/10.1007/978-3-540-74484-9_63
4. Staples, M., Niazi, M.: Experiences using systematic review guidelines. J. Syst. Softw. **80** (9), 1425–1437 (2007)
5. Lisboa, L.B., Garcia, V.C., Lucrédio, D., et al.: A systematic review of domain analysis tools. Inf. Softw. Technol. **52**(1), 1–13 (2010)
6. Kitchenham, B.A., Charters, S.: Guidelines for performing systematic literature reviews in software engineering (version 2.3). Technical report, EBSE Technical Report EBSE-2007-01, Keele University and Durham University (2007)
7. Dyba, T., Dingsoyr, T., Hanssen, G.K.: Applying systematic reviews to diverse study types: an experience report. In: Proceeding of the first international symposium on empirical software engineering and measurement(ESEM), pp. 225–234 (2007)
8. Wohlin, C.: Guidelines for snowballing in systematic literature studies and a replication in software engineering. In: Proceedings of the 18th International Conference on Evaluation and Assessment in Software Engineering, p. 38. ACM (2014)
9. Zimmermann, A., Lorenz, A., Oppermann, R.: An operational definition of context. In: Kokinov, B., Richardson, D.C., Roth-Berghofer, T.R., Vieu, L. (eds.) CONTEXT 2007. LNCS (LNAI), vol. 4635, pp. 558–571. Springer, Heidelberg (2007). https://doi.org/10.1007/978-3-540-74255-5_42
10. Bettini, C., Brdiczka, O., Henricksen, K., et al.: A survey of context modelling and reasoning techniques. Pervasive Mob. Comput. **6**(2), 161–180 (2010)
11. Hong, J., Suh, E., Kim, S.J.: Context-aware systems: a literature review and classification. Expert Syst. Appl. **36**(4), 8509–8522 (2009)

12. Peng, R., Lai, H.: DRE-specific wikis for distributed requirements engineering: a review. In: 2012 19th Asia-Pacific Software Engineering Conference (APSEC), vol. 1, pp. 116–126. IEEE (2012)

13. Khan, H.H., bin Mahrin, M.N.: Situational requirement engineering: a systematic literature review protocol. In: 2013 IEEE Conference on Open Systems (ICOS), pp. 123–126. IEEE (2013)

14. Yang, Z., Li, Z., Jin, Z., Chen, Y.: A systematic literature review of requirements modeling and analysis for self-adaptive systems. In: Salinesi, C., van de Weerd, I. (eds.) REFSQ 2014. LNCS, vol. 8396, pp. 55–71. Springer, Cham (2014). https://doi.org/10.1007/978-3-319-05843-6_5

15. Boudaa, B.: Towards a model-driven requirements specification of context-aware services. In: 2014 Tenth International Conference on Signal-Image Technology and Internet-Based Systems (SITIS), pp. 194–200. IEEE (2014)

16. Dalpiaz, F., Giorgini, P., Mylopoulos, J.: Adaptive socio-technical systems: a requirements-based approach. Requirements Eng. **18**(1), 1–24 (2013)

17. Ismail, I., Moussa, F.: User requirements deduction in a pervasive environment. In: NGMAST: IEEE International Conference on Next Generation Mobile Application, Services and Technologies (2010)

18. Wurdel, M., Burghardt, C., Forbrig, P.: Supporting ambient environments by extended task models. In: Mühlhäuser, M., Ferscha, A., Aitenbichler, E. (eds.) AmI 2007. CCIS, vol. 11, pp. 131–138. Springer, Heidelberg (2008). https://doi.org/10.1007/978-3-540-85379-4_16

19. Pasquale, L., Spoletini, P., Pometto, D., Blasi, F., Redaelli, T.: Requirements engineering meets physiotherapy: an experience with motion-based games. In: Doerr, J., Opdahl, A. (eds.) REFSQ 2013. LNCS, vol. 7830, pp. 315–330. Springer, Heidelberg (2013). https://doi.org/10.1007/978-3-642-37422-7_23

20. Ramdane-Cherif, A., Hina, M.D., Tadj, C., et al.: Analysis of a new ubiquitous multimodal multimedia computing system. In: 2007 Ninth IEEE International Symposium on Multimedia, ISM 2007, pp. 161–168. IEEE (2007)

21. Sun, J., Liu, F., Zhang, H., Liu, L., Yu, E.: Understanding the diversity of services based on users' identities. In: Mouratidis, H., Rolland, C. (eds.) CAiSE 2011. LNCS, vol. 6741, pp. 612–626. Springer, Heidelberg (2011). https://doi.org/10.1007/978-3-642-21640-4_45

22. Desmet, B., Vallejos, J., Costanza, P., De Meuter, W., D'Hondt, T.: Context-oriented domain analysis. In: Kokinov, B., Richardson, D.C., Roth-Berghofer, T.R., Vieu, L. (eds.) CONTEXT 2007. LNCS (LNAI), vol. 4635, pp. 178–191. Springer, Heidelberg (2007). https://doi.org/10.1007/978-3-540-74255-5_14

23. Ahmad, A., Rahman, M.A, Afyouni, I., et al.: Towards a mobile and context-aware framework from crowdsourced data. In: 2014 The 5th International Conference on Information and Communication Technology for The Muslim World (ICT4 M), pp. 1–6. IEEE (2014)

24. Ruiz-López, T., Noguera, M., RodríGuez, M.A.J., et al.: REUBI: a requirements engineering method for ubiquitous systems. Sci. Comput. Program. **78**(10), 1895–1911 (2013)

25. Ali, R., Dalpiaz, F., Giorgini, P., Souza, V.E.S.: Requirements evolution: from assumptions to reality. In: Halpin, T., Nurcan, S., Krogstie, J., Soffer, P., Proper, E., Schmidt, R., Bider, I. (eds.) BPMDS/EMMSAD -2011. LNBIP, vol. 81, pp. 372–382. Springer, Heidelberg (2011). https://doi.org/10.1007/978-3-642-21759-3_27

26. Saavedra, R., Ballejos, L., Ale, M.: Software requirements quality evaluation: state of the art and research challenges. In: Proceedings of 14th Argentine Symposium on Software Engineering, Cordoba, Argentina (2013)

27. Kim, J.-H., Kim, S.-C.: Adaptive smart vehicle middleware platform for aspect oriented software engineering. In: Park, J.J.H., Arabnia, H.R., Kim, C., Shi, W., Gil, J.-M. (eds.) GPC 2013. LNCS, vol. 7861, pp. 659–664. Springer, Heidelberg (2013). https://doi.org/10.1007/978-3-642-38027-3_71

28. Ali, R., Dalpiaz, F., Giorgini, P.: Reasoning with contextual requirements: detecting inconsistency and conflicts. Inf. Softw. Technol. **55**(1), 35–57 (2013)

29. Zhang, M., Selic, B., Ali, S., Yue, T., Okariz, O., Norgren, R.: Understanding uncertainty in cyber-physical systems: a conceptual model. In: Wąsowski, A., Lönn, H. (eds.) ECMFA 2016. LNCS, vol. 9764, pp. 247–264. Springer, Cham (2016). https://doi.org/10.1007/978-3-319-42061-5_16

30. Liu, W., Feng, Z.: Requirement uncertainty analysis for service-oriented self-adaptation software. In: Lei, Jingsheng, Wang, Fu Lee, Li, Mo, Luo, Yuan (eds.) NCIS 2012. CCIS, vol. 345, pp. 156–163. Springer, Heidelberg (2012). https://doi.org/10.1007/978-3-642-35211-9_20

31. Raji, A., Dhaussy, P.: Use cases modeling for scalable model-checking. In: 2011 18th Asia Pacific Software Engineering Conference (APSEC), pp. 65–72. IEEE (2011)

32. Vrbaski, M., Mussbacher, G., Petriu, D., et al.: Goal models as run-time entities in context-aware systems. In: Proceedings of the 7th Workshop on Models@ run. time, pp. 3–8. ACM (2012)

33. Riahi, I., Riahi, M., Moussa, F.: XML in formal specification, verification and generation of mobile HCI. In: Jacko, J.A. (ed.) HCI 2011, Part III. LNCS, vol. 6763, pp. 92–100. Springer, Heidelberg (2011). https://doi.org/10.1007/978-3-642-21616-9_11

34. Sitou, W., Spanfelner, B.: Towards requirements engineering for context adaptive systems. In: 2007 31st Annual International Computer Software and Applications Conference, COMPSAC 2007, vol. 2, pp. 593–600. IEEE (2007)

35. Kofod-Petersen, A., Cassens, J.: Modelling with problem frames: explanations and context in ambient intelligent systems. In: Beigl, M., Christiansen, H., Roth-Berghofer, T.R., Kofod-Petersen, A., Coventry, K.R., Schmidtke, H.R. (eds.) CONTEXT 2011. LNCS (LNAI), vol. 6967, pp. 145–158. Springer, Heidelberg (2011). https://doi.org/10.1007/978-3-642-24279-3_17

36. Ruiz-López, T., Rodríguez-Domínguez, C., Noguera, M., Rodríguez, M.J.: A model-driven approach to requirements engineering in ubiquitous systems. In: Novais, P., Hallenborg, K., Tapia, D., Rodríguez, J. (eds.) ISAmI 2012. AINSC, vol. 153, pp. 85–92. Springer, Heidelberg (2012). https://doi.org/10.1007/978-3-642-28783-1_11

37. Canchi, S., Durán, J.E.: Functional requirements modelling for interactive tv applications. In: Fricker, S.A., Schneider, K. (eds.) REFSQ 2015. LNCS, vol. 9013, pp. 254–261. Springer, Cham (2015). https://doi.org/10.1007/978-3-319-16101-3_17

38. Xiong, J., Fan, J., Li, Y.: A layered context reference model for context/situation middleware. In: 2008 Seventh International Conference on Grid and Cooperative Computing, GCC 2008, pp. 15–21. IEEE (2008)

39. Sengupta, S., Dasgupta, R.: Use of semi-formal and formal methods in requirement engineering of ILMS. ACM SIGSOFT Softw. Eng. Notes **40**(1), 1–13 (2015)

40. Soares, F., Araújo, J., Wanderley, F.: VoiceToModel: an approach to generate requirements models from speech recognition mechanisms. In: Proceedings of the 30th Annual ACM Symposium on Applied Computing, pp. 1350–1357. ACM (2015)

41. Leonardi, C., Sabatucci, L., Susi, A., Zancanaro, M.: Design as intercultural dialogue: coupling human-centered design with requirement engineering methods. In: Campos, P., Graham, N., Jorge, J., Nunes, N., Palanque, P., Winckler, M. (eds.) INTERACT 2011, Part III. LNCS, vol. 6948, pp. 485–502. Springer, Heidelberg (2011). https://doi.org/10.1007/978-3-642-23765-2_34

42. Klimek, R.: Preference models and their elicitation and analysis for context-aware applications. In: Gruca, D.A., Czachórski, T., Kozielski, S. (eds.) Man-Machine Interactions 3. AISC, vol. 242, pp. 353–360. Springer, Cham (2014). https://doi.org/10.1007/978-3-319-02309-0_38

43. Yang, Z., Jin, Z.: Modeling and specifying parametric adaptation mechanism for self-adaptive systems. In: Zowghi, D., Jin, Z. (eds.) Requirements Engineering. CCIS, vol. 432, pp. 105–119. Springer, Heidelberg (2014). https://doi.org/10.1007/978-3-662-43610-3_9

44. Nakagawa, H., Ohsuga, A., Honiden, S.: Constructing self-adaptive systems using a kaos model. In: 2008 Second IEEE International Conference on Self-Adaptive and Self-Organizing Systems Workshops, SASOW 2008, pp. 132–137. IEEE (2008)

45. Ali, R., Dalpiaz, F., Giorgini, P.: A goal modeling framework for self-contextualizable software. In: Halpin, T., Krogstie, J., Nurcan, S., Proper, E., Schmidt, R., Soffer, P., Ukor, R. (eds.) BPMDS/EMMSAD -2009. LNBIP, vol. 29, pp. 326–338. Springer, Heidelberg (2009). https://doi.org/10.1007/978-3-642-01862-6_27

46. Lapouchnian, A., Mylopoulos, J.: Modeling domain variability in requirements engineering with contexts. In: Laender, A.H.F., Castano, S., Dayal, U., Casati, F., de Oliveira, J.P.M. (eds.) ER 2009. LNCS, vol. 5829, pp. 115–130. Springer, Heidelberg (2009). https://doi.org/10.1007/978-3-642-04840-1_11

47. Ali, R., Dalpiaz, F., Giorgini, P.: A goal-based framework for contextual requirements modeling and analysis. Requirements Eng. 15(4), 439–458 (2010)

48. Morandini, M., Migeon, F., Gleizes, M.-P., Maurel, C., Penserini, L., Perini, A.: A goal-oriented approach for modelling self-organising MAS. In: Aldewereld, H., Dignum, V., Picard, G. (eds.) ESAW 2009. LNCS (LNAI), vol. 5881, pp. 33–48. Springer, Heidelberg (2009). https://doi.org/10.1007/978-3-642-10203-5_4

49. Yu, L., Glenstrup, A., Zhang, Y., et al.: Goal-driven context-aware service composition. In: 2010 5th International Conference on Pervasive Computing and Applications (ICPCA), pp. 342–347. IEEE (2010)

50. Qureshi, N.A, Perini, A., Ernst, N.A., et al.: Towards a continuous requirements engineering framework for self-adaptive systems. In: 2010 First International Workshop on Requirements@ Run. Time (RE@ RunTime), pp. 9–16. IEEE (2010)

51. Qureshi, N.A., Jureta, I.J., Perini, A.: Towards a requirements modeling language for self-adaptive systems. In: Regnell, B., Damian, D. (eds.) REFSQ 2012. LNCS, vol. 7195, pp. 263–279. Springer, Heidelberg (2012). https://doi.org/10.1007/978-3-642-28714-5_24

52. Vilela, J., Castro, J., Pimentel, J.: A systematic process for obtaining the behavior of context-sensitive systems. J. Softw. Eng. Res. Dev. 4(1), 2 (2016)

53. Sun, W., France, R.B., Ray, I.: Supporting iterative development of robust operation contracts in UML requirements models. In: 2011 IEEE 13th International Symposium on High-Assurance Systems Engineering (HASE), pp. 9–16. IEEE (2011)

54. Al-alshuhai, A., Siewe, F.: An extension of the use case diagram to model context-aware applications. In: 2015 SAI Intelligent Systems Conference (IntelliSys), pp. 884–888. IEEE (2015)

55. Almutairi, S., Bella, G., Abu-Samaha, A.: Specifying security requirements of context aware system using UML. In: 2012 Seventh International Conference on Digital Information Management (ICDIM), pp. 259–265. IEEE (2012)

56. Al-alshuhai, A., Siewe, F.: An extension of UML activity diagram to model the behaviour of context-aware systems. In: 2015 IEEE International Conference on Computer and Information Technology; Ubiquitous Computing and Communications; Dependable, Autonomic and Secure Computing; Pervasive Intelligence and Computing (CIT/IUCC/DASC/PICOM), pp. 431–437. IEEE (2015)

57. Santos, E., Pimentel, J., Castro, J., Finkelstein, A.: On the dynamic configuration of business process models. In: Bider, I., Halpin, T., Krogstie, J., Nurcan, S., Proper, E., Schmidt, R., Soffer, P., Wrycza, S. (eds.) BPMDS/EMMSAD -2012. LNBIP, vol. 113, pp. 331–346. Springer, Heidelberg (2012). https://doi.org/10.1007/978-3-642-31072-0_23

58. Zhu, J., Pung, H.K., Oliya, M., et al.: A context realization framework for ubiquitous applications with runtime support. IEEE Commun. Mag. **49**(9), 132–141 (2011)

59. Huang, J., Yang, H., Xu, L., et al.: Supporting context—Aware service evolution with a process management requirements model. In: 2011 IEEE International Conference on Service-Oriented Computing and Applications (SOCA), pp. 1–8. IEEE (2011)

60. Mcheick, H.: Modeling context aware features for pervasive computing. Procedia Comput. Sci. **37**, 135–142 (2014)

61. Ahmad, A., Rahman, M.A., Afyouni, I., et al.: Towards a mobile and context-aware framework from crowdsourced data. In: 2014 The 5th International Conference on Information and Communication Technology for The Muslim World (ICT4M), pp. 1–6. IEEE (2014)

62. Dzvonyar, D., Krusche, S., Alkadhi, R., et al.: Context-aware user feedback in continuous software evolution. In: Proceedings of the International Workshop on Continuous Software Evolution and Delivery, pp. 12–18. ACM (2016)

63. Jørgensen, J.B., Tjell, S., Fernandes, J.M.: Formal requirements modelling with executable use cases and coloured Petri nets. Innovations Syst. Softw. Eng. **5**(1), 13–25 (2009)

64. Huang, P.C., Kuo, Y.H.: A reliable context model for context-aware applications. In: 2008 IEEE International Conference on Systems, Man and Cybernetics, SMC 2008, pp. 246–250. IEEE (2008)

65. Bencomo, N.: Requirements for self-adaptation. In: Lämmel, R., Saraiva, J., Visser, J. (eds.) GTTSE 2011. LNCS, vol. 7680, pp. 271–296. Springer, Heidelberg (2013). https://doi.org/10.1007/978-3-642-35992-7_7

66. Wiesner, S., Gorldt, C., Soeken, M., Thoben, K.-D., Drechsler, R.: Requirements engineering for cyber-physical systems. In: Grabot, B., Vallespir, B., Gomes, S., Bouras, A., Kiritsis, D. (eds.) APMS 2014, Part I. IAICT, vol. 438, pp. 281–288. Springer, Heidelberg (2014). https://doi.org/10.1007/978-3-662-44739-0_35

67. Yang, Z., Li, Z., Jin, Z., Chen, Y.: A Systematic literature review of requirements modeling and analysis for self-adaptive systems. In: Salinesi, C., van de Weerd, I. (eds.) REFSQ 2014. LNCS, vol. 8396, pp. 55–71. Springer, Cham (2014). https://doi.org/10.1007/978-3-319-05843-6_5

68. Zhao, T., Zhao, H., Zhang, W.: A preliminary study on requirements modeling methods for self-adaptive software systems. In: Proceedings of the 5th Asia-Pacific Symposium on Internetware, p. 3. ACM (2013)

Issues of Using Function Point Analysis Method for Requirement Changes During Software Development Phase

Jalal Shah[✉] and Nazri Kama

Advanced Informatics School, Universiti Teknologi Malaysia,
Kuala Lumpur, Malaysia
engrjalalshah@yahoo.com, mdnazri@utm.my

Abstract. Software go through changes at all stages of Software Development Life Cycle (SDLC). Accepting a large amount of changes may raise the time and cost of the software. While denying changes may rise customer dissatisfaction. An effective change acceptance decision helps software project manager to decide whether to accept or reject these changes. Software effort estimation is one of the methods that helps software project manager in an efficient change acceptance decision. Several software effort estimation techniques have been introduced to date and Function Point Analysis (FPA) is one of them. FPA method is used for measuring the size and complexity of a software by calculating the functionality that the system provides its user. Many studies highlighted that FPA method is used for early phases of SDLC as compared to software development phase. During software development phase software artifacts are in inconsistent states. Therefore, it is a challenging task for software project manager to estimate the amount of required effort for a change request during software development phase. In this paper we have used FPA method in a case study for requirement changes during software development phase. This study has highlighted the main concerns of using FPA method for requirement changes during software development phase.

Keywords: Software development phase
Software requirements change management · Function Point Analysis
Software effort estimation

1 Introduction

In traditional methodologies, software project manager is having the opportunity to accept or reject changes. On the other hand agile methodologies, give high priority of accepting changes throughout Software Development Life Cycle (SDLC) as compared to the traditional methodology [1]. Mostly software failure reasons are due to the change of requirements. Software project's success or failure depends upon the project manager that how he responds on these changes [2, 3]. Numerous studies have emphasized the significance of the software project manager role in a project's success or failure especially in managing the changes in software projects. In software project management process the most common causes of project failure are estimation

© Springer Nature Singapore Pte Ltd. 2018
M. Kamalrudin et al. (Eds.): APRES 2017, CCIS 809, pp. 156–163, 2018.
https://doi.org/10.1007/978-981-10-7796-8_12

mistakes, ambiguous project goals, objectives and requirement changes during the project. A successful software project manager manages these changes and gives good reason for the change acceptance decisions [4, 5]. Likewise introducing software changes during software development phase, may need to identify the impact of these changes on software artifacts and estimates the required effort.

Software effort estimation is an important approach that helps software project manager in making an effective change approval decision. Software efforts estimation is the process of predicting the most accurate amount of effort required to develop or maintain software based on a large number of changing variables [3]. The estimation of required efforts for requirement changes can be done in many ways, some of them are: Expert Judgment [6], Estimation by Analogy [7], Impact Analysis [8], Source Lines of Code (SLOC) [9] and Function Point Analysis (FPA) [10]. It has been a continuous research because there are still many views and debates in getting an accurate effort estimation result. All techniques showed that they can be useful to estimate effort and cost of software, but not any of them every time provides an accurate estimation result [11].

The estimation of required efforts for the requirement changes can be calculated once the software size is measured. Software size can be measured by using different methods two of them are: SLOC and FPA. In SLOC the number of lines used for source instruction or coding are counted while FPA method is used for measuring the size and complexity of a software by calculating its functionality that system provides the user.

FPA method was introduced by Albert in 1970s. He wanted to develop a method for software size measurement that is independent of technology and can measure software size in early phases of SDLC as compared to SLOC, which can measure software size once the task of coding is completed [12].

Many studies highlighted the importance of FPA method for software effort estimation. FPA method estimates the efforts in the early phases of SDLC or for maintenance phase based on pre-defined requirements [10]. During software development phase software artifacts are in inconsistent states. Such as, some of the artifacts are fully developed, some are partially developed and some are not developed. Therefore it is a challenging task for software project managers to estimate the required efforts for a change request during software development phase [13].

In this paper we have used FPA method in a case study for requirement changes during software development phase. The outcome of this study has highlight the main issues of using FPA method for requirement changes during software development phase.

This paper covers following sections. Section 2 shows the related work, Sect. 3 shows the method that is used during the case study, Sect. 4 shows the evaluation of the study, Sect. 5 contains the discussion and finally Sect. 6 is the conclusion and future scope.

2 Related Work

There are two closely related keywords involved in this research namely: Software Effort Estimation and Function Point Analysis.

2.1   Software Effort Estimation

Software effort estimation is the method of predicting how much work and how many hours of work are needed for the completion of a software project. Software effort estimation results can be used in project plans, budgets, iteration plans, investment analysis, bidding rounds and risk management.

In the literature different categories of software effort estimation are discussed [14, 15]. while some of them are very famous and used widely i.e. Expert Judgement [16]; Estimation by Analogy [17, 18]; Function Point Analysis [19]; Regression Analysis [20]; and Model Based [21].

Expert judgement is a common method that is used till date. Most of the project managers select expert judgment effort estimation because of its flexibility and less complexity as compared to other formal methods. At present there is not a single effort estimation method that claims for 100% accurate results. Therefore expert judgement effort estimation is a good choice for software project managers [16].

Effort estimation through Analogy, uses the knowledge or information that is gained from previously developed projects of similar type. The idea behind analogy-based effort estimation is the prediction of required efforts for a specific project on the bases of the past information of similar projects. Perhaps due to simplicity and flexibility, analogy-based estimation is frequently used as hybrid model for combination with other approaches to increase its performance and accuracy such as, particle swarm optimization (PSO), grey relational analysis (GRA), outlier elimination technique, principle component analysis (PCA), regression and rough set theory [22].

In the early days, Source Lines of Code (SLOC) was used for the calculation of software size and efforts estimation in software projects. In this method the estimation can be performed by counting the source lines of code. Furthermore, it is only possible once the task of coding is completed. In addition, studies indicate that the significance of SLOC is reduced for larger scale of development projects and using of different programming languages create different values of estimation. Therefore using SLOC for getting accurate estimation results in software projects could be a challenge [18, 19]. Later on Allan Albrecht introduced Function Point Analysis (FPA) to solved the estimation problems faced during estimation by SLOC [23].

2.2   Function Point Analysis

Function Point Analysis FPA approach is developed by Allan Albrecht in 1979. FPA is the method of measuring size and complexity of software by calculating the functionality, that the system provides to its end user [23]. The main goals of FPA are: (1) To calculate the functionality that is provided to the end user. (2) To perform estimation that is independent of technology.

In FPA approach Function Points (FPs) of a software project are calculated by the number of transactions, file types, general system characteristics and their complexity. However several steps are required for the calculation of FPs [10, 24].

First, calculating Unadjusted Function Points (UFP) by adding Internal Logical Files ILF, External Interface Files EIF, External Output EO, External Input EI and External inquiries EQ with their complexity (low, medium, or high) [24].

Secondly, calculating Value Adjustment Factor VAF from fourteen General System Characteristics (GSC) [24]. A scale is used from 0 to 5 to rate the degree of influence for each GSC. Whereas, 0 = Not present or no Influence, 1 = Incidental influence, 2 = Moderate influence, 3 = Average influence, 4 = Significant influence and 5 = Strong influence throughout. Once the 14 GSCs have assigned values regarding to their degree of influence. The next step is the calculation of VAF shown in the Eq. 1 [24].

$$VAF = 0.65 + \left[\left(\sum_{i=1}^{n} Ci \right) * 0.1 \right] \qquad (1)$$

So after getting the VAF the final value of FPs can be calculated from the Eq. 2 [24].

$$FPs = UFP * VAF \qquad (2)$$

3 Evaluation

This section describes the method of evaluating our case study. During this process four main evaluation factors are considered. These factors are; (1) Case selection, (2) Evaluation metrics, (3) Data collection and analysis, and (4) Evaluation results.

3.1 Case Study

To verify FPA method for software requirement changes during software development phase. We have applied the method in one case study i.e. Payroll System (PS). PS is a software development project assigned to the postgraduate students of software engineering at Advance Informatics School (AIS), at University Teknologi Malaysia (UTM). We have used FPA method in four phases, whereas each phase is representing a different development progress state in software development life cycle as shown in the Table 1.

Table 1. Case studies

Case study	Development progress	States of software artifacts
Phase 1	Analysis	Software requirements specification is completed
Phase 2	Design	Software design is completed
Phase 3	Coding	Some classes are partially developed
Phase 4	Testing	All classes are developed

3.2 Evaluation Metric

An evaluation metric has been used for evaluating the change effort prediction results produced by the software change effort estimation which is the Magnitude of Relative Error (MRE). It has calculated a rate of the relative errors in both cases of over-estimation or under-estimation as shown in equation.

$$MRE = \frac{[\text{Actual Results} - \text{Estimated Results}]}{\text{Actual Results}}$$

3.3 Data Collection and Analysis

During data collection the following items such as; (1) Change Request Form (2) System Integration Test Report (3) User Acceptance Test Report (4) Software Requirements and Software Design Document, (5) Source Code, and (6) Progress Report have been collected from case selection.

The data collection from the experiment have been analyzed based on the project ID, change request ID, change request type, estimated effort result, actual effort and the magnitude of the relative error (MRE) between the estimation effort and the actual effort for each change request.

In our case study i.e. Payroll System (PS). We have selected fifteen change requests (CR) in four phases with three Change Types (CTs) i.e. Addition, Modification, and Deletion during software development phase as shown in Table 2.

Table 2. Change requests

CTs	Phase 1	Phase 2	Phase 3	Phase 4
CT1-Addition	CR1 CR2	CR5	CR8 CR9	CR12
CT2-Deletion	CR3	CR6	CR10	CR13 CR14
CT3-Modification	CR4	CR7	CR11	CR15

4 Evaluation Results

Table 3 shows the experiment result of the selected case software project. The table indicates the effort estimation produced by the actual implementation effort and MRE value (percentage of discrepancy between estimated effort and actual implementation effort) sorted by the Project ID and Change Request ID. These all 15 change requests were introduced to the case selection software project during the software development phase.

5 Discussion

To review the results of our study we have come up with some issues while using FPA approach for estimating software size for change requests during software development phase. The main issues are: (1) tracking of change request in software artifacts and (2) the impact of change request on software artifacts.

Table 3. Experiment results

Project ID	Change request ID	Change type	Change request phase	Estimated effort (man/month)	Actual implementation effort (man/month)	MRE (%)
Project 1 (water fall)	C1	CT-A	Analysis	0.195	1.1	0.822%
	C2	CT-A	Analysis	0.292	0.35	7.36%
	C3	CT-D	Analysis	0.195	0.025	69.20%
	C4	CT-M	Analysis	0.292	0.0275	7.73%
	C5	CT-A	Design	0.195	0.175	11.91%
	C6	CT-D	Design	0.074	4.95	2.10%
	C7	CT-M	Design	0.103	0.4	4.65%
	C8	CT-A	Coding	0.133	0.025	100.00%
	C9	CT-A	Coding	0.292	0.0125	92.80%
	C10	CT-D	Coding	0.195	1	9.11%
	C11	CT-M	Coding	0.123	0.023	4.347%
	C12	CT-D	Testing	0.190	0.210	0.869%
	C13	CT-D	Testing	0.21	0.023	8.130%
	C14	CT-D	Testing	0.390	0.250	0.56%
	C15	CT-M	Testing	0.292	0.75	4.80%

5.1 Tracking of Change Request in Software Artifacts

In FPA approach there is no formal way of tracking the change requests in software artifacts. While during the implementation of change requests in the following case studies i.e. CS2, CS3 and CS4. We faced the issue of tracking the change request in software artifacts. We performed the traceability of change requests in software artifacts manually. The process of traceability in software artifacts was repeated for every change request and it was a time taking process. As we used it for small project but it will be very difficult if FPA approach uses for big software projects for requirements change during software development phase.

5.2 Impact of Change Requests on Software Artifact

The second issue faced during this study was the impact of change requests on software artifacts. While accepting or rejecting a change request it is necessary for software project manager to know the impact of that change request on software artifacts. Whereas FPA approach cannot predict the impact of change requests on software artifacts. So, it becomes critical for software mangers to accept or reject a change request while using FPA approach for requirements change during software development phase.

6 Conclusion and Future Work

This paper has presented a case study for software requirements change during software development phase using FPA. Generally, FPA approach uses in early stages of SDLC for the measurement of the functionalities that the system provides to its end users. While in this paper we used FPA approach during the software development phase when the software artifacts were in inconsistent states. As we used FPA during software development phase hence we have faced some issues during FPs count. The main issues were: (1) Tracking of a change request in software artifacts and (2) Impact of a change request on software artifacts. However, we used FPA approach during software development phase in the case study and it was only possible because the software we used as a case study was a small software and we tracked the change requests manually. While it is challenging to use FPA approach for requirement changes during software development phase. On the other hand, FPA approach can be applied if it is integrated with change impact analysis. So as a future work we recommend that the integration of FPA approach with change impact analysis can be useful for effort estimation during software development phase.

Acknowledgements. This research is funded by Research University Grant, Vote No: 16H68 under Universiti Teknologi Malaysia.

References

1. Meli, R.: Measuring change requests to support effective project management practices. In: ESCOM Conference (2001)
2. Sharma, A., Kushwaha, D.S.: Estimation of software development effort from requirements based complexity. Procedia Technol. **4**, 716–722 (2012)
3. Kama, N., Halmi, M.: Extending change impact analysis approach for change effort estimation in the software development phase. In: WSEAS International Conference, Proceedings. Recent Advances in Computer Engineering Series (2013)
4. Lam, W., Shankararaman, V.: Requirements change: a dissection of management issues. In: Proceedings 25th EUROMICRO Conference. Informatics: Theory and Practice for the New Millennium, vol. 2, pp. 244–251 (1999)
5. Bano, M., Imtiaz, S., Ikram, N., Niazi, M., Usman, M.: Causes of requirement change - a systematic literature review. In: 16th International Conference on Evaluation and Assessment in Software Engineering (EASE 2012), pp. 22–31 (2012)
6. Jorgensen, M., Boehm, B., Rifkin, S.: Software development effort estimation: formal models or expert judgment? IEEE Softw. **26**, 14–19 (2009)
7. Chinthanet, B., Phannachitta, P., Kamei, Y., Leelaprute, P., Rungsawang, A., Ubayashi, N., et al.: A review and comparison of methods for determining the best analogies in analogy-based software effort estimation. In: Presented at the Proceedings of the 31st Annual ACM Symposium on Applied Computing, Pisa, Italy (2016)
8. Khurana, P., Tripathi, A., Kushwaha, D.S.: Change impact analysis and its regression test effort estimation. In: 2013 IEEE 3rd International Advance Computing Conference (IACC), pp. 1420–1424 (2013)
9. Longstreet, D.: Fundamentals of Function Point Analysis. Longstreet Consulting, Inc., Blue Springs (2002)

10. Hira, A., Boehm, B.: Function point analysis for software maintenance. In: Presented at the Proceedings of the 10th ACM/IEEE International Symposium on Empirical Software Engineering and Measurement, Ciudad Real, Spain (2016)
11. Peixoto, C.E.L., Audy, J.L.N., Prikladnicki, R.: The importance of the use of an estimation process. In: Presented at the Proceedings of the 2010 ICSE Workshop on Software Development Governance, Cape Town, South Africa (2010)
12. Kaur, M., Sehra, S.K.: Particle swarm optimization based effort estimation using function point analysis. In: International Conference on 2014 Issues and Challenges in Intelligent Computing Techniques (ICICT), pp. 140–145 (2014)
13. Sufyan, B., Nazri, K., Saiful, A., Faizura, H.: Using static and dynamic impact analysis for effort estimation. IET Softw. **10**, 89–95 (2016)
14. Jorgensen, M., Shepperd, M.: A systematic review of software development cost estimation studies. IEEE Trans. Softw. Eng. **33**, 33–53 (2007)
15. Suri, P.K., Ranjan, P.: Comparative analysis of software effort estimation techniques. Int. J. Comput. Appl. (0975–8887) **48** (2012)
16. Jorgensen, M.: Practical guidelines for expert-judgment-based software effort estimation. IEEE Softw. **22**, 57–63 (2005)
17. Li, J., Ruhe, G., Al-Emran, A., Richter, M.: A flexible method for software effort estimation by analogy. Empir. Softw. Eng. **12**, 65–106 (2007)
18. Shepperd, M., Schofield, C., Kitchenham, B.: Effort estimation using analogy. In: Proceedings of the 18th International Conference on Software Engineering, pp. 170–178 (1996)
19. Yinhuan, Z., Beizhan, W., Yilong, Z., Liang, S.: Estimation of software projects effort based on function point. In: 4th International Conference on Computer Science and Education (ICCSE 2009), pp. 941–943 (2009)
20. Garcia, C.A.L., Hirata, C.M.: Integrating functional metrics, COCOMO II and earned value analysis for software projects using PMBoK. In: Presented at the Proceedings of the 2008 ACM Symposium on Applied Computing, Fortaleza, Ceara, Brazil (2008)
21. Attarzadeh, I., Mehranzadeh, A., Barati, A.: Proposing an enhanced artificial neural network prediction model to improve the accuracy in software effort estimation. In: Fourth International Conference on Computational Intelligence, Communication Systems and Networks (CICSyN), pp. 167–172 (2012)
22. Bardsiri, V.K., Jawawi, D.N.A., Bardsiri, A.K., Khatibi, E.: LMES: a localized multi-estimator model to estimate software development effort. Eng. Appl. Artif. Intell. **26**, 2624–2640 (2013)
23. Albrecht, A.J.: AD/M productivity measurement and estimate validation. IBM Corporate Information Systems, IBM Corporation, Purchase, NY (1984)
24. Longstreet, D.: Function points analysis training course. SoftwareMetrics.com, October 2004

Understanding Uncertainty of Software Requirements Engineering: A Systematic Literature Review Protocol

Ahmad M. Salih, Mazni Omar[(✉)], and Azman Yasin

Human-Centered Computing Research Lab, School of Computing,
Universiti Utara Malaysia, UUM, 06010 Sintok, Kedah, Malaysia
ahmad_mahdi@ahsgs.uum.edu.my,
{mazni,yazman}@uum.edu.my

Abstract. Requirements engineering uncertainty is considered as one of the main problems in software industry. It can complicate early decisions on requirements and architecture and might expose the software project to significant risks. Continuous effort by researchers has resulted in a largely grown body of work on uncertainty in software requirements. In this paper, a systematic literature review protocol is presented to investigate the research literature on approaches deals with uncertainty in software requirements engineering. Requirements management was widely studied on the uncertainty in software requirement engineering. Results showed that review and analyses approach are most widely approaches dealt with requirements uncertainty and some were briefly explained. Further research is required on the identification of prominent causes of software requirements uncertainty and the solution to cope with such causes.

Keywords: Requirements engineering · Requirements uncertainty
Systematic literature review

1 Introduction

Software requirements engineering is a highly incremental and iterative endeavour where uncertainty can exist at multiple stages of the development process. For software systems to be accepted by stakeholders or users, their requirements need to be properly captured, analysed and then prioritised [1]. Uncertainty is regarded as one of the key problems in software industry. Typically, it happens when the designers do not have the complete, consistent and accurate information needed to decide during the software development lifecycle [2]. Uncertainty in requirements can be about stakeholder goals and their priorities, alternatives impact on these goals, cost, feasibility, and duration of implementing alternatives. It may also include future changes in stakeholder goals, technological environments and business context as well as uncertainty of whether the right questions about decisions can be asked [3]. It is useful to plainly express the uncertainty in requirements engineering to simplify its resolution by further elicitation

© Springer Nature Singapore Pte Ltd. 2018
M. Kamalrudin et al. (Eds.): APRES 2017, CCIS 809, pp. 164–171, 2018.
https://doi.org/10.1007/978-981-10-7796-8_13

or decision making and capturing such uncertainty-reduced decisions and elicitation of information [4]. Uncertainty can complicate early decisions of requirements and architecture and may expose software projects to significant risks. Highlighting the need to appropriate approaches of requirements engineering and software cost estimation can disclose uncertainty rather than hiding it [3].

The rest of this paper is organised as follows; Sect. 1 gives an introduction to the uncertainty in software requirements. The background is briefly presented in Sect. 2. A literature review on the methodology employed to conduct this study is fully described in Sect. 3. Then a brief explanation of data synthesis is presented in Sect. 4, while the results and discussion are explained in Sect. 5. Finally, the conclusion and future work are derived in Sect. 6.

2 Background

Requirements engineering is the first step in software development life cycle. Thus, it is obvious that requirements engineering is a very significant task to develop the software projects [5]. Requirement uncertainty [6] denotes that requirements are unknown until they are practically used and come from software requirements that create an unclear problem. Typical outcomes of requirements uncertainty are inadequate project planning, continual changes in project, problems in configuration, defects, and total customer dissatisfaction because of not being rponsiblees or do not obtain the expected product [7].

Ebert and De Man [7] had analysed in their study on how to handle requirements uncertainty and they showed that a definite degree of uncertainty is part of any project risk, which determines the proposition value. They looked into techniques that address early symptoms of project that indicate a number of uncertainties derived from heavy delays in the project. In addition, Voola and Babu [8] introduced a novel approach for requirements uncertainty prioritisation called Requirements Uncertainty Prioritisation Approach (RUPA). In this approach, the basic prioritisation technique numerical assignment was shaped as an extensive numerical assignment through probability distribution and grade intervals.

So far, no systematic review study was conducted on summarising the research trends and categorising the employed approaches of requirements engineering activities. Thus, this study aims to investigate the approaches in dealing uncertainty in software requirements engineering by conducting a systematic literature review. A systematic literature review (SLR) approach is a formalised, iterative process whereby researchers systematically investigate a set of literature in order to document knowledge on a specific topic [9, 10]. The significance beyond utilising SLR, in contrast to more common ad-hoc approach use, is that it gives the researchers more confidence that they have cited as much pertinent information as possible [11]. To be effective, SLR should be in line with the overall study goal, which is to categorise the used approaches of uncertainty requirements engineering activities.

3 Research Method

The SLR is a well-defined approach used to identify, assess and interpret all pertinent studies related to particular research questions, topics area or interesting phenomenon. SLR is referred to as secondary studies. The analysed studies are referred to as primary studies [12]. After the inception of SLR in 2004, it became a widespread methodology in software engineering to further explore about the respective domain. SLR is considered as an Evidence-Based Software Engineering (EBSE) practice [13]. The approach proposed by [9] is adapted to undertake this research.

3.1 Research Questions

The main objective of this systematic literature review is to review the current research works in the literature of uncertainty in software requirements engineering with focus on the approaches used. The research question is:

What are the most used approaches in requirements engineering activities that deal with requirements uncertainty?

3.2 Search Strategy

After identifying the research goals and questions, a formal search strategy was constructed and the analysis all available empirical materials related to the SLR objectives was initiated. Activities that are pertaining to the search strategy are comprised of search terms, literature resources and search process as clarified in the following sub-sections:

Search Terms
The subsequent steps adapted from [12] are employed to build this study search terms:

1. Derive the main terms from the study's research questions.
2. Identify the alternative synonyms and spellings for the main terms.
3. Identify the keywords in pertinent papers or books chapters.
4. Employ the Boolean OR to incorporate alternative synonyms and spellings.
5. Employ the Boolean AND to connect the main terms.

   The main resulted search terms are:
   ("software requirements" OR "requirements engineering") AND (uncertainty OR variability OR changing OR ambiguous OR ambiguity OR fuzzy OR vague OR unclear OR volatility OR inconsistency OR incompleteness).

Literature Resources
The primary list of sources databases is developed by using the following explained in selection criteria [14].

Search Process
The SLR process recommends searching several lists of databases libraries that can be completely accessed to ensure thorough retrieval of the relevant studies [10], this list is then reviewed. The final sources is depicted in Table 1.

Table 1. Sources list

Databases	ACM Digital Library, IEEE Xplore, Springer Verlag, Google Scholar, ScienceDirect, CiteSeerX
Additional sources	Reference lists from primary studies

The search string is composed of each database manually to get as much as possible related studies based on the search functionality provided via that database. In each database, the search is treated as a process of learning and experimentation [9].

Included and Excluded Studies

The inclusion and exclusion criteria are defined to choose the pertinent studies. Firstly, extracted papers will be tested with the exclusion criteria. The paper is excluded if such paper meets any one of the exclusion criteria. The rest of papers are tested with inclusion criteria as proposed in [14].

Studies Selection Procedure

The preliminary collection of possible primary studies had retrieved over 2,000 papers which was reduced to 705 based on reviewing the title, abstract, and keywords sections. Then, this search was extended to comprise the Conclusion section if the title, keywords and abstract did not provide enough information which then narrowed down the total number of papers to 299. All the studies were inspected to find repeated publications so as to avoid any study replication, that is when the same study is published in different publications channels, even though by different authors, whereby only the broadest or recent study will be included in the review. Then, all selected studies were reviewed against a detailed criteria group that was applied for all publications and which finally remained as 167 studies. Table 2 shows the number of identified studies during the last round of this SLR.

Table 2. Number of the identified studies during the last round

Database	Retrieved	Included	Excluded
ACM	65	26	39
CiteSeerX	11	4	7
Google Scholar	54	27	27
IEEE	73	45	28
Science Direct	19	15	4
Springer Link	48	34	14
Reference List	29	16	13
Total	299	167	132

Quality Assessment Criteria
The quality assessment of the selected studies has employed to guide the clarification of the synthesis results as well as to define the strength of the elaborated inferences [9]. The quality of every accepted study was assessed based on the criteria depicted in in [9].

4 Data Synthesis

The data synthesis aims at aggregating the data from the chosen studies to answer the research questions. Different strategies were used to synthesise the extracted data pertaining to the research questions. The data were tabulated in a manner that was consistent with the study questions. Some visualisation tools, such as bar chart and tables, were used to enhance the presentation of the results. Based on the synthesis, conclusions and recommendations for future work were derived.

5 Results and Discussion

This section introduces the results related to the research questions and discusses them briefly.

5.1 Distribution of Studies Based on Publication Channel Type

Table 3 illustrates the distribution of papers based on the publication channels' type.

Table 3. Distribution of publication channels

Publication channel type	No.
Conference proceedings	74
Journals	55
Workshops	16
Symposium	9
Book chapters	7
Technical report	2
Forums	2
Newsletter	2
Total	167

This table shows that conference proceedings are the widest publication channel with 74 channels because experience reports are mostly published in conferences, followed by journals with 55 and workshops 16.

5.2 The Most Used Approaches

Figure 1 shows that approaches that deal with software requirements uncertainty are widely varied in nature and scope.

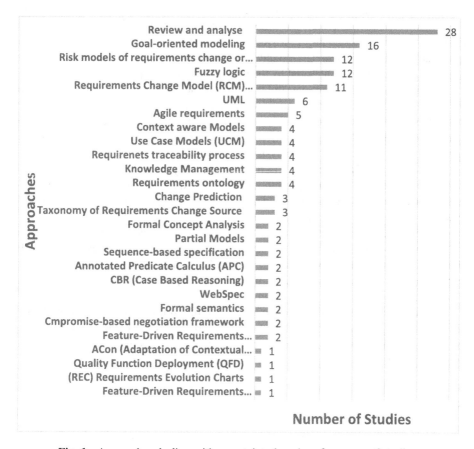

Fig. 1. Approaches dealing with uncertainty based on frequency of studies.

Review and analysis approach is the most widely used for dealing uncertainty of requirements. It is useful in analysing and categorising the most prevailing methods and techniques that handle the requirements uncertainty. Goal-oriented modelling can describe the intension of stakeholders and systems requirements as clearly as possible to cope with requirements uncertainty. Change and volatile are the prevailing causes for requirements uncertainty and are frequently associated with risks, therefore, risk models can be considered as the effective approach in dealing with them. The fuzzy logic method was used to calculate the weights of the factors that relate to causes of requirements uncertainty, such as requirements changes, requirements volatility, requirements vague and so on. For changing requirements, the requirements change models (RCM) developments were employed to handle changes in requirements, which was one of the main reasons for requirements uncertainty.

6 Conclusion and Future Work

The main goal of this study is to systematically investigate the research literature for the uncertainty in software requirements engineering, summarising the research trends, and categorising the used approaches and requirements engineering activities in studies published between 2003 and 2016. During the systematic review process, many questions had arose. Keele in [9] provided a set of employed guidelines to conduct this systematic literature review. These guidelines provided steps to formulate the research questions that were to be answered by the review and a review protocol was developed.

Requirement management was the most studied activity for uncertainty in software requirement engineering, since requirements uncertainty can occur during the software development life cycle. Managing this uncertainty is necessary to successfully develop a software system. Other important activities are requirements modelling, requirements specifications and requirements analysis.

Review and analysis approach is the most broadly used because it is useful in categorising the most prevailing methods and techniques that deal with the requirements uncertainty. Goal-oriented modelling can define stakeholders' intension and systems requirements as clearly as possible to cope with the requirements uncertainty. Risk models can be considered as the effective approach in dealing with change and volatile which causes uncertainty in requirements and are frequently associated with risks. Clearly much more work is needed in the formalisation of using traditional approaches to deal with uncertainty in software requirements engineering and in developing new approaches for that purpose.

Future works are needed to further investigate on prominent causes of uncertainty in software requirements identification and the solution to cope with such causes. Additionally, the relationship between topics and application domain for the software systems must be explored and analysed systematically.

References

1. Perini, A., Susi, A., Ricca, F., Bazzanella, C.: An empirical study to compare the accuracy of AHP and CBRanking techniques for requirements prioritization. In: Fifth International Workshop on 2007 Comparative Evaluation in Requirements Engineering CERE 2007, pp. 23–35 (2007)
2. Ziv, H., Richardson, D., Klösch, R.: The uncertainty principle in software engineering. In: Proceedings of the 19th International Conference on Software Engineering ICSE 1997 (1997)
3. Letier, E., Stefan, D., Barr, E.T.: Uncertainty, risk, and information value in software requirements and architecture. In: Proceedings of the 36th International Conference on Software Engineering, pp. 883–894 (2014)
4. Salay, R., Chechik, M., Horkoff, J., Di Sandro, A.: Managing requirements uncertainty with partial models. Requirements Eng. **18**, 107–128 (2013)
5. Saha, S.K., Selvi, M., Buyukcan, G., Mohymen, M.: A systematic review on creativity techniques for requirements engineering. In: 2012 International Conference on Informatics, Electronics & Vision (ICIEV), pp. 34–39 (2012)

6. Liu, W., Feng, Z.: Requirement uncertainty analysis for service-oriented self-adaptation software. In: Lei, J., Wang, F.L., Li, M., Luo, Y. (eds.) NCIS 2012. CCIS, vol. 345, pp. 156–163. Springer, Heidelberg (2012). https://doi.org/10.1007/978-3-642-35211-9_20
7. Ebert, C., De Man, J.: Requirements uncertainty: influencing factors and concrete improvements. In: Proceedings of the 27th International Conference on Software Engineering, pp. 553–560 (2005)
8. Voola, P., Babu, A.V.: Requirements uncertainty prioritization approach: a novel approach for requirements prioritization. Softw. Eng. Int. J. (SEIJ) **2**, 37–49 (2012)
9. Keele, S.: Guidelines for performing systematic literature reviews in software engineering. Technical report, Ver. 2.3 EBSE Technical report. EBSE, ed. (2007)
10. Kitchenham, B.: Procedures for performing systematic reviews, Keele University, Keele, UK, vol. 33, pp. 1–26 (2004)
11. Brereton, P., Kitchenham, B.A., Budgen, D., Turner, M., Khalil, M.: Lessons from applying the systematic literature review process within the software engineering domain. J. Syst. Softw. **80**, 571–583 (2007)
12. Kitchenham, B., Pretorius, R., Budgen, D., Brereton, O.P., Turner, M., Niazi, M., Linkman, S.: Systematic literature reviews in software engineering–a tertiary study. Inf. Softw. Technol. **52**, 792–805 (2010)
13. Dybä, T., Kitchenham, B., Jorgensen, M.: Evidence-based software engineering for practitioners. Softw. IEEE **22**, 58–65 (2005)
14. Walia, G.S., Carver, J.C.: A systematic literature review to identify and classify software requirement errors. Inf. Softw. Technol. **51**, 1087–1109 (2009)

Automation

Constructing a Goal Model from Requirements Descriptions Based on Extraction Rules

Hironori Shimada[✉], Hiroyuki Nakagawa, and Tatsuhiro Tsuchiya

Graduate School of Information Science and Technology,
Osaka University, Suita-Shi, Osaka, Japan
{h-simada, nakagawa, t-tutiya}@ist.osaka-u.ac.jp

Abstract. A goal model, which is one of the common requirements models, has advantages of formalizing and visualizing results of requirements analysis. The model regards a requirement as a goal, and the root goal that is achieved by system execution should be decomposed to precondition goals. Current systems are large and complexed, so that there are a lot of requirements to be implemented. Therefore it is difficult to extract all goals and construct an elaborated goal model manually. In this paper we propose a process to support constructing goal models from requirements descriptions written in a natural language. In the proposed process, extraction rules are used to extract goals from requirements descriptions and then to construct a goal model from the goals. To evaluate our process, we applied the process to two system descriptions to construct goal models. The results show that the proposed process extracted appropriate goals and successfully assembled these goals in a goal hierarchy. We also report preliminary results of automating the proposed process.

Keywords: Goal models · Requirements analysis · Natural languages

1 Introduction

Requirements elicitation and analysis are conducted in the very early phase of software development. The failure of these processes may result in much additional cost, as it can require rework of the whole development process. The Chaos report [21] lists the factors of project failures. The top three factors are incomplete requirements, lack of user involvement, and lack of resources. The first factor of incomplete requirements means that the analysts could not grasp requirements correctly. The second factor, lack of user involvement is insufficient communication with users. From the report, requirements issues including the first and second factors are the largest issues with software development. Moreover, current systems have many requirements, so that extracting all requirements is difficult and labor intensive. Aiming to visualize and place requirements structurally, a goal model can be used. A goal model is one of requirements models and has advantages of goal and refinement formalization [8] and reusability [10, 14]. Furthermore, a goal model is used to develop self-adaptive systems [5, 17, 19]. Though a goal model has these advantages, it can be large and complexed even for small problems [14].

© Springer Nature Singapore Pte Ltd. 2018
M. Kamalrudin et al. (Eds.): APRES 2017, CCIS 809, pp. 175–188, 2018.
https://doi.org/10.1007/978-981-10-7796-8_14

In this paper, we propose an approach to facilitate extracting requirements and constructing a goal model. Specifically, we propose a process of goal model construction from requirements descriptions. Our goal model construction process consists of three steps: decomposition, goal extraction, and integration. In the goal extraction step, extraction rules are applied to elicit goals from requirements descriptions. To validate the proposed process, we evaluate the results of applying our process to two example systems. We also implemented a tool that enables to automatically extract goals to validate whether the extraction rules are properly applied. This paper makes two main contributions:

(1) We provide extraction rules that enables us to construct a preliminary goal model at low cost. Some rules called keyword-based rules generate goals without understanding contents of requirements descriptions.
(2) The extraction rules can be applied to find implicit goals in the requirements descriptions. Some rules generate a partial goal model with complementing such goals.

The rest of the paper is organized as follows. Section 2 explains the concept of goal model and presents related work on requirements models. In Sect. 3, we explain our process of constructing a goal model in detail. In Sect. 4, we evaluate our process. In Sect. 5, we discuss the evaluation results. Section 6 presents partial automation of our process. Finally, Sect. 7 concludes our study and mentions future work.

2   Background and Related Work

2.1   Goal Model

A goal model is a requirements model and has proven to be useful for correct understanding of requirements. Figure 1 illustrates an example of a goal model. In a goal model, requirements are treated as goals that must be achieved. A goal model is constructed through iterative refinement of goals. The root goal of the model represents the purpose of system implementation and each goal is decomposed into precondition goals. The relationship between a parent goal and child goals is described either by AND-refinement or OR-refinement links. An AND-refinement link represents that the parent goal is achieved when all its child goals are achieved. On the other hand, the OR-refinement link represents that the parent goal is achieved when at least one of the child goals. A leaf goal is assigned to an actor, which is responsible for achieving the goal. Leaf goals that are connected with users are called expectations. Entities represent data or objects. Our approach focuses on extracting goals and connecting them with refinement links in order to visualize the requirements structurally. In this paper we use KAOS [7, 12] as a goal model notation; but our proposed process does not depend on this particular notation and can be used with other notations, such as i* [23] and NFR [15].

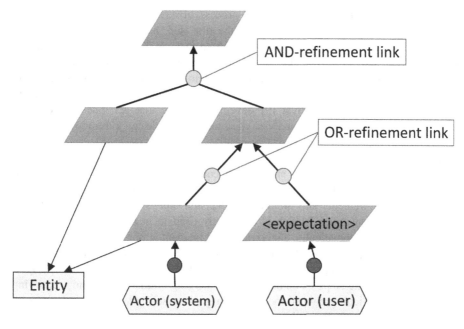

Fig. 1. Example of a goal model.

2.2 Related Work

2.2.1 Goal Model Construction

Several studies have been conducted on the topic of goal model construction. Cleland-Huang et al. [6, 18] proposed an automatic process of eliciting quality concerns and constructing a Softgoal Interdependency Graph (SIG) from a requirements specification by using the techniques of machine learning and data mining. In the first step of the process, a generic goal model is structured and requirements are connected to the relative goals of the model. Next, the requirements are clustered and qualities are mapped to the clusters. Finally, quality hierarchies are generated and attached to the leaf nodes of the model. The techniques of clustering and mapping, used in the second step, can be used to automate our approach. Weber-Jahnke and Onabajo [22] proposed a process of mining security goals and analyzing a security goal model, and implemented the tool that supports execution of the process. For goal mining, goal annotation from Natural Language regulations is executed as the first step. Next, goal annotation structures are analyzed and incompleteness of the constructed goal model is detected. Thirdly, annotated concepts hierarchization and arrangement (e.g. combining or decomposing synonyms) are performed. Finally, goal models are analyzed semantically to validate consistency of the goal model. Our approach focuses on constructing a goal model; therefore these approach complementary.

Other related studies try to automate the construction of other requirements models. Thakur and Gupta [20] implemented a tool that automatically constructs a sequence diagram from a use case specification written in a natural language. The tool parses a specification and identifies domain objects, then it visualizes a sequence diagram.

Arora et al. [3] proposed the automatic process of extracting a domain model by extending the existing extraction rules. In the first step, natural language processing (NLP) is applied to requirements. The second step extracts dependencies at a semantic level from the results of NLP. Finally, a domain model is constructed by using the extended extraction rules. This dependency extraction technique could be integrated in our approach to summarize goal descriptions; but we leave the integration for future work. Deeptimahanti and Sanyal [9] developed a tool that generates some UML models, i.e., use-case diagram, analysis class model, and design class model.

2.2.2   Analyzing Goal Model

There are studies that focus on analyzing a constructed goal model, not only construction of a goal model. Busari and Letier [4] proposed a modeling language and tool RADAR for requirements and architecture decision analysis. RADAR generates an AND/OR refinement graph, which is commonly used in goal-oriented requirements engineering, and automatically analyzes the refinement graph to create a decision graph. Nakagawa et al. [16] introduced the process of control loop extraction from a goal model to detect impacts of changes in software evolution. A control loop is extracted through the steps of adding entities, merging similar goals, and identifying prime goals. By eliciting control loops from a goal model, independent system components are defined mechanically.

3   Our Approach

3.1   Overview

Figure 2 illustrates the overview of our process. Since the objective of our study is formalization or reuse of requirements descriptions, we assume that the input requirements description is a complete version and grammatically correct. Our construction process consists of three steps:

> **Step 1. Decomposition:** The description is decomposed into fragments of requirements description. We assume that requirements descriptions can be decomposed into lists of sentences as fragments. This decomposition makes it easier to construct partial goal models.
> **Step 2. Goal extraction:** After the decomposition, extraction rules are applied to each requirements description to extract goals and generate structures of models. These rules are explained in more detail in Sect. 3.2. Then a partial goal model is constructed from each requirements description.
> **Step 3. Integration:** Finally, these goal models are integrated into one goal model. In this step, analysts refine the goal model, such as shorten goal descriptions.

3.2   Extraction Rules

In this paper, we propose extraction rules to elicit goals from sentences in a requirements description. These rules also help to construct a hierarchical goal model. Table 1 lists the extraction rules and their keywords. The extraction rules we have developed

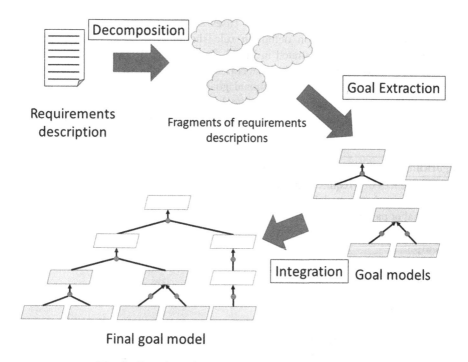

Fig. 2. Overview of our goal model construction process.

are classified into two types: *context-based* and *keyword-based*. *Context-based rules* require analysts to understand the context of sentences when they apply the rules. On the other hand, *keyword-based rules* are the rules for extracting goal descriptions when a keyword is found in a sentence. Algorithm 1 represents the algorithm of extraction rule execution.

The context-based rules are composed of exception definition, listing flattening and parent goal definition rules.

Table 1. Extraction rules.

Context-based rules	
• Exception definition	
• Listing flattening	
• Parent goal definition	
Keyword-based rules	**Keywords used in rules**
• Demonstrative replacement	"it", "its", "they", "theirs",…
• Clause extraction	"after", "before", "and", "or"
• Example extraction	"for example", "for instance", "following", "such as"
• Case extraction	"if", "when", "in particular"
• Alternative case extraction	"alternatively", "instead"
• In-bracket description extraction	"(", ")", "[", "]", "{", "}"

(A) **Exception definition**: If exceptional cases are not described in a requirements description, the exception definition rule should be applied. An example of applying this rule is illustrated in Fig. 3. The rule first lets us construct an "exceptional" goal or partial goal model corresponding to the exceptional cases. After that, the rule connects the exceptional goal models and the goal model for the normal case to a newly added parent goal. Here, the parent goal is generated with no description. In this paper, we name the goal with no description blank goal. Analysts replace these blank goals with suitable goals.

Algorithm 1. Extraction rules execution

1: S: sentences of a requirements description
2: G: generated goal model
3: g: goal or partial goal model
4: **input**: S
5: **output**: G
6:
7: apply the listing fattening rule to S
8: **for all** s in S **do**
9:     // s is a sentence of S
10:     **if** keywords are included in s **then**
11:         apply corresponding keyword-based rules
12:         $g \leftarrow$ a constructed partial goal model or a goal that represents s itself
13:     **end if**
14:     apply the parent goal definition rule to g
15:     merge g into G
16: **end for**
17: apply the exception definition rule to G

(B) **Listing flattening:** If a listing expression is found in a requirements description, goals that represent the items are generated in a one-to-one fashion and connected to a parent goal (blank goal) with AND-refinement or OR-refinement links. The selection of refinement links depends on relationship among generated goals.

(C) **Parent goal definition:** As described above, parent goals that are generated mechanically have no description. Such a goal is replaced with the goal that represents a common topic in child goals by analysts.

The keyword-based rules are composed of demonstrative replacement, clause extraction, example extraction, case extraction, alternative case extraction and in-bracket description extraction rules.

(A) **Demonstrative replacement:** In order to prevent from losing the context of a target sentence, this rule is applied and demonstratives are replaced with the word that they refer to before other rules are applied. Figure 4 shows the case where the rule is applied. The keyword "it" should be replaced with the word "the system".

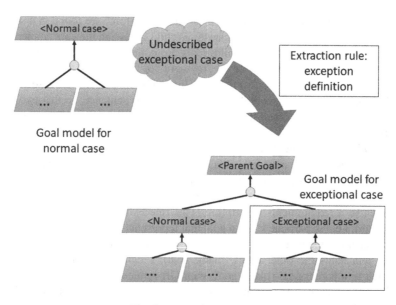

Fig. 3. Exception definition.

After the system determines a number is wrong,
it prints an error message.

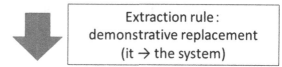

Extraction rule:
demonstrative replacement
(it → the system)

After the system determines a number is wrong,
the system prints an error message.

Extraction rule:
clause extraction

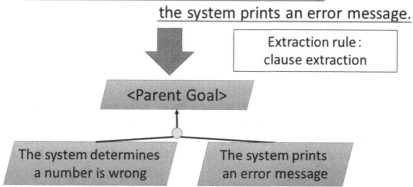

Fig. 4. Demonstrative replacement and clause extraction.

(B) **Clause extraction:** If keywords such as "after", "before" are found in a sentence, this rule is applied to extract two clauses as child goals and they are connected to a parent goal (blank goal). The child goals are connected to the parent goal with AND-refinement links but when the keyword "or" is found in the sentence, child goals are connected with OR-refinement links. Figure 4 shows the case where the rule is applied. The keyword "after" is found in the sentence, so that two clauses (the clauses are underlined in the figure) are elicited as goals and connected to a parent goal (blank goal).

(C) **Example extraction:** This rule extracts examples in sentences as goals and connects them to a parent goal (blank goal) with an AND-refinement link.

(D) **Case extraction:** If keywords such as "if", "when", "in particular" are found in a sentence, we can regard that the sentence represents a particular case in a scenario written in a requirements description. This rule extracts the sentence except the keyword, i.e. "in particular", as a goal that represents the particular case. This rule also generates the goal that represents the sentence itself as a particular case and a goal represents the other cases (blank goal). Finally, generated goals are connected to a parent goal (blank goal) with OR-refinement links.

(E) **Alternative case extraction:** When one of the keywords, "alternatively" and "instead", is found in a target sentence, we can regard that the sentence represents an alternative case. The rule generates two goals. One is the goal that represents the alternative case; the other is the goal that represents the other case (blank goal). Finally, these two goals are connected to a parent goal (blank goal) with OR-refinement links.

(F) **In-bracket description extraction:** This rule is applied when an in-bracket description appears in a sentence. If the description in the bracket is a sentence or clause, the description is extracted as an independent goal.

4 Evaluation

To evaluate our process, we manually applied the process to requirements descriptions of two systems: a meeting scheduling system [11] (1,074 words) and an ATM system [2] (749 words). Figure 5 shows a part of the constructed model for the meeting scheduling system. We evaluate the constructed goal models with respect to two research questions: *RQ1: Does the process extract appropriate goals?* and *RQ2: Does the process exercise known refinement patterns?*

RQ1: Does the process extract appropriate goals? We compared the constructed model to the model presented in [11]. As a result, extracted goals are placed in the upper part of the goal model in [11]. This fact demonstrates that general goals were extracted by our process in this case study. There are some goals that were not extracted by our process, but they can be extracted if we further refine the extracted goals.

RQ2: Does the process exercise known refinement patterns? There are some well-know refinement patterns [11]. We checked which refinement patterns occurred during the course of constructing the goal models. From the result listed in Table 2,

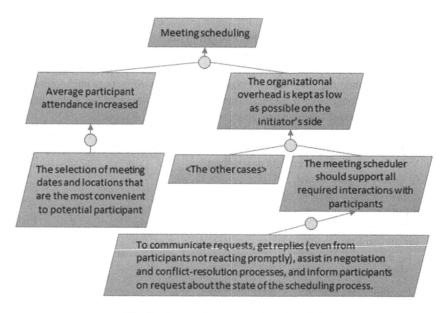

Fig. 5. A part of constructed goal model.

decomposition-by-case pattern was found in the goal model of the meeting scheduling system. In the goal model of ATM system, three patterns were observed: milestone-driven refinement pattern, decomposition-by-case pattern, and divide-and-conquer pattern. The result indicates our process can construct appropriate goal models. On the other hand, the other three patterns, namely, guard-introduction, unmonitorability-driven refinement and uncontrollability-driven refinement patterns, were not observed in the case studies. The reason for this is that they all require domain knowledge, such as knowledge of the actors who are responsible for meeting the goals.

Table 2. Appearance of refinement patterns.

Refinement pattern	Meeting Scheduling	ATM
Milestone-driven refinement pattern	–	✓
Decomposition-by-case pattern	✓	✓
Guard-introduction pattern	–	–
Divide-and-conquer pattern	–	✓
Unmonitorability-driven refinement pattern	–	–
Uncontrollability-driven refinement pattern	–	–

5   Discussion

Our approach outputs a goal model from a requirements description, but the goal model is too spread horizontally because it is insufficiently hierarchized. To solve this problem, we should introduce a new step when the analysts determine hierarchical relationship between fragments of requirements descriptions. Another possible way of further decomposition is to develop other extraction rules. There is possibility that other terms can be used as keywords for keyword-based rules. In this paper, our approach was used to process two requirements descriptions that are well known and simple in requirements engineering. We need to conduct more experiments using requirements descriptions that consists of a large amount of text. Furthermore, an experiment for usability of goal model is needed to guarantee quality of the model.

Algorithm 2. Automatic (a part of) keyword-based rules execution

---

1: S: sentences of a requirements description
2: G: generated goal model
3: g: goal or partial goal model
4: **input**: S
5: **output**: G
6: **for all** s in S **do**
7:      // s is a sentence of S
8:      **if** keywords are included in s **then**
9:          apply corresponding extraction rules
10:         $g \leftarrow$ a constructed partial goal model
11:     **else**
12:         $g \leftarrow$ a goal that represents s itself
13:     **end if**
14:     merge g into G
15: **end for**

---

6   Automation

In this section, we describe our attempt to automate the application of some of the proposed extraction rules. Figure 6 illustrates the overview of the automatic process. The process consists of three steps. In the first step, a parse tree is obtained from requirement descriptions. We use Stanford CoreNLP [13] to detect grammatical components from requirements descriptions and to elicit the components as goal descriptions. In the second step, the extraction rules are applied to the parse tree. This results in a goal model. In the last step, the goal model is visualized. We use Graphviz [1] for this purpose. Algorithm 2 represents the pseudo code of an algorithm of the process. For each sentence in the input of requirements description, if keywords are included in the sentence, corresponding extraction rules are applied and a partial goal model is constructed. On the other hand, if no keywords are included in the sentence, the process regards the sentence as a goal. Finally, the partial goal models or the goals are merged into a final goal model.

Figure 7 illustrates the automated process of applying the case extraction rule. First, the tool searches the parse tree and finds keyword "in particular". The tool then extracts the part following the keyword ("X" in Fig. 7) as a goal and adds tentative goals labeled "Specification" and "The other cases" in Fig. 7. The tentative goals should be replaced with concrete description by analysts. According to the case extraction rule, the parent

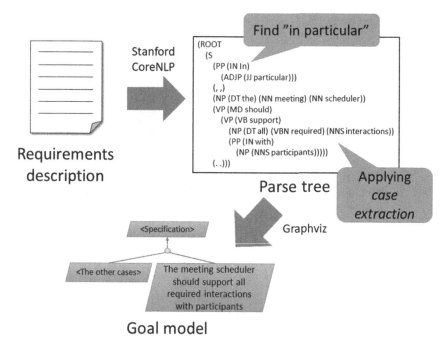

Fig. 6. Automation process of applying extraction rules.

node and child nodes should be connected by AND-refinement links. Our current implemented tool automates the following rules: *clauses extraction, example extraction,* and *case extraction.* Figure 8 shows the goal model automatically obtained from the meeting scheduling system. For comparison purposes, we focus on and enlarge the particular part that corresponds to part of the manually constructed model in Fig. 5. The corresponding part of the latter model is shown at the lower left of Fig. 8. In both automatic and manual construction, the rule *case extraction* was used for refinement.

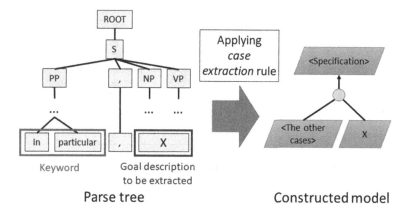

Fig. 7. Automated process of applying the *case extraction* rule.

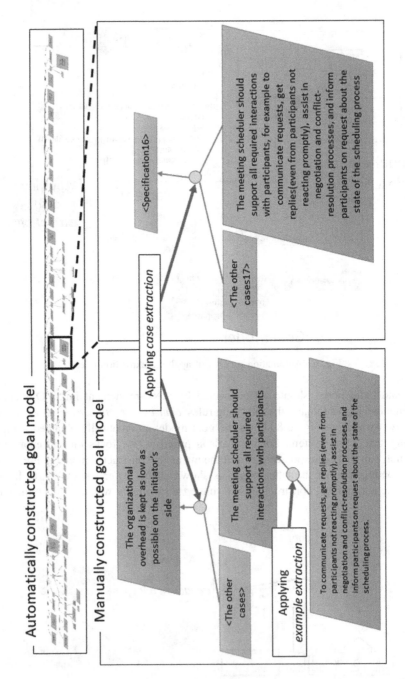

Fig. 8. Comparing an automatically constructed goal model to a manually constructed goal model.

However, the rule *example extraction* was not applied automatically, resulting in the difference of the two models. This is because the current tool is intentionally designed not to apply this rule unless it can clearly determine that the phrase "for example" qualifies the whole clause or sentence. Extending the scope of automatic rule application deserves future work.

7 Conclusion

In this paper, we proposed a process that supports constructing a goal model from requirement description written in a natural language. Our approach is composed of the three steps: decomposition of a requirements description, goal extraction, integration of partial goal models. In the goal extraction process, extraction rules are used to extract goals from a requirements description and then to construct a partial goal model. To evaluate our process, we constructed goal models of two systems based on our process. The results showed that our process successfully extracted general goals and constructed effective models. Furthermore, we automated the application of some extraction rules and demonstrated that a partial goal model was actually constructed in an automatic manner. In future work, we plan to solve following issues: *simplification*, *hierarchization* and *responsibility identification*. Simplification shortens descriptions of goals. Current extraction rules generate goals without summarization of goal descriptions. It makes the goal model too large and complicated to understand. For readability of a goal model, goal description simplification can be an effective improvement. As described in Sect. 5, constructed goal models need to be more hierarchical. Therefore, fragment hierarchization should be included in future. Responsibility identification means the discovery of associations between goals and actors. Each goal in a goal model should be decomposed into goals repeatedly until each leaf goal can be associated with an actor. A goal model with sufficient decomposition guarantees that each goal has its own actor.

References

1. Graphviz. http://www.graphviz.org/
2. Requirements statement for example ATM system. http://www.math-cs.gordon.edu/courses/cs211/ATMExample/Requirements.html
3. Arora, C., Sabetzadeh, M., Briand, L., Zimmer, F.: Extracting domain models from natural-language requirements: approach and industrial evaluation. In: Proceedings of the ACM/IEEE 19th International Conference on Model Driven Engineering Languages and Systems (MODELS 2016), pp. 250–260. ACM, New York (2016)
4. Busari, S.A., Letier, E.: Radar: a lightweight tool for requirements and architecture decision analysis. In: Proceedings of the 39th International Conference on Software Engineering (ICSE 2017), pp. 552–562 (2017)
5. Cailliau, A., van Lamsweerde, A.: Runtime monitoring and resolution of probabilistic obstacles to system goals. In: 2017 IEEE/ACM 12th International Symposium on Software Engineering for Adaptive and Self-Managing Systems (SEAMS), pp. 1–11, May 2017

6. Cleland-Huang, J., Settimi, R., Zou, X., Solc, P.: The detection and classification of non-functional requirements with application to early aspects. In: 14th IEEE International Requirements Engineering Conference (RE 2006), pp. 39–48, September 2006

7. Dardenne, A., van Lamsweerde, A., Fickas, S.: Goal-directed requirements acquisition. Sci. Comput. Program. **20**(1–2), 3–50 (1993)

8. Darimont, R., van Lamsweerde, A.: Formal refinement patterns for goal-driven requirements elaboration. In: Proceedings of the 4th ACM SIGSOFT Symposium on Foundations of Software Engineering (SIGSOFT 1996), pp. 179–190 (1996)

9. Deeptimahanti, D.K., Sanyal, R.: Semi-automatic generation of UML models from natural language requirements. In: Proceedings of the 4th India Software Engineering Conference (ISEC 2011), pp. 165–174. ACM (2011)

10. Duran, M.B., Pina, A.N., Mussbacher, G.: Evaluation of reusable concern-oriented goal models. In: 2015 IEEE International Model-Driven Requirements Engineering Workshop (MoDRE), pp. 1–10, August 2015

11. van Lamsweerde, A.: Requirements Engineering From System Goals to UML Models to Software Specifications. Wiley, New York (2009)

12. Letier, E.: Reasoning about agents in goal-oriented requirements engineering. Ph.D. thesis, University of Louvain (2001)

13. Manning, C.D., Surdeanu, M., Bauer, J., Finkel, J., Bethard, S.J., McClosky, D.: The Stanford CoreNLP natural language processing toolkit. In: Association for Computational Linguistics (ACL) System Demonstrations, pp. 55–60 (2014)

14. Mussbacher, G., Amyot, D., Araujo, J., Moreira, A., Weiss, M.: Visualizing aspect-oriented goal models with AoGRL. In: Second International Workshop on Requirements Engineering Visualization (REV 2007), p. 1, October 2007

15. Mylopoulos, J., Chung, L., Nixon, B.: Representing and using nonfunctional requirements: a process-oriented approach. IEEE Trans. Softw. Eng. **18**(6), 483–497 (1992)

16. Nakagawa, H., Ohsuga, A., Honiden, S.: A goal model elaboration for localizing changes in software evolution. In: 2013 21st IEEE International Requirements Engineering Conference (RE), pp. 155–164, July 2013

17. Nakagawa, H., Ohsuga, A., Honiden, S.: Gocc: a configuration compiler for self-adaptive systems using goal-oriented requirements description. In: Proceedings of the 6th International Symposium on Software Engineering for Adaptive and Self-Managing Systems (SEAMS 2011), pp. 40–49 (2011)

18. Rahimi, M., Mirakhorli, M., Cleland-Huang, J.: Automated extraction and visualization of quality concerns from requirements specifications. In: 2014 IEEE 22nd International Requirements Engineering Conference (RE), pp. 253–262, August 2014

19. Souza, V.E., Lapouchnian, A., Angelopoulos, K., Mylopoulos, J.: Requirements-driven software evolution. Comput. Sci. **28**(4), 311–329 (2013)

20. Thakur, J.S., Gupta, A.: Automatic generation of sequence diagram from use case specification. In: Proceedings of the 7th India Software Engineering Conference (ISEC 2014), pp. 20:1–20:6. ACM, New York (2014)

21. The Standish Group: The Standish Group Report Chaos (1995)

22. Weber-Jahnke, J.H., Onabajo, A.: Mining and analysing security goal models in health information systems. In: 2009 ICSE Workshop on Software Engineering in Health Care, pp. 42–52, May 2009

23. Yu, E.S.K.: Towards modelling and reasoning support for early-phase requirements engineering. In: Proceedings of the Third IEEE International Symposium on Requirements Engineering, pp. 226–235 (1997)

New Requirements Elicited from Accidents of Train Control System Simulated by Modelica

Wen Zhong, Yan Wang, and Xiaohong Chen[(✉)]

Shanghai Key Laboratory of Trustworthy Computing,
East China Normal University, Shanghai, China
xhchen@sei.ecnu.edu.cn

Abstract. Although train control system (TCS) is regarded relatively safe, accidents still happened from time to time. In this paper, we propose a simulation based approach to elicit new requirements from accidents and then modify the TCS to provide a more reliable and safer system. A Modelica system model is constructed to describe the structure and interactions of TCS according to the continuous behavior and discrete fault event of TCS devices. A Modelica accident model is also defined based on the system model in order to predict accidents. These Modelica models are simulated in Open Modelica until all scenarios (paths) are covered. By analyzing the simulation results which indicate the causes of accidents, we elicit new requirements, and modify the original system model. Simulation is used again to show that these modifications could effectively avoid such accidents. A case study is provided to validate our approach.

Keywords: Requirements elicitation · Accidents · Train control system
Modelica simulation

1 Introduction

With the rapid development of high-speed railway traffic in China, more and more people choose to take high-speed railway travel. Once an accident happens, it will lead to severe loss of life and property. Therefore, the safety of railway transportation is a critical issue in today's train control system (TCS) highlighted in many countries and governments especially in China.

However accidents still happen from time to time. For example, in 2011, two high-speed trains collided with each other on the Yongwen railway line. The front train D3115 stopped due to a track fault and it took more than 7 min to turn to onSight mode. Unfortunately, train D3115 was hit by train D301 from the rear, which resulted in 40 people killed and at least 192 people injured.

Current approaches used for analyzing accidents can be divided into two types: informal and formal approaches. Informal approaches include fault tree analysis (FTA) [1], failure mode and effect analysis (FMEA) [2], hazard and operability study [3], event tree analysis [4] and so on. They are used to analyze risks, causes or consequences. Based on the analysis, the software engineers modify safety

© Springer Nature Singapore Pte Ltd. 2018
M. Kamalrudin et al. (Eds.): APRES 2017, CCIS 809, pp. 189–204, 2018.
https://doi.org/10.1007/978-981-10-7796-8_15

requirements for system. Formal approaches, such as model checking, are used to detect undesired failure modes [5–8]. The input of model checking is some specifications such as property constraints. Those approaches rely on the specifications given before and do not contain dynamic analysis.

However, the above approaches are not suitable for the TCS because TCS is a classic hybrid system that contains continuous behavior and discrete events. Discrete events include device faults which happen unexpectedly in TCS and may lead to accidents. The informal approaches do not support continuous behavior modeling. In addition, TCS is a large and complex system, which makes formal methods difficult to be applied. Therefore, in this paper, we propose to use the simulation based approach to predicate the accidents in the train control system, and analyze the causes of accidents to elicit new requirements for avoiding similar accidents. According to the characteristics of TCS which integrates continuous behaviors and discrete events, Modelica and its supporting tool Open Modelica [9] are chosen for simulation, and based on the simulation results, accident causes are found and used to elicit a new requirement accordingly. At last, modifications of system models are given to avoid such accidents. We validate our modification by experiment.

The rest of this paper is organized as follows. Section 2 introduces the TCS and Modelica; Sect. 3 presents overview of our approach; Sect. 4 describes the process of constructing system model in Modelica; in Sect. 5, we use an example to show how to elicit new requirements from simulation results and locate them in the related system model; related works are presented in Sect. 6; and Sect. 7 concludes the paper and puts forward the future work.

2 Preliminaries

TCS, which consists of a set of traffic controls and train operation controls, is the core system in the railway transportation system. In this paper, we simplify the TCS and consider interaction scenario among train, light, track and control center. The interaction scenario is described as follows: (1) Train sends a signal to the control center before entering a track. (2) Control center receives the signal and then sends a signal to the track to check the occupancy situation. (3) The track receives the signal and returns a signal of occupancy situation. (4) Control center receives the signal from track and sends a signal to the light to control it turn green or red based on the occupancy information of the track. (5) Train sends a signal to the light to check the light state. (6) Light sends a signal of state information to train. (7) If the state of light is green, train sends a signal to the track to enter it. (8) Then control center sends a signal to light to make it turn red. (9) Train sends a leaving signal to track after leaving the track. (10) Then control center sends signal to light to make it turn green. (11) In the step 7, if the state of light is red, train will return to step 1.

Modelica [10–12] is a non-proprietary, object-oriented, equation based language to conveniently model complex physical systems. In the following we will clarify some basic knowledge of Modelica language.

Class. The fundamental structuring unit. Class contains declaration, equation and algorithm section. Declaration represents the elements belonging to class. Equation and algorithm define the behavior of class. There are seven restricted classes with specific names, such as *model*, *type*, *connector* and so on. A *model* definition is the most generic type of definition in Modelica.

Declaration. Variables, parameters and instances of class can be contained in declaration section. The basic syntax for a variable declaration is simply the "type" of the variable followed by the name of the variable, e g., "Real x".

Equation and Algorithm. Physical behavior of a class is described by equations. Equations are declarative and acausal and they express an equality relation between two expressions. Algorithm is imperative and can be used to express sequence of assignment statements and iteration.

3 Overview of Our Approach

The main idea of our approach is to find new requirements of TCS based on model simulation results. Two models, system model and accident model, are required. In our case study, system model includes 4 component models and 1 system composition model. It describes the structure and behaviors of TCS as well as the interaction scenario. Accident model is used to investigate that accident happens in which situation.

Our approach works as follows. Firstly, system and accident models are constructed. Then, by using the Open Modelica, we get the simulation results and analyze the results to check whether the property specification (like distance < 0) is met. If met, we try to elicit new requirements based on simulation results and modify the original model to avoid the accidents and guarantee the safety of TCS. Figure 1 shows the framework of our approach.

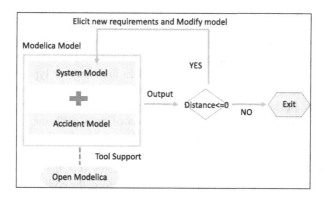

Fig. 1. Framework of our approach.

3.1 System Model

Based on the interaction scenario of TCS in Sect. 2, we describe the structure of system and information delivered among components. As shown in Fig. 2, the composition of system model includes train, track, light and control center. The first thing is to construct each component model which describes their behaviors and other information. These components interact with each other. For example, train receives signals from track and light respectively. These signals include the color of light and fault information. Meanwhile, the control center receives signals from the track which contains the information of occupancy situation and fault. Based on these signals, control center makes the light turn red or green. Control center also receives signals of train's position and speed. We combine these isolated component models together in a system model based on interaction scenario and simulate all these models in Open Modelica. The exact models in Modelica will be explained in the next section.

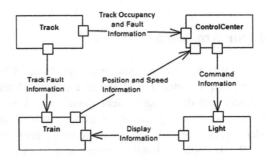

Fig. 2. Composition and interactions of system.

3.2   Accident Model

Through investigation, we find derailment, collision and fire to property and personnel are primary accidents in railway system. Collision is divided into two types: rear-end collision and head-on collision. According to rail accident investigation reports from China, the speed and the speed difference are great in a very serious collision or derailment accident. Therefore, we argue that the severity level of collision or derailment accident is related to the speed and speed difference. The severity level of other accidents such as fire and explosion are related to fire range or type. We list all the accident types and level in Table 1. The smaller the number is and the greater the accident level is. In this paper, we consider one type of accident: rear- end collision.

Position is a significant factor in the situation of train collision. In the Wenzhou railway "7.23" high-speed railway accident, it is too late for the rear train to take emergency brake. In this paper, we define *distance* as the position difference between the front and rear train. A collision accident indicates that the position difference between two trains is less than or equal to zero. Therefore, the collision accident model is defined as follows:

$$distance = position(t_1) - position(t_2) <= 0 \tag{1}$$

where t_1 is the front train and t_2 is the rear train. When variable *distance* meets the formula during simulation, collision accident happens.

Table 1. Accident Type and Level.

Accident Type			Level
Rear-end Collision	The speed of both trains is between 100 km/h and 200 km/h	50 < Speed difference < 100	2
		0 < Speed difference < 50	3
	The speed of both trains is between 20 km/h and 100 km/h	40 < Speed difference < 80	3
		0 < Speed difference < 40	4
	The speed of both trains is less than 20 km/h	0 < Speed difference < 20	5
Head-on Collision	The speed of both trains is between 100 km/h and 200 km/h	50 < Speed difference < 100	1
		0 < Speed difference < 50	2
	The speed of both trains is between 20 km/h and 100 km/h	40 < Speed difference < 80	2
		0 < Speed difference < 40	3
	The speed of both trains is less than 20 km/h	0 < Speed difference < 20	4
Derailment	The speed of train is between 100 km/h and 200 km/h		2
	The speed of train is less than 100 km/h		3
Fire	Out of control		2
	Under control		3
Explosion	Chemicals explosion		1
	Physics explosion		2

4 System Modeling

According to Sect. 3, TCS includes 4 components that are train, light, track and control center. In this section, we will present how to construct Modelica model of them in detail.

4.1 Train

The key part of a train is the onboard software, mainly onboard vital computer units and automatic train protection (ATP). It works as follows: according to the received information, such as proceed signal, stop signal, over speed signal and so on, the onboard software make a judgment on the value of train's acceleration in the next time unit while ensuring train operation safety. Meanwhile, its movement process conforms to the law of physical movement. In physical area, velocity is the derivation of position and acceleration is the derivative of velocity. We mainly consider position, velocity and acceleration property of train.

The exact decision tree of acceleration is as follows. Firstly, the onboard software judges whether the train is in a running state. If train is running, then onboard software judges the signals it receives. If light color is not green or the track is in error, the train must decelerate. Otherwise, onboard software judges whether the speed of train reaches maximum speed. If it reaches, then acceleration of train should be set zero. Otherwise, train keeps accelerating. Figure 3 shows the decision tree.

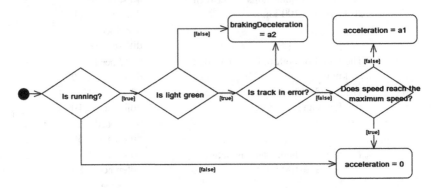

Fig. 3. Decision tree of acceleration in Train.

In addition, departure time is used to specify the time when train leaves station and request time specifies the time when train sends a request to enter into a track. Due to the physical property of the train, there are many limitations. For example, the acceleration could not be infinite great. It has maximum acceleration. Similarly, we have maximum braking deceleration. Moreover, considering the property of track, when running on the track, the speed of train must less than maximum limited speed of track in order to void derailment.

Based on the above information, we declare variable v, a and *trainPositon* to represent the velocity, acceleration and position of train respectively when constructing train Modelica model. Also, we define the parameter *startTime* representing the departure time and *requestTime* representing the request time. Parameters $a1$, $a2$, *length* and *maxConstSpeed* represent maximum braking deceleration, maximum acceleration, length of train and maximum limited speed of track respectively. In the equation section, we use equations *der (trainPosition) = v* and *der (v) = a* to represent behaviors of train. Finally, the train Modelica model is obtained as shown in Fig. 4(a).

4.2 Light

Light (short for signal light) which erects beside track passes information related to the state of track to train. Light does not contain any behavior and the only function of it is to display red color or green color. Light may encounter a fault and then display the wrong color. Whether and when the fault occurs are unknown.

For modeling, we declare a variable *isGreen* and define its type boolean. If the value of *isGreen* is "true", then it means the color of light is green. Otherwise, it is red.

```
model Train
  Real v;
  Real a;
  Real train Position;
  parameter Modelica.SIunits.Time
startTime;
  parameter Modelica.SIunits.Time request
Time;
  parameter Real a1;
  parameter Real a2;
  parameter Real maxConstSpeed;
  parameter Real length;
  ......
equation
  der(train Position) = v;
  der(v) = a;
  if time >= startTime and time <= request
  Time and isAcc and not isError or time >=
  request Time and isAcc and isGreen and
  not isError then
    a = a2;
  elseif time >= request Time and not isStop
  and (not isGreen or isError) then
    a = a1;
  else
    a = 0;
  end if;
  ......
algorithm
  when v >= maxConstSpeed then
    isAcc = false;
  elsewhen v < maxConstSpeed then
    isAcc = true;
  end when;
  when v > 0 then
    isStop = false;
  elsewhen v <= 0 then
    isStop = true;
  end when;
end Train;
```

(a) Train

```
model Light
  Boolean isGreen;
  Boolean isRedError;
  Boolean isGreenError;
  Boolean doGreen;
  Real random1;
  Real random2;
......
equation
  if doGreen and not isRedError or isGreenError then
    isGreen = true;
  else
    isGreen = false;
  end if;
algorithm
// Generate a random and to judge whether a fault occurs
when time > 50 then
  state1 :=Modelica.Math.Random.Generators.
             Xorshift64star.initialState(localSeed1, globalSeed1);
  (random1, state1) := Modelica.Math.Random.Generators.
             Xorshift64star.random(state1);
end when;
  if random1 >= 0.5 then
    isRedError := true;
  else
    isRedError := false;
  end if;
// Generate a random and to judge whether a fault occurs
when time > 60 then
  state2 :=Modelica.Math.Random.Generators.
             Xorshift64star.initialState(localSeed2, globalSeed2);
  (random2, state2) :=Modelica.Math.Random.Generators.
             Xorshift64star.random(state2);
end when;
if random2 >= 0.5 then
  isGreenError := true;
else
  isGreenError := false;
end if;
end Light;
```

(b) Light

Fig. 4. Key code of Train, Light in Modelica.

Boolean variables *isRedError* and *isGreenError* represent two different types of display faults. For example, if the value of variable *isRedError* is "true", it means that the light displays red all the time. Besides, we define two variables *random1* and *random2*, and use Modelica random generator function to generate random number between 0 and 1. If *random1* is greater than 0.5, then the value of *isRedError* is "true". Otherwise, it is "false". The relation between *random2* and *isGreenError* is similar. Finally, we get the light Modelica model as shown in Fig. 4(b).

4.3 Track

Track enables trains to move by providing a dependable surface for their wheels to roll upon. Similar to light, track does not contain any behavior. It only has two states which are occupied and unoccupied. By detecting the absence of train, the occupancy situation of track is collected. Track may encounter a fault such as broken rail, power supply failure and so on. Unlike light fault, we does not distinguish the type of track fault. Whether and when the fault occurs are unknown.

In track model, we define two variables *isOccupied* and *isTrackError*. Variable *isOccupied* represents the occupancy state of track. When the value of *isOccupied* is "true", it means that the track is occupied. Otherwise, track is clear. Variable *random* is defined to indicate the occurrence of fault. We use Modelica random generator function to generate the value of *random*. If the value of *random* is greater than 0.5, then fault occurs. Otherwise, fault does not occur. Parameter *length* is defined to represent the length of track. Finally, the track model is obtained as shown in Fig. 5(a).

```
model Track
  Boolean isOccupied;
  Boolean isTrackError;
  parameter Real length;
  ......
algorithm
//Generate a random
when time > 60 then
    state1 := Modelica.Math.Random.Generators.Xorshift64star.
        initialState(localSeed1, globalSeed1);
    (random1, state1) := Modelica.Math.Random.Generators.
        Xorshift64star.random(state1);
end when;
//To judge whether a fault occurs
if random1 >= 0.5 then
  isTrackError := true;
else
  isTrackError := false;
end if;
  ......
end Track;
```

(a) Track

```
model ControlCenter
  Boolean doGreen;
  .......
equation
  if not isOccupied and not isTrackError then
    doGreen = true;
  else
    doGreen = false;
  end if;
  doGreenOut = doGreen;
end ControlCenter;
```

(b) Control Center

```
model TCS
  Train t1 (requestTime = 30);
  Train t2 (startTime = 50, requestTime = 80);
  Track track;
  Light light;
  ControlCenter cc;
  Real distance;
  Boolean isCollision;
equation
  //Train receive light signal
  connect(t1.lightIn, light.lightOut[1]);
  connect(t2.lightIn, light.lightOut[2]);
  //Control center receives train position signal
  connect(t1.positionOut[2], cc.positionIn[1]);
  connect(t2.positionOut[2], cc.positionIn[2]);
  //Control center receives train speed signal
  connect(t1.speedOut,cc.speedIn[1]);
  connect(t2.speedOut,cc.speedIn[2]);
  //Train receives track fault signal
  connect(track.errorOut[1], t1.errorIn);
  connect(track.errorOut[2], t2.errorIn);
  //Control center receives track fault signal
  connect(track.errorOut[3], cc.errorIn);
  //Control center receives track occupancy signal
  connect(track.occupOut, cc.occupIn);
  //Light receives display command
  connect(cc.doGreenOut, light.doGreenIn);
  distance = t1.trainPosition - t2.trainPosition;
  if distance <= 0 then
      isCollision = true;
  else
      isCollision = false;
  end if;
end TCS;
```

(c) TCS

Fig. 5. Key Code of Track, Control Center, TCS in Modelica.

4.4 Control Center

Control center calculates the command based on signals from track and then sends the command to light to the control light. The signals received from track include the occupancy state of track and track fault. If track is not occupied and does not encounter a fault, then control center sends a command to the light to make light turn green. Otherwise, it sends command to light to make light turn red in order to prevent train from entering into track.

We define variable *doGreen* to represent the command sent to light. The type of varible *doGreen* is boolean. If the value of *doGreen* is "true", it makes light turn green. Otherwise, light turns red. In addition, variables *isOccupied* and *isTrackError* represent signals received from track. Finally, we get the control center Modelica model as shown in Fig. 5(b).

4.5 System Composition

TCS includes all the component models and describes the interaction among these components. In system model, according to the accident model, we pay attention to the distance between two trains. If distance is less than or equal to zero, it means that two trains collide with each other.

We declare instances *t1* and *t2* of Train model, instance *track* of Track model, instance *light* of Light model and instance *cc* of Control Center model respectively. Variable *distance* is defined to represent distance between *t1* and *t2* and the equation is *distance* = *t1.trainPosition* − *t2.trainPosition*. We use variable *isCollision* to represent the collision accident. If *distance* is less than or equal to zero, the value of *isCollision* is "true". Otherwise, the value is "false". In Modelica, a connect statement is used to describe data exchanging among components. Therefore, we use 11 connect statements to represent interactions among components. Finally, we get the TCS Modelica model as Fig. 5(c) shows.

5 Simulation and New Requirements Elicitation: A Case Study

5.1 Simulation Scenarios

In this paper, we assume that only light or track will encounter a fault. The occurrence of light fault is random. In normal situation, light works well and display the right color corresponding to the actual state of track. However, when a fault occurs, light may display the color that opposite to the right color. For example, it displays green color even though there is a train in the track. Therefore, for light, it has three situations which are "*Normal*","*Should be green but red*" and "*Should be red but green*". Similarly, the occurrence of track fault is unexpected. There are multiple types of track faults but in this paper we do not distinguish these faults. So track has two situations which are "*Normal*" and "*Fault*".

We combine the three light situations and two track situations, and then get six scenarios. However, in some situations, train may not receive the track fault signal and then run as normal. For example, in Wenzhou "7.23" high-speed railway accident, the rear train did not detect the track fault and finally the two trains collide with each other. We take this situation into consideration and assume that the rear train did not receive the fault signal. Combining this situation with the three light situations, we gets another three scenarios. Finally, we get nine scenarios. They are conducted respectively to check whether there is a collision accident.

5.2   Train Control System Simulation Settings

According to the domain knowledge of railway system and data materials searched, we set the parameters of simulation as shown in Table 2.

Table 2. Initial Parameter Settings for Simulation

Model	Parameter	Value
Train	maximumConstantSpeed	200 km/h
	braking deceleration	-1 m/s^2
	acceleration	2 m/s^{-2}
	length	400 m
	requestTime	30 s after Departure
Train t1	startTime	0 s
Train t2	startTime	50 s
Track	length	8000 m

In addition, in order to simulate the occurrence of light fault and track fault, a random function is defined. We assume that the fault occurs when the random number is greater than 0.5. The fault occurrence time is important and decides whether the accident happens. In this paper, an assumption is proposed that the light fault occurs after Train t1 entering the track and the track fault occurs when Train t1 has been entered and Train t2 has not yet entered the track. According to the nine scenarios above, we assume that Train t1 can always detect the track error and Train t2 cannot detect the track error in some scenarios.

Based on these parameters setting, we simulate the model in Open Modelica and try to find out whether the accident happens.

5.3   Analyzing Simulation Results

All the Modelica models are simulated in the simulation tool Open Modelica and we get all the simulation results. Table 3 shows nine scenarios as well as the results.

From Table 3, we find that only in scenario 6 and 9, Train t1 and Train t2 collide with each other. In these two scenarios, the light fault makes light turn green and green color represents proceed signal. In scenario 6, although the rear Train t2 has detected the track fault and braked immediately, collision accident occurred because the distance

Table 3. Scenarios and Simulation Results. (t1: front train, t2: rear train)

Light	Track	Result
1. Normal	Normal	t1, t2 are normal
2. Should be green but red	Normal	t1 enters Track normally, t2 cannot enter Track
3. Should be red but green	Normal	Both t1,t2 can enter Track but not collide
4. Normal	Fault	t1 takes emergency brake, t2 cannot enter Track
5. Should be green but red	Fault	t1 takes emergency brake, t2 cannot enter Track
6. Should be red but green	**Fault**	**Both t1, t2 take emergency brake but collide with each other**
7. Normal	Fault (t2 did not detect)	t1 takes emergency brake, t2 cannot enter Track
8. Should be green but red	Fault (t2 did not detect)	t1 takes emergency brake, t2 cannot enter Track
9. Should be red but green	**Fault (t2 did not detect)**	**t1 takes emergency brake, t2 runs normally, t1, t2 collide with each other**

between the two trains is too close. As shown in Fig. 6, the line of t1 represents the position of train t1 and the line of t2 represents the position of train t2. We can find that the line of t1 and line of t2 coincide in the final period. In scenario 9, t2 did not detect the track fault and keeps running at a full speed. Therefore, it collides with t1 directly. Scenario 9 is similar to scenario 6, so we will not discuss it particularly because of the limitation of pages.

In both scenarios, proceed signal is a risk factor because it makes Train t2 keep running in an unsafe situation. Normally, when in an unsafe situation, it is better for a train to stop in order to avoid accident. Even though Train t2 takes emergency brake in

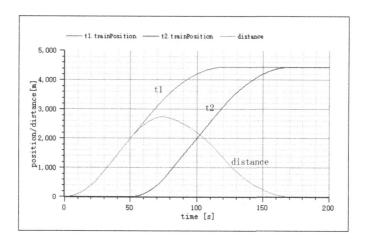

Fig. 6. Simulation results of Scenario 6.

scenario 6, accident happens because the distance between two trains is too short for the rear train to stop. So distance is a significant factor we should take into consideration.

5.4   Eliciting and Locating New Requirements

We analyze the causes of the collision accident based on the simulation results and find out new safety requirements. In some extreme situations, multiple faults occur at the same time. For example, in Wenzhou "7.23" high-speed railway accident, the cause of the accident is the equipment failure which results from lightning. The signal light maintains green state and the track circuit sends signals abnormally at the meantime. The front train D3115 detected the track fault and then ATP enforces the train to stop. Meanwhile, because of the track fault, D3115 cannot turn to OnSight mode. Unfortunately, the rear train D301 did not detect the track fault so that ATP did not work automatically. It is too late for driver to take emergency brake to avoid the collision accident.

In these situations, distance between two trains and the speed of rear train are both significant. In scenario 6, the distance is too short for the rear train to stop. Therefore, we consider setting a safe distance to prevent rear train from colliding with front train Safe distance is calculate based on some parameters. Assuming that the rear train does not slow and runs at speed v, then in the worst case where the front train has stopped, it needs time t to accelerate to v with acceleration a. During this period, the running distance of rear train is $v*t$. The length of train is 400 meters. Finally, the safety distance should be equal or greater than $v*t + 400$.

According to the analysis of this problem, we reconsider the original requirements of ATP – "*Once detected environment failure such as track error, ATP automatically takes emergency brake to protect train. The train turns to OnSight mode after 2 min*". In an extreme situation where collision and derailment risk exist at the same time, train should compare the level of two different accidents and choose a less severe accident situation. In addition, the front train and rear train should take different measures to avoid accidents. The new requirement is as follows:

Once detected environment failure such as track error, ATP automatically takes emergency brake to protect train. If two different accidents exits at the same time, ATP should compare the level of these accidents and chooses a less severe accident. When in the situation where collision accident level is greater than derailment level, the front train stops decelerating if the rear train does not slow down until the distance between two trains is less than the safe distance. The rear train must decelerate.

Based on the new requirement, safe distance and speed are key factors we should pay attention to. Speed is the main property of train and is controlled by the acceleration. Therefore, we locate the new requirement in train model and add a new decision tree of acceleration. The new decision process is parallel with the original one. Train must conduct the new decision process when in a situation where the level of collision accident is greater than derailment accident (Fig. 7).

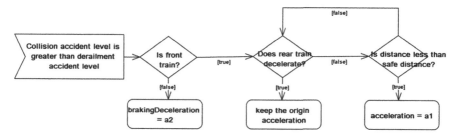

Fig. 7. Modification: Decision tree of acceleration in the Train model

5.5   Modification of System Model

The train model is modified based on the new requirements we presented above. At first, we add the comparison rules in model and define two variables *collisionLevel* and *derailmentLevel* to represent accident level. A new variable *isBrake* represents the state of other train, for example, if the train is a front train, then the other train is rear train. Also, safe distance is added to prevent accidents. Modification of train model is shown in Fig. 8.

```
if time >= startTime and time <= requestTime and isAcc and not isError or time >= requestTime and isAcc and
isGreen and not isError or
    id == 0 and not isBrake and trainPosition - positionIn < safeDistance and collisionLevel > derailme Level then
// Decision of acceleration in front train
        a = 2;
elseif time >= requestTime and not isStop and (not isGreen or isError) or  //Decision of acceleration in front
                                                                              train
    id == 1 and isBrake and positionIn - trainPosition < safeDistance then
        a = -1;
else
        a = 0;
end if;
```

Fig. 8. Modification of Train Modelica model.

We simulate the modified models in the Open Modelica and find that the two trains will not collide with each other in scenario 6 and 9. In scenario 6, as shown in Fig. 9, compared to its former results, the line of t2 always down below the line of t1. This means that there will not be a collision accident. In addition, distance between two trains is always greater than safe distance after train t2 leaves station.

Of course, our simulation is not the same process in real world. In real world, the response of equipment takes time while in Modelica simulation it does not take any time. However, the response time will not influence the prediction of accidents it is very short.

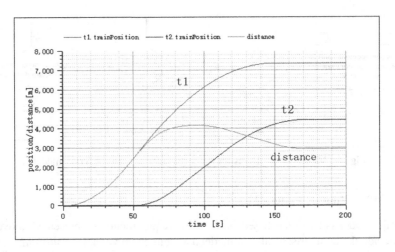

Fig. 9. Result of scenario 6 after modification.

6 Related Work

Accidents analysis has been researched for many years and divided into two types: informal approach and formal approach. Based on informal approach, Lu et al. [13] propose a method extending traditional fault tree analysis with temporal and fault characteristics to determine which fault need to be eliminated urgently. Helmer et al. [14] apply software fault tree approach to requirements analysis of an intrusion detection system. By analyzing the ways in which the system can reach an unsafe state, SFTA assists in changing requirements. In railway industry, Kim and Yoon [15] propose a model of accident causation and constructed a sequence of events leading to an accident/incident. By analyzing the accident causation model, it is useful to explain how an accident occurs. But these methods do not support dynamic analysis.

Formal methods can improve accident analysis by emphasizing the importance of precision in definitions and descriptions, and providing notations for describing and reasoning about certain aspects of accidents. Vernez et al. [16] proposed colored Petri nets for accident modeling and then conducted a risk analysis. Petri nets model the accident event in order to get safety data. In paper [17], Tomoya Yamaguchi et al. combine requirements mining, model checking and simulation-based verification for industrial automotive systems. Model checking is used find unit-level counterexamples while simulation is used to find system-level counterexamples. Requirement mining is used to find formulas that system satisfies for all possible inputs. However, Tomoya Yamaguchi only focuses on the requirements that already exist.

To sum up, the limited use of informal methods become evident while analyzing dynamic processes with time constraints. For instance, informal methods cannot model the physical properties of system such as speed, velocity and so on. For formal methods, such as model checking, the biggest limitation is state explosion. When the system is large and complex, the size of model will become very large. It cannot be solved by the model checking methods. So all these formal and informal methods are not suitable for the real-time rail transit systems. Compared with those methods, our work can dynamically model the accident and take time into consideration when modeling. Also, as our approach is based on simulations, there is no limitation in complex system. By analyzing the accidents results, our work can elicit and locate requirements in system model.

7   Conclusion

Ensuring the safety of TCS is of great importance. Our paper presents a simulation based approach to elicit new requirements from accidents and then locate them in model. The new requirements help us to modify the system model to avoid accidents and a case study is provided to verify our approach. The main contributions include:

(1) Considering continuous and discrete characteristics of TCS system, we use Modelica to construct system model as well as accident model. Through simulation, the accidents and corresponding causes are found;
(2) By analyzing simulation results, we elicit requirements and locate the new requirements on the system model, and make the corresponding modifications.

However, our work of requirements elicitation is done manually and the comparison of accident level is simple in our case study. Therefore, we will work further to find an automatic way to elicit and locate requirements based on accident results. In addition, a more complicate situation which contains the other accident types should be considered.

Acknowledgements. This paper is partially supported by the projects funded by the NSFC No. 61472140, 61572195 and, NSFC Key Project 61332008, and SHEITC160306.

References

1. Stamatelatos, M., Vesley, W.: Fault Tree Handbook with Aerospace Applications (Draft). Nasa Office of Safety & Mission Assurance Nasa Headquarters Washington DC (2002)
2. Ravi Sankar, N., Prabhu, B.S.: Modified approach for prioritization of failures in a system failure mode and effects analysis. Int. J. Qual. Reliab. Manag. **18**(3), 324–336 (2001)
3. Dunjó, J., Fthenakis, V., Vílchez, J.A., et al.: Hazard and operability (HAZOP) analysis. a literature review. J. Hazard. Mater. **173**(1), 19–32 (2010)
4. Ericson, C.A.: Event tree analysis. In: Hazard Analysis Techniques for System Safety, pp. 223–234 (2005)
5. Chiappini, A., Cimatti, A., Porzia, C., Rotondo, G., Sebastiani, R., Traverso, P., Villafiorita, A.: Formal specification and development of a safety-critical train management system. In: Felici, M., Kanoun, K. (eds.) SAFECOMP 1999. LNCS, vol. 1698, pp. 410–419. Springer, Heidelberg (1999). https://doi.org/10.1007/3-540-48249-0_35
6. Cimatti, A.: Industrial Applications of Model Checking. In: Cassez, F., Jard, C., Rozoy, B., Ryan, M.D. (eds.) MOVEP 2000. LNCS, vol. 2067, pp. 153–168. Springer, Heidelberg (2001). https://doi.org/10.1007/3-540-45510-8_6

7. Cimatti, A., Pieraccini, P.L., Sebastiani, R., Traverso, P., Villafiorita, A.: Formal specification and validation of a vital communication protocol. In: Wing, J.M., Woodcock, J., Davies, J. (eds.) FM 1999. LNCS, vol. 1709, pp. 1584–1604. Springer, Heidelberg (1999). https://doi.org/10.1007/3-540-48118-4_34

8. Hinchey, M.G., Bowen, J.P. (eds.): Industrial Strength Formal Methods in Practice. Formal Approaches to Computing and Information Technology. Springer, London (1999). https://doi.org/10.1007/978-1-4471-0523-7

9. https://www.openmodelica.org/

10. http://book.xogeny.com/

11. Fritzson, P.: Principles of Object-Oriented Modeling and Simulation with Modelica 2.1. Wiley, New Jersey (2010)

12. Tiller, M. (ed.): Introduction to Physical Modeling with Modelica. Springer, Boston (2012). https://doi.org/10.1007/978-1-4615-1561-6

13. Lu, Y., Peng, Z., Miller, A., et al.: Timed fault tree models of the China Yongwen railway accident. In: 2014 8th Asia Modelling Symposium (AMS), pp. 128–133. IEEE (2014)

14. Helmer, G., Wong, J., Slagell, M., et al.: A software fault tree approach to requirements analysis of an intrusion detection system. Requirements Eng. 7(4), 207–220 (2002)

15. San Kim, D., Yoon, W.C.: An accident causation model for the railway industry: Application of the model to 80 rail accident investigation reports from the UK. Saf. Sci. 60, 57–68 (2013)

16. Vernez, D., Buchs, D., Pierrehumbert, G.: Perspectives in the use of coloured Petri nets for risk analysis and accident modelling. Saf. Sci. 41(5), 445–463 (2003)

17. Yamaguchi, T., Kaga, T., Seshia, S.A.: Combining requirement mining, software model checking and simulation-based verification for industrial automotive systems. In: Conference on Formal Methods in Computer-Aided Design. FMCAD Inc., pp. 201–204 (2016)

Author Index

Printed in the United States
By Bookmasters